GOLF
THE ULTIMATE GUIDE

GOLF

THE ULTIMATE GUIDE

LONDON ■ NEW YORK
MUNICH ■ MELBOURNE ■ DELHI

Editor	Satu Fox
Art Editor	Katie Cavanagh
US Editor	Jacqueline Hornberger
US Associate Managing Editor	Allison Singer
Producers (Pre-production)	Rebecca Fallowfield, Luca Frassinetti
Producer (Print Production)	Mandy Inness
Jacket Designer	Mark Cavanagh
Jacket Design Development Manager	Sophia M.T.T.
Managing Editor	Stephanie Farrow
Managing Art Editor	Lee Griffiths

DK India

Project Editor	Rupa Rao
Editor	N. Visalam
Art Editors	Priyanka Singh, Heena Sharma
DTP Designer	Sachin Gupta, Vijay Kandwal
Managing Editor	Kingshuk Ghoshal
Managing Art Editor	Govind Mittal
Pre-production Manager	Balwant Singh
Production Manager	Pankaj Sharma

First American Edition, 2014

Published in the United States by
DK Publishing

345 Hudson Street, New York, New York 10014

14 15 16 17 18 10 9 8 7 6 5 4 3 2 1

193206—September/2014

Published in Great Britain by Dorling Kindersley Ltd.

A catalog record for this book is available from the
Library of Congress.

ISBN 978-1-4654-2444-0

DK Books are available at special discounts when purchased
in bulk for sale promotions, premiums, fund-raising, or
educational use. For details, contact: DK Publishing Special
Markets, 345 Hudson Street, New York, New York 10014 or
SpecialSales@dk.com

Content previously published in *Eyewitness Companions: Golf*

Printed and bound in China by Leo Paper Products Ltd.

Discover more at **www.dk.com**

Contents

Golf—The Game

Golf has so much to offer, no matter what your age, gender, or background. As well as taking fresh air and exercising, there is the opportunity to meet new friends, the chance to explore beautiful golf courses, and the physical and mental challenges of developing your skills as a player.

The origins of golf

Nobody is entirely sure where the first golf shot was actually played, but St. Andrews in Scotland is widely regarded as the home of golf. Some historians believe that people were playing golf along the West Sands—a stretch of sand dunes along the coast from St. Andrews—as early as the 12th century, but this fact has never been substantiated.

Shrouded in mystery

Some historians believe a game very similar to golf was played by the Chinese many centuries ago—nobody is quite sure exactly when. Others liken it to the Flemish game of *chole*, in which balls made from beechwood were hit with iron-headed sticks against a tree or a door. There could also be a link to the medieval Dutch game *kolven*, which was played on ice with a ball about the size of a baseball, and depicted by the artist Aert van der Neer (*see* below). Other scholars believe that golf is a form of the 11th-century French game *jeu de mail*, also known as pall-mall. If you look at paintings by early 17th-century artists, in which both *chole* and *kolven* are depicted, it is easy to see why these games are widely considered to be the direct forerunners of golf. However, golf is known to have been played in Scotland in the first half of the 15th century, two hundred years earlier, which destroys this argument.

The only hard fact in this quagmire of theories and rumors is that the first printed reference to golf is in 1457, in a parliamentary decree issued by James II of Scotland. This stated that "fute-ball and golfe be utterly cryit doune, and nocht usit" ("football and golf should be utterly cried down and not used"), in effect, he tried to ban the game. James was concerned that too many of his countrymen were honing their swings on the golf course when they should have been practicing their archery. A sweetly struck iron was unlikely to repel the English invaders, whereas a straight arrow might.

⏵⏵ **The game of *kolven*** Aert van der Neer depicts the Dutch entertaining themselves with *kolven* played on ice, a game thought by some to be a forerunner to golf.

◀◀ **Early playing days**
The traditions of the Bruntsfield Links Golfing Society date back to 1761, when the members played over Bruntsfield Links in the shadow of Edinburgh Castle.

The Scottish game

It is ironic that a game that was loathed and abhorred by the Scottish leadership became its national treasure and has now spread worldwide. The Scottish game has today conquered all corners of the globe.

It was not long before the Scottish hierarchy became hooked on the game they once dreaded. James IV of Scotland married the daughter of Henry VII of England, and in 1513 had a set of clubs made by an artisan in Perth, for a match he later played against the Earl of Boswell. Golf had suddenly become a royal, as well as an ancient, game.

Mary Queen of Scots played golf, and is rumored to have played shortly after the murder of her husband, Lord Darnley, an incident that is often cited as a sign of her insensitivity. After Elizabeth I died without an heir, and the Scottish Stuarts assumed the English throne in 1603, golf spread throughout the UK because James I (James VI of Scotland) was an avid golfer. He was adamant that, as long as there had been due religious observance, anyone could enjoy playing sports on a Sunday.

James I and his descendants—Charles I, Charles II, and James II of England—were all avid golfers. In fact, Charles I was in the middle of a game on Leith Links in Scotland when news of a rebellion in Ireland was brought to him. There are records of a match played by James II and his shoemaker against two noblemen from England. The king and his Scottish shoemaker, named Paterstone, won the game. The latter was rewarded for his prowess with enough money to build a house in Edinburgh.

The advent of golf clubs

Until the 18th century, golf was a fairly haphazard pursuit. People did not pay to play, because there was no one to pay. Most of the courses were on common land, owned by whole communities. There were no greenkeepers employed to look after the courses and there were no formal rules—players just decided the format of the match on the day. All games were match play (see p.46), with wagers being agreed between parties. Scorecards had yet to be invented.

> **DID YOU KNOW?**
>
> There is a stained-glass window in Gloucester Cathedral, England, dating from around 1340, that shows a man resembling a golfer. The English claim that this is undeniable proof that golf is a sport that they invented. However, most early cultures have games involving a ball and a stick.

>> **Musselburgh links**
By 1859, when this scene was painted, golf was becoming a popular pastime along the Scottish east coast.

The first golf club to be formed was the Honourable Company of Edinburgh Golfers in 1744, which was first based in Leith on the east coast of Scotland. The club has since moved, first to Musselburgh in 1836, and then to their final and more upmarket residence at Muirfield, in 1891. The first golf holes at Leith were all well over 400 yards (365m). Taking into account the sort of equipment they were using at the time, the distances must be the equivalent to well over 600 yards (550m) today.

Nothing was standardized in these early days and for many years, courses had different numbers of holes: for example, 22 at St. Andrews, 12 at

△ **Royal approval**
As golf's popularity spread around Britain, so did the demand for well-made equipment—fit for a prince.

Prestwick, five at Leith, six at Perth, and 25 at Montrose. In 1764, William St. Clair of Roslin, captain of both the Leith and St. Andrews golf clubs, organized the first four holes at St. Andrews to be compressed into two, bringing the total to 18 holes. This soon became the standard, particularly since the Society of St. Andrews Golfers was so influential in the development of the game. The club changed its name in 1834 to the Royal & Ancient Golf Club (R&A), and this has since become the governing authority of golf, alongside the US Golf Association (USGA).

During the 19th century, holes became a standard 4¼in (10.8cm) in diameter, which happened to be the width of an implement at Musselburgh that was used to cut holes. Greens were very rough and bumpy during this time, because lawnmowers did not exist, making the act of putting a tricky business.

>> **Golf clubs** By the 1900s, makers began producing irons with grooves on the faces for greater distances. This coincided with the introduction of the modern ball in 1905.

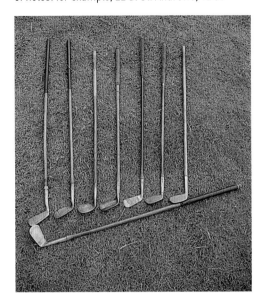

Popular appeal

Until the 1850s, the game was only played by a few rich and privileged people. This changed with the introduction of the gutta percha (a saplike material which is malleable when boiled in water) ball, or "gutty." Until this time, the ball was a "feathery" made from goose or duck feathers. Featheries were expensive to make and could not be hit great distances.

The gutty was first used in 1856 and it flew much greater distances, rolled much straighter, and lasted longer than the feathery. It could also be remolded if it became damaged during play.

Very soon it became cheaper and therefore easier to play the game. In 1850, before the gutty was invented, there were 17 clubs in Britain and a dozen or so known golf courses. By 1890, there were 387 clubs and 140 different courses. Lytham & St. Anne's was founded in 1886, St. George's in 1887, Portrush in 1888, and Birkdale in 1889.

Golf grows more popular

The growth of railroads across Britain in the 1880s and 1890s contributed greatly to the spread of the game. At last, people could get away from the cities and reach the seaside easily. And the seaside happened to be fertile ground for the building of golf courses. In the early 20th century, places like North Berwick, along the Firth of Forth, and even Machrihanish, on the Mull of Kintyre in northern Scotland, were towns where the rich and famous spent their vacations.

The explosion of golf in the latter part of the 19th century is also reflected in the proliferation of golf publications. In 1890, only a dozen or so books

⏶ **Changing fashions**
In the 1860s, tweed jackets, vests, and cravats were the golfing attire of the day.

⏴ **Taking refreshments**
From the 1840s, Old Daw Anderson ran a mobile refreshment stall at St. Andrews dispensing ginger beer on hole 4. The hole is still called "Ginger beer" to this day.

⏶ Scottish golf pioneer
Old Tom Morris was one of the first golf professionals in the mid- to late 19th century.

about golf had been written. By 1900 there were many more, and today, hundreds are published every year, on everything from the changing technology of the golf ball to the delights of the golf courses of Morocco. Golf also has a proud literary tradition. Bernard Darwin, Grantland Rice, and Peter Dobereiner were all outstanding writers on the subject of golf, and P. G. Wodehouse's *Golf Omnibus* is still regarded by many as one of the funniest golf books ever written.

During the 19th century, the game had spread throughout the world, reaching outposts of the British Empire such as the Royal Calcutta Golf Club in India, which was established as early as 1829. British expatriates working abroad were largely responsible for taking the game to new countries, with courses being built in Far Eastern countries such as Hong Kong and Thailand in the 1890s.

Royal Melbourne, founded in 1891, is the oldest golf club in Australia. The oldest in South Africa is the Royal Cape Golf Club, which was established in 1885 in Cape Town. In South America, the Buenos Aires Golf Club was founded in 1878, and Sao Paulo in Brazil some 12 years later. The first club to open in North America was in Montreal in 1873, and clubs in Quebec and Toronto were soon to follow.

Golf in the US

The most important and significant development of all was the arrival of golf in the US in the late 19th century. This is generally attributed to a Scotsman named John Reid. He was living and working in New York in the 1880s, when he asked a friend named Robert Lockhart to bring him some clubs and balls on a visit back to Scotland. Lockhart went to Old Tom Morris' shop in St. Andrews to buy the golf equipment. Following the purchase of five more sets of clubs, on February 22, 1888, Reid, Lockhart, and a few friends played three roughly designed holes near Reid's house. On November 14 that same year, Reid and his friends drew up a constitution for their club in New York, which

DID YOU KNOW?

Old Tom Morris (1821–1908) was known as the Grand Old Man of Golf, having influenced the game for nearly 87 years. He became involved in golf course design and construction, and designed the New Course at St. Andrews. His portrait now hangs in the clubhouse of the R&A.

≪ Broadening appeal
By 1890, when this picture was taken, not only had golf spread far and wide, but the game had become much more organized and the rules were more formalized.

⏫ **Professional job** Modern-day pros, such as Jack Nicklaus, here winning the 1980 US Open, have little in common with early professional golfers, who were often snubbed by clubs.

Much of the course-building and design was based on the principle of quantity rather than quality, and few of the layouts compared favorably with the great British links courses. As the golf writer Peter Dobereiner stated: "The game which had started as an informal knock-about on the sandy turf of a Scottish fishing town 450 years previously was now full-grown and under new management."

Looking back today, it is extraordinary to think that professionals at clubs were regarded as second-class citizens at the beginning of the 20th century, and were not even allowed to enter clubhouses. As recently as 1923, when Walter Hagen finished runner-up to Arthur Havers at Royal Troon, Hagen refused to attend the presentation ceremony in the clubhouse, as a protest against the fact that he and his fellow pros were not allowed into the clubhouse during the championship.

Some professionals began their careers as caddies, just as some, such as Seve Ballesteros, have done in recent times. The word caddie comes from the French *cadet*, which means the son of a nobleman, and many of the early caddies were young boys who carried the bags of gentlemen for a small tip.

Evolution of the swing

Originally, golfers played in their everyday clothes such as tight tweed jackets and ties for the men, and long skirts and hats for the women. Tight jackets restricted the movement of the swing, and with early hickory-shafted clubs, a very full, flat slashing swing seemed necessary. Players gripped clubs in the palms of their hands, with both thumbs gripping the club, a grip that is today known as the "baseball grip."

Jersey's Harry Vardon had a very upright swing, which was copied by many. He also popularized, though did not invent, the Vardon grip, which is when the little finger of the right hand overlaps the first finger of the left for the right-hander, and vice versa for the left-hander. In this way, the hands work together as one unit, giving more consistency to the strike.

Famous golfers have gripped the club in different ways over the years. Jack Nicklaus, who has very small hands, has always used an interlocking grip. Gene Sarazen had his left thumb hanging free

was appropriately called St. Andrews Golf Club. The first properly designed golf course in the US was built by Willie Dunn from Musselburgh at Shinnecock Hills (see pp.242–3) on Long Island, and it has played host to the US Open (see p.194) in recent years. In 1891, Dunn laid out 12 holes there, and later added nine holes for the women. The two courses were amalgamated in time for the first US Open, which was held at Shinnecock Hills in 1896.

Although Reid, Lockhart, and Dunn were among the first Scotsmen to emigrate to the US and spread the gospel of golf, they were certainly not the last. They started a trend that hundreds followed. People from Scotland traveled to the US to teach the game to new recruits; they were hired to build and design new golf courses; and they became clubmakers and greenkeepers. In 1890, Reid's course in New York was the only one in the US. By 1896, this figure had grown to 80, and by 1900 there were an astonishing 982.

outside the shaft. Harry Vardon cupped his left wrist, holding it bent throughout the swing. This method was something that Bobby Jones copied in the 1920s, although he was much more fluid through the ball than Vardon, and made sure his hands were always slightly ahead of the ball.

Byron Nelson developed a swing with a one-piece takeaway—hands, arms, and shoulders moving the club back together—with his left arm rigidly straight. Close to impact, he had a lot of leg action. Nelson's terrific success in the 1940s (he won 11 consecutive tournaments in 1945, and a total of 18 events) meant that many copied his swing.

Ben Hogan wrote one of the first great instruction books, *The Modern Fundamentals of Golf*, in which he highlights the importance of the "swing plane." If you imagine a wheel resting against your shoulders, with the base of the wheel where the ball is, Hogan's theory was that this is the path your clubhead should ideally take.

With the advent of players such as Ernie Els, the swing has changed once again. Whereas previously teachers emphasized the swing, with the ball "getting in the way" of the clubhead, today's youngsters are taught to swing hard directly at the ball.

⌃ **Modern clothing**
Loose-fitting, comfortable clothes that will not impede the swing are the order of the day for today's golfers.

« **Quality equipment**
Amateur players can not only copy and practice the techniques of the top pros, they are also able to use the same equipment as their heroes.

Golf **Equipment**

Investing in the right gear can help you enjoy your game of golf more and improve your performance. There is a huge range of different equipment available depending on your personal preference, and while you don't need the most expensive clubs, bags, or gloves, it is useful to know what is available.

Basic gear

Despite its humble origins in the 15th century, modern golf equipment includes everything from radio-controlled carts and laser-guided putting gadgets to electronic yardage devices, but clubs and balls are still the essential hardware. Golfers are advised to select equipment that suits their individual requirements, but should remember that, for all the marketing claims, there is no substitute for practice.

Golf clubs

Clubs divide broadly into four categories: pear-shaped woods (or "metalwoods") for tee and long shots (a driver is the No. 1 wood); thinner metal irons for approach play; hybrid designs that combine features of both irons and woods for longer fairway play; and putters, for use on and around the green.

For any round of golf, the rules allow you to take a maximum of 14 clubs around the course with you. These are numbered—as a general rule, the lower the number of the club you use, the farther you will hit the ball.

Golfers starting out should consider opting for a half set of clubs, which ought to be more than sufficient for most playing requirements in the early stages of the game. Typically, this would consist of a 1 and 3 wood; 3, 5, 7, and 9 irons;

and a putter. This selection of clubs will usually be enough to provide a broad shot selection to cover most situations.

Golf balls

The basic specifications of golf balls, including size, weight, and initial velocity, are tightly regulated by the United States Golf Association (USGA) and the Royal and Ancient Golf Club (R&A) in the UK, but there is no standard golf ball. For any given swing speed, different constructions, materials, and dimple designs create subtly different levels of spin that affect both distance and control. New players to the game tend to favor harder-covered, lower-spinning balls that go slightly farther and are least susceptible to deviation in flight. Similarly, softer-covered, higher-spinning balls can be used by more experienced players to shape their shots and control the ball more effectively on the greens.

There is no limit to the number of balls with which a player can start a round, but it is against the rules to restock a bag with balls during a game.

Bags and carts

Golf bags and carts have come a long way since the early days when caddies carried bundles of hickory-shafted clubs under their arms. Modern bags range from thin "pencil" styles designed for a half set (of perhaps two woods, four irons, and a putter), through to larger diameter tops with various types of dividers to provide easy access to a full set.

Carts save golfers from carrying a heavy load and have replaced the caddie at most courses. Powered carts, especially, are now transforming the enjoyment of the game for all age groups, with hands-free models controlled by a small remote.

» **Set of irons** A full set of clubs is normally built around a set of nine irons, as shown here, supplemented by three woods and a putter to provide the maximum choice of shot.

Golf clothing

A round of golf typically involves a walk of 4–6 miles (6–10km), so it is vital to wear comfortable shoes that also support your feet during the swing. You should also wear comfortable, reasonably loose-fitting clothing that enables you to swing your club freely. However, all clothing must conform to golf etiquette (*see* p.52), which usually means no jeans, shirts without collars, or untailored shorts. A rain suit is essential, preferably one with a breathable lining, as well as shoes for wet weather, and winter gloves.

« Standard golfing gear Comfort is the watchword with golfing apparel, but the clothes you wear must conform to the rules at most golf clubs. Be prepared for any weather by carrying a golf umbrella, and a cap to shield your eyes from the sun. A glove improves grip.

Drivers

The largest, longest, and most powerful club in the bag, the driver has always been at the forefront of cutting-edge technology. Over the last 15 years, traditional handmade persimmon wood has given way to progressively larger heads made from steel, titanium, and lightweight graphite composites, which help golfers of all abilities to achieve greater distance and more control in their game.

⌃ **Using a driver**
Golfers looking for maximum distance will use their drivers on perhaps 14 tee shots on a typical 18-hole course.

Choosing a driver

The driver is usually the most expensive single club to purchase and should be chosen carefully according to head size, head materials, and loft, as well as the type and flex of the shaft.

Head size and materials

Most golfers benefit from using a driver with an oversize titanium head, and volumes in the 400cc–460cc range (double that of early 1990s designs). This size promotes confidence at address and genuine performance benefits at impact.

Large, thin-walled clubfaces are less resistant to twisting when struck away from the central sweet spot (optimum hitting point) and this results in straighter shots. The deeper and wider body has a lower center of gravity, which helps the ball to get airborne on a higher trajectory to achieve a greater distance.

Driver lofts

The loft (the angle the clubface hits the ball to elevate it) of the driver clubface should vary according to the type of player. Powerful pros and long-driving champions can manage very steep lofts as low as five degrees, but only because their swing speeds of over 120mph (190km/h) generate adequate lift at impact. At the other extreme,

juniors, seniors, and ladies with swing speeds of less than 80mph (130km/h) will only maximize their distance with lofts of at least 15 degrees—which is technically a 3-wood rather than a driver. Loft options typically come in the 9- to 11-degree range, with the majority of handicap golfers—those with swing speeds of around 90mph (145km/h)—advised to opt for at least 10.5 degrees.

≫ **Driver names** The marketing of the traditional No. 1 wood has been transformed by colorful names such as Big Bertha, Powersphere, and Ignite.

Shaft design
Shafts are made from either steel or, increasingly, graphite which is lighter, enabling the driver to be swung faster

Head design
The shaft joins the clubhead at the neck, or hosel

Face design
Because of its steep loft, the driver does not need grooves to grip the ball—although most models have them for appearance

TRAMPOLINE EFFECT

As drivers increased in size in the mid-1990s the ball was being hit farther because the thin faces flexed at impact and rebounded to give the ball a trampoline effect. This has led to formal limits on a driver's coefficient of restitution (COR), which measures the energy transfer from club to ball. Pros must now conform to a maximum COR of 0.83, but amateurs have more leeway.

Driver shafts

Almost all drivers now come with lightweight graphite shafts, which can be swung faster than steel shafts in order to achieve greater distance on drives. Meanwhile, different shaft flex options, such as Regular, Stiff, and Ladies, are designed to complement the force of an individual's swing (*see* p.34). Traditionally 43–4in (109–12cm) in length, driver shafts measuring 45–6in (114–17cm) are now widely used to deliver a bigger, and hence faster, clubhead arc. Although these shafts are longer than those used until recently, they should not generally compromise a comfortable posture. Players of shorter stature may find longer shafts more difficult to use.

Wilson Deep Red Maxx Drivers with very deep faces, like the Wilson Deep Red Maxx, often perform best when striking the ball high in the face—a feature that has led to tee pegs getting progressively longer. This is to allow the player to address the ball with the optimum area of the face.

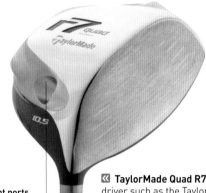

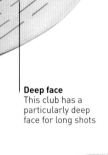

Weight ports
This club features adjustable weight ports for personal customization

Deep face
This club has a particularly deep face for long shots

TaylorMade Quad R7 Using a driver such as the TaylorMade R7 Quad, golfers can experiment with four external weight bolts to customize the club to their preferred shape of shot. The rules of golf stipulate that this cannot be done during a round on a course.

Graphite section
The rear crown of this club features a lightweight graphite section

Wilson Pro Staff Peaking at 300cc in volume, steel drivers are some 25 percent smaller than titanium models. But some players prefer the discipline and aesthetics of a more compact head, such as the one on this Wilson Pro Staff.

Callaway ERC Fusion In the quest for ever lighter and stronger materials, golf scientists have turned to graphite, which is some 30 percent lighter than titanium. The Callaway ERC Fusion started a trend by combining both materials into one head design.

Trying a driver

Golfers should always try out clubs thoroughly before buying them, and many manufacturers now offer demonstration days. Contact the club professional at your local course for more information.

The pro will be able to advise on the type of shaft that best suits a player and also point out specific features, such as the angle of the face.

Most handicap golfers slice their drives and are advised to opt for a face that is "closed" by one or two degrees. Again, a club professional can offer help on such technical details.

Similarly, because of the variety of weighting configurations in today's drivers, the optimum hitting point—the sweet spot—is not always directly in the middle of the face. On deep-faced drivers, the sweet spot might be higher.

Titanium
This titanium face flexes into the graphite crown for more power

Sweet spot
This is extra wide to give a greater hitting area

◀◀ **Yonex Cyberstar Powerbrid** The sound a driver makes at impact is described as "feel" and all players experience it differently. The titanium and graphite Yonex Cyberstar Powerbrid was designed after polling hundreds of Japanese golfers for their preferences.

◀◀ **Nike Ignite** Developed for Tiger Woods using a strong titanium derivative, the Nike Ignite has a face that extends in one large section around the crown of the head to effectively widen the central sweet spot.

Short hosel
This device allows weight to be repositioned elsewhere in the head

Diamond
This club features a tough diamond face insert

◀◀ **Callaway Big Bertha** With both the earliest steel Big Bertha and the later titanium Great Big Bertha, Callaway pioneered the use of the short hosel (where the shaft fits into the clubhead). The weight saved could then be redirected to the sole, to lower the center of gravity of the club for greater height on the drive.

◀◀ **Diamond Touch DR4E** When searching for a driver with their preferred feel and feedback, golfers can experiment with face inserts that range from soft-feeling plastic to 12-carat industrial diamond, which is one of the world's hardest materials.

Driver distance

The result of any golf shot depends on three factors: the speed at which the ball leaves the clubhead, the launch angle of the ball, and the rate of spin on the ball. The relationship between these three variables is such that two golfers of the same handicap can generate very different distances, depending on their individual styles of swing. As a rough guide, average golfers with a 90mph (145km/h) swing manage around 210 yards (190m)—not the 250 yards (230m) some claim. The average tour pro with a 110mph (175km/h) swing hits the ball some 285 yards (260m)—around 30 yards (27m) farther than in 1968. This is due to a combination of modern ball and club technology, as well as improved player fitness and better course conditioning.

Dome
The dome of this clubhead deflects the shock of impact

» Mac Powersphere The need to transfer the maximum possible energy from head to ball has led to some elaborate designs. Mac's dome-shaped cavity is designed to reflect the shock waves at impact back to the face for a more efficient contact with the ball, while reducing the damaging vibrations that travel back up the shaft to the player's hands and arms.

Face
The clubhead transfers the additional energy to the ball at impact

V-FOIL technology
The low center of gravity with the V-FOIL technology produces a more accurate and higher launch drive

400cc
This figure specifies the volume of the clubhead

Offset face
The offset face is designed to help golfers who slice their shots

« MacGregor Eye-O-Matic
MacGregor's titanium driver features alignment markings named after the distinctive Eye-O-Matic plastic insert formerly found on their famous persimmon woods. Meanwhile, genuine wooden drivers are now the domain of a few specialized clubmakers.

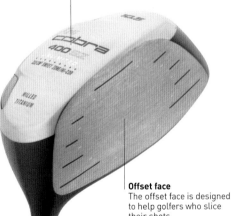

« King Cobra Reflecting the demand for subtly different clubhead options, the Cobra SZ drivers come in several sizes, including 400cc and 440cc. The 400SZ model (pictured) has a face slightly set back (or offset) from the line of the shaft to help players who tend to slice.

Irons

Whether you are a pro or a beginner, irons represent the largest and most important element of a golfer's equipment and should be chosen very carefully. Buying decisions should include the choice between blades and cavity backs, cast or forged materials, and various wedge options.

⏶ **Using an iron** US prodigy Michelle Wie demonstrates the downward blow required for irons to generate backspin, resulting in the ideal ball flight and control.

The numbering system

Irons usually come in sets of nine, with seven clubs numbered from 3 to 9, plus a pitching wedge (PW) and a sand wedge (SW). Moving up through the numbers, the shaft becomes progressively shorter, and the face more lofted (less steep), to match the length of approach shot to the green. Additional clubs can be chosen according to an individual player's priority, but other clubs will have to be sacrificed to keep to the 14-club maximum. The 1 and 2 irons are mainly favored by more experienced players as an alternative to fairway woods, while the less commonly used gap (GW) and lob (LW) wedges increase the options around the green.

Iron lofts

Most sets of irons feature lofts (the degree of angle of a club face) that increase in mainly 3- to 4-degree increments, reducing the distance by about 10 yards (9m), though this relationship varies with the low numbers and the wedges.

When choosing a set of irons, golfers should note that there is no standard that dictates the precise angle for each iron between manufacturers. Indeed, iron lofts have tended to be a few degrees lower (steeper) in recent years to offset the trend in heavy sole weighting, which itself promotes a higher ball flight.

❱❱ **Iron** Heads are either cast or hand-forged. Irons feature thin, grooved faces of varying lofts. Designs range from "muscleback" blades (which subtly concentrate some weight directly behind the hitting area), through to those with very deep cavity backs.

Shaft design
Most players (especially professionals) claim that steel shafts keep the head more stable than graphite shafts when striking the ground through impact

Face design
Grooves act like the tires on a car, letting water and debris escape, and allowing enough spin to be imparted on the ball for lift and control

---

DISTANCE GUIDES—IRONS

Here is a rough guide to how an average player might select their irons in a typical set according to the length of approach shot to the green.

Iron number	Distance	Loft
1	200 yards	16°
2	190 yards	18°
3	180 yards	22°
4	170 yards	23°
5	160 yards	26°
6	150 yards	30°
7	140 yards	34°
8	130 yards	38°
9	120 yards	42°
PW	110 yards	46°
SW	90 yards	56°

Blade irons

The weight distribution in the clubhead must complement a player's individual skill level and style of swing. There are two basic head design concepts, starting with the traditional blade. This is distinguished by a smooth rear, where weight is evenly spread behind the face of the club or slightly concentrated behind the hitting area in a "muscleback" design. Blades are favored by players who can shape their ball flight. They do this by exploiting the weight characteristics that make this type of club more sensitive to sidespin.

Cavity back irons

In contrast to the blade, the cavity back iron has weight concentrated at the edges of the club—the heel, the toe, and, especially, the sole. As with perimeter-weighted drivers, cavity back irons are most appreciated by beginners, as the sole weighting helps the ball become airborne, while

---

PROGRESSIVE WEIGHTING

Rather than forcing golfers to choose between cavity backs or blades, some manufacturers offer both concepts within a single set. These invariably emphasize a forgiving, deep cavity in the harder-to-hit long irons (low numbers) before moving to more traditional bladed irons at the short end where the margin of error is less. There are many variations on this concept, including the Three-In-One sets like the Nike Pro Forged Combo (shown below).

---

the heel-and-toe bias makes the club more stable, delivering less unwanted sidespin. Missing the sweet spot on a blade by ¼in (0.6cm) reduces hitting distance by some 9 percent—almost 17 yards (16m) on a 180 yard (165m) shot—with this margin reduced by judicious weighting.

» Nike Pro Forged Combo mid-iron
The need for "game improvement" features diminishes as clubs get less lofted. The 5, 6, and 7 irons have more weight directly behind the ball, while a shallow cavity still provides some helpful perimeter weighting.

Blade weighting
Simple blade weighting for the wedge replaces cavity features of the long- and mid-irons

» Nike Pro Forged Combo long-iron The set features a pronounced cavity back design only in the 2, 3, and 4 irons where lofts are steeper, shafts are longer, and the required sweeping type of golf swing all contribute to a wide margin for error.

» Nike Pro Forged Combo pitching wedge All clubs from the 8-iron through to the sand wedge in the same set are designed as pure blades, encouraging even average golfers to develop their shot-making creativity. All golfers generate more backspin as lofts get flatter and shafts get shorter, making the ball easier to control and perimeter weighting far less important.

Cast or forged irons?

Traditionally, irons are hand-forged from steel ingots, resulting in dense clubheads. Some golfers insist that these both strike the ball more consistently and provide superior feedback in terms of impact sound and vibrations up the shaft. However, tests suggest that most players cannot distinguish them from mass-produced cast clubs made from molten steel shaped in wax molds. With the more expensive forgings normally associated with blade designs and castings with cavity backs, the debate is more about the performance of the different weighting methods than the actual materials used. Meanwhile, manufacturing techniques have recently improved to allow the development of forged cavity backs. These enable the modern golfer to experiment with all the various design permutations available.

» Mizuno MP-37 3 iron Bladed long irons are favored by more experienced players precisely because their unbiased weighting makes the club more sensitive to off-center hits. This allows sidespin to be more easily imparted in order to shape ball flight with fades and draws.

» Mizuno MP-37 wedge With traditional blades, every club in this set features the same unbiased weighting philosophy that appeals to precise shot-makers. Despite the rise in cavity backs, all but a handful of golf's Major championships have been won with blades.

» Nike Slingshot 4 iron In a novel variation on progressive weighting, the Slingshot irons feature a rear weight bar whose position varies with each club to deliver the most efficient center of gravity.

» Nike Slingshot sand wedge The weight bar in the rear cavity gradually rises throughout the Nike set, culminating in the more neutrally weighted sand wedge.

Offset heads

A common fault of the average player is failure to keep the hands ahead of the ball at impact to deliver a sufficiently descending blow. This affects the flight of the ball and nearly always results in a shorter shot than intended. One remedy for this problem is offset irons, in which the leading edge of the blade is set slightly back from the vertical line of the shaft. This feature can also help players who slice the ball, because of the physics of the offset head design, which helps the toe of the face close slightly at impact. Most cavity backs come with progressive offset, starting at around ¼in (5mm) in the long irons where it is most needed, and reducing to a more subtle ¹⁄₁₆in (1mm) in the short irons where shot-making is easier.

THE SAND WEDGE

The sand wedge is distinctive for its bulbous sole that drops below the level of the leading edge of the clubface. This bounce greatly helps when escaping from bunkers as it helps the blade glide through the sand—rather than digging in. Pioneered by Gene Sarazen in 1932, the amount of bounce can be chosen according to a player's requirements. Less proficient golfers, or those tackling fine sand in seaside bunkers, should ask for at least a 10-degree bounce angle.

Nick Faldo preferred very little bounce on his sand wedge, making bunker play more challenging, but the same club is more playable from tight fairway lines.

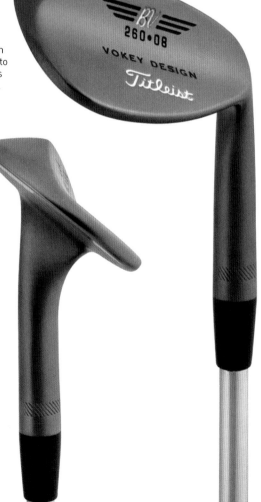

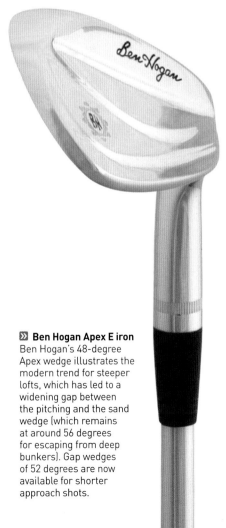

» Vokey 60-degree wedge
Highly lofted lob wedges are gradually being used more for delicate approach shots that need to stop quickly, such as over greenside bunkers or to plateau greens where there is very little green to work with.

Bulbous sole
The wide, fat sole helps the clubhead glide through the sand

» Vokey 56-degree wedge
High-lofted wedges with shiny chrome finishes can cause distracting reflective glare for the player. Hence the trend in exotic finishes such as beryllium copper, black, "oil can," and "rust." Meanwhile, because of the 14-club limit, modern multiwedge systems require other clubs in the bag, of the player's choosing, to be sacrificed.

» Ben Hogan Apex E iron
Ben Hogan's 48-degree Apex wedge illustrates the modern trend for steeper lofts, which has led to a widening gap between the pitching and the sand wedge (which remains at around 56 degrees for escaping from deep bunkers). Gap wedges of 52 degrees are now available for shorter approach shots.

Putters

The pros' old adage that "you drive for show, but putt for dough" reflects the fact that the putter is arguably one of the most important—and certainly the most used—golf clubs. Even average golfers can usually match the 36 putts per round expected on an 18-hole course, while only top pros regularly take less than 30.

⌃ Using a putter Most top golfers recommend a pendulum action from the shoulders, with no breaking (forward or backward action) of the wrists that is so often responsible for inconsistent putting.

Choosing a putter

Despite the plethora of modern designs, putters should be chosen according to their weighting, alignment features, and feel, as described opposite.

Weighting

Putters divide broadly into three basic categories: blade, heel-and-toe, and mallet. As with irons (see pp.24–9), some argue that blade putters (where weight is again equally distributed behind the face) encourage a more grooved, repeatable stroke, as the face is more prone to twisting if not hit right in the center. Heel-and-toe weighting, as the term suggests, counters this common problem by moving weight to the edges of the face for an effectively larger sweet spot (see p.22). Mallets have deeper bodies that bring weight back from the face to encourage a flowing, accelerating stroke, while also offering the most scope for alignment features.

Alignment features

Arguably the most important factor is alignment, as nothing else matters if you do not aim in the right direction. Scientists estimate that just a one-degree misalignment on a 6ft (1.8m) putt leads to a 1in (2.5cm) error from the center of cup. To help golfers square up, putters feature everything from simple notches and colorful stripes to perpendicular sight lines and golf-ball-sized spheres on the top of the clubhead.

THE MYTH OF THE "FLAT STICK"

Contrary to popular belief, putter-faces are not vertical and typically sport 3 to 5 degrees of loft. This is needed to help the ball out of small depressions on the green and to get it rolling with the necessary topspin to keep its line as quickly as possible after impact. As a general guide, the more bumpy the greens, the greater the loft recommended. Often overlooked is how matching the loft to an individual's stroke can improve performance. For example, Colin Montgomerie has experimented with 8 degrees of putter loft to compensate for his hand action, which effectively de-lofts the face when his putter-face strikes the ball.

» Putter The rules allow only putters to have grips with flat sides, as opposed to cylindrical ones like those of other clubs. Some golfers find this feature helps them place their hands consistently, and assists them in swinging square to the target line.

Shaft length
The standard length is 34–36in (86–91cm). Longer "broom handle" and "belly" putters will become obsolete after 2016 because it will be illegal for the player to anchor the top of the putter in the midriff or under the chin

Head design
Most models are variations on the themes of simple blade, deeper-bodied mallet, or heel-and-toe where weight is concentrated at these points. Steel, copper, and aluminum are among the most popular materials

Face design
Faces often feature a central insert of a different material, usually for a soft feel at impact

>> **Ping Anser** The Ping brand revolutionized golf by introducing heel-and-toe weighting in the 1960s. Models like the Anser, the A-Blade, and My Day won dozens of Major championships in the hands of players such as Tom Watson, Seve Ballesteros, and José Maria Olazabal. The basic concept, which balances the weight of the head, can help beginners and average players.

Heel-and-toe
This weighting concept reduces twisting of the putter's face

Bent shaft
The shaft bend should suit the player's lie angle

Mallet head
Weight set back from the face encourages a smooth stroke

>> **Ram Zebra** Mallet putters are larger and traditionally heavier, which can help when putting on slow greens. Some versions of the Zebra feature sole weights which can be adjusted according to the speed of the greens.

The feelgood factor

As with all clubs, personal choice is vital when buying a putter, and golfers should choose one whose shape, size, and feel instills confidence. Jack Nicklaus won the 1986 Masters with a huge-headed MacGregor Response putter, while Paul Azinger used Natural Golf's The Thing, with a face barely the size of a coin, to win the 1992 PGA Tour Championship.

Feel in putting is largely manifested as sound, with some golfers preferring the duller tones of a softer head material, such as copper, aluminum, or a synthetic insert—rather than the sharp click of steel. The combination of putter-face and golf ball is crucial. Harder two-piece balls will create a much brighter sound.

Meanwhile, top putter designers such as Titleist's Scotty Cameron suggest that weaker flex shafts can improve the feel of a putter. Unlike other clubs, putters are not normally available in other flex options, but players can test out different types, which are easily fitted by their local club pro.

>> **Titleist blade** Sleek blade putters may be the antithesis of some modern elaborate designs, but they have been favored down the years by such putting giants as Bobby Jones, Jack Nicklaus, Ben Crenshaw, and Phil Mickelson.

PROTECTING YOUR PUTTER

The putter is the most delicate club in the bag, along with the driver, whose large head and graphite shaft also need special protection. The trend is toward precision-milled putter-faces engineered to the smallest measurement, as well as soft-feeling, often expensive, inserts. So it is advisable to use a putter headcover to prevent the club from being damaged as it is replaced in the bag after using it for putting.

Pitch fork
This tool is essential for repairing pitch marks

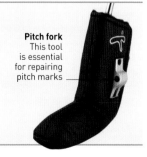

☑ **Rossa Monza** This insert mallet uses its deep body to house an elaborate alignment aid. A pair of bright red, synthetic titallium pipes are set either side of an extended white sight line, perpendicular to the face. They encourage the correct square stance at address.

Offset hosel
This type of hosel helps to encourage a more effective stroke

Face insert
This provides a soft feel on contact with the ball

⌃ **Mizuno Tourstyle T301** This heel-and-toe weighted Mizuno club illustrates how some putters have a kink in the hosel where the shaft joins the head. This offset feature encourages the hands to be ahead of the ball at the point of impact, and helps develop the correct upward stroking motion to give topspin.

⏵⏵ **Odyssey White Hot Two-Ball** Modern high-tech designs are increasingly blurring the distinction between the traditional categories of putterhead. While this Odyssey Two-Ball has the deep body of a mallet, most of the weight is concentrated directly behind the hitting area for an extra-solid feel on central hits.

Insert revolution

Distinctive inserts in the optimum hitting area have multiplied over the past decade, with a wide variety of both natural and synthetic materials, each offering a slightly different sound and feel at impact. Since Nick Faldo won the 1996 Masters with a plastic insert and, the following year, Tiger Woods won with an intricate alloy of 12 different metals, the putter market has been transformed. Most famous are Odyssey's black and white thermoplastic inserts, which many players find softer than traditional steel. The inserts help them to be less tentative with their strokes—especially on fast greens. Some players claim that soft faces allow beneficial topspin to be worked into the stroke.

Meanwhile, in the elusive quest for perfect feel, face inserts now come in ever more exotic materials, including gold plate, platinum, tungsten, nickel, copper, and aluminium—some manufacturers even use 12-carat industrial diamonds.

ALIGNMENT MARKINGS

Traditionally, putters have featured lines, dots, arrows, and triangles to help golfers align the face toward the hole. More recently, the phenomenally successful Odyssey Two-Ball uses the philosophy that, being a round object, the golf ball is easier to line up with other circles.

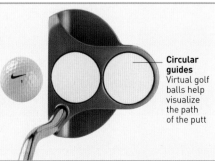

Circular guides
Virtual golf balls help visualize the path of the putt

Ben Hogan Big Ben The Big Ben, designed by putter designer Bob Bettinardi for the Ben Hogan company, is another intricate modern mallet. The large hourglass shape is useful for alignment, while the aluminum body—drilled with holes into a honeycomb structure—ingeniously keeps down the overall weight.

T-shapes
Lining up with the T-shaped graphic on the head encourages square alignment

Hollows
These sections allow the weight to be distributed to the edges of the head

Head holes
Honeycomb holes keep down the weight in the large body

Shaft position

While choosing a putter involves many subjective decisions, the position of the shaft on the head should ideally be chosen to suit a player's style of stroke.

Shafts and hosels set near to the heel are good for players with open-to-closed strokes (taking the putter inside on the backswing). Conversely, those with a more robotic, straight-back-and-through action often prefer center-shafted models geared to a simpler swing path. Finally, carefully engineered face-balanced putters may not have a center shaft, but perform as if they do. To assess face-balancing in a putter, hold the base of the shaft across the palm of the hand while the face points horizontally toward the sky.

MacGregor MK5 MOI The MOI name refers to the high Moment Of Inertia—the technical term for the low resistance to twisting that the face enjoys courtesy of the central holes that concentrate weight at the edges.

Gooseneck
The extreme bend in the shaft allows it to join the center of the body to maximize clubhead stability

TOPSPIN SYSTEMS

Designers use various methods to reduce skidding in the early stages of a putt, and get the ball rolling with beneficial topspin.

Steel horseshoe
This back weight device contains 75 percent of the putter's weight to encourage a smooth, true roll, producing putts that—in theory—roll directly on the intended line

Titleist Futura Scotty Cameron, Titleist's putter designer, rewrote the rules of putterhead design with the Futura by combining the seemingly contradictory elements of blade (thin face), mallet (deep body), and heel-and-toe weighting (heavy tungsten plugs) into one space-age package. Again, circles form the primary alignment aid, while the eye-catching, curved rear section dramatically lowers the center of gravity (see left).

Fairway woods and utilities

With their range of generous lofts, fairway woods are widely favored over the hard-to-hit long irons, while utility clubs such as rescues and hybrids offer great versatility for all players.

Choosing fairway woods

The most common strategy when choosing a wood is to supplement the driver (the No. 1 wood) with two traditional fairway woods—usually the 3 and 5. With lofts of 15 and 21 degrees, respectively, the 3 and 5 should be regarded as equivalent to the 1-iron and 3-iron in terms of the overall distances they will hit. However, by virtue of their greater carry and less roll, woods are ideal for long shots over hazards and approaches to heavily bunkered greens.

The image of the humble 5-wood was transformed at the 1976 Masters, when Ray Floyd played Augusta National's par-5s in a record 14-under-par.

⌃ **Using a fairway wood** Suzann Pettersen demonstrates how professionals as well as amateurs can benefit from high-flying wood designs.

A range of woods

With most golfers finding woods slightly easier to hit than irons, manufacturers began to offer them in steadily higher loft options. Some fairway wood ranges take in 7, 9, 11, and even 13-woods, which broadly offer high-flying alternatives to the 4, 5, 6, and 7-irons. Indeed, many sets of irons now start at the 4, 5, or even 6-iron, in order to encourage the replacement of hard-to-hit long irons with the corresponding fairway woods. They are mainly directed at amateurs, but Lee Trevino (7-wood) and Vijay Singh (9-wood) are among the top pros who have successfully exploited high-lofted woods in their careers.

While some sets of golf clubs consist entirely of woods, even players who have difficulty with irons will benefit from the greater control of higher-spinning iron shots on at least the shorter approach shots.

FAIRWAY WOODS OR LONG IRONS

Most golfers find fairway woods inherently easier to hit than long irons, partly because the sweeping type of swing required with wide-soled woods is less exacting than the downward blow associated with irons. Moreover, in the thin head of an iron, clubmakers cannot place the center of gravity much more than 1in (2.5cm) back from the face. With fairway woods, they can double that, delivering a higher launch angle which gets the ball up quicker— a great benefit for slow swingers.

While lightweight titanium dominates the oversize driver market, smaller-headed fairway woods are still made mainly of steel. This is because a more compact head provides less friction with the ground, while the golf ball is more effectively aligned with the sweet spot (see p.22) of a shallower face.

» **Fairway wood** With the term drivers referring to woods with lofts of up to some 12 degrees, fairway woods follow on sequentially, with the most popular lofts of 13, 15, 17, 19, and 21 degrees each delivering progressively shorter distances.

Shaft design
As with irons, fairway wood shafts get shorter as lofts increase— though some hybrids fit slightly longer shafts in certain heads for a little extra distance

Head design
Reduces in size as loft increases (a 9-wood is smaller than a 3-wood)

Face design
Shallow faces are best from tight, bare lies; deeper faces allow more potential for tee shots

Utilities

These clubs cover a wide category, and all have unconventional specifications, especially designed for greater versatility than that provided for in a traditional set. They also have special features for certain recovery situations.

Rescue clubs can be traced back to the 18th century, when rutting irons were used to get out of rabbit holes and wagon tracks on early golf courses. In modern times, landmark designs like the Cobra Baffler and the metal TaylorMade Raylor pioneered small, shallow-headed woods that are ideal for playing from the rough. Many have aerodynamic soles, or thin rails, that reduce the turf drag that a wider sole can suffer at impact.

Very similar to rescue clubs are hybrids, which, as the name suggests, are the result of combining various design concepts to create user-friendly alternatives to the traditional fairway wood. The term usually refers to a combination of a metalwood and an iron. Intriguing variations on the hybrid theme involve mixing and matching head size, loft, and shaft length. A number of manufacturers now offer such combinations.

Bore-thru shaft
This feature provides extra head stability

Titleist fairway wood The Pro Trajectory 980 fairway metals adopt the classic pear-shaped heads found on traditional wooden clubs. However, the modern internal weighting system is configured for a low center of gravity, promoting a higher, and more efficient, ball flight.

Shallow face
This makes the club ideal for playing from tight, bare lies

Big Bertha 13-wood The extreme loft of the Big Bertha 13-wood is a practical alternative to irons on short approach shots. Callaway transformed the market for fairway woods and hybrids in the 1990s with clubs such as the Heavenwood and Divine 9.

Wide sole
This feature and 21-degree loft make this club very user-friendly

Mizuno Fli-Hi 21 degree While most hybrids are more wood than iron, some reverse the emphasis, for example, the Mizuno Fli-Hi. Sometimes called driving irons, the design of these clubs allows shot-makers to work the ball, but with a higher flight than that offered by a conventional iron of the same loft.

Sonartec MD The versatility of the hybrid was illustrated by Todd Hamilton during the 2004 Open. He used his 17-degree Sonartec MD for several tee shots and long fairway approaches, as well as the final deft pitch-and-run that set up the winning putt.

Shafts and grips

The shaft is often called the engine of the golf club, because it harnesses the energy set up in the swing and releases it at impact. Almost all clubs come in various shaft options, allowing players to choose the flex, weight, and material that suits their particular swing.

The role of the shaft

The shaft should ideally deliver the clubhead to the ball at the greatest possible speed—even if, in almost all cases, even in the professional game, the club is actually slowing down at impact.

The best shafts have a flex that keeps deceleration to a minimum to avoid losing energy and distance in the shot. Accurate shaft fitting is a complex task, but a basic understanding of a player's style of swing will greatly help when experimenting with different shafts.

Flex fitting

The flex is normally available in five different categories of increasing stiffness: Ladies (L), Amateur (A), Regular (R), Stiff (S), and Extra Stiff (X). The simplest guideline is to choose a flex according to swing speed, with the ratings broadly applicable to golfers with 70–110mph (110–175km/h) swings in 10mph (16km/h) increments. Most golf stores have simple radar gadgets for estimating swing speed.

While swing speed is a useful guide, it does not always take into account the stress, or load, put on a shaft that the choice of flex should complement. For example, a golfer with a quickly accelerating hand action may bend the shaft more, and therefore require a stiffer shaft, than a player achieving the

VIBRATION DAMPENING

Shaft companies constantly look for ways to reduce the shock waves transmitted to the hands and arms at impact. Graphite shafts tend to dampen vibration better than standard steel, though True Temper's ingenious internal "plug" in their Sensicore range absorbs two-thirds of the vibrations of regular steel.

Coiled plug
This internal device reduces unwanted frequencies

same speed with a smoother swing. As an example, the ultra-powerful John Daly won the 1991 USPGA Championship playing with regular flex shafts.

Some elaborate systems can measure a player's load profile, though simply comparing the same club in a few different flexes with the help of a golf pro is the most practical solution.

As a rough guide: low, weak shots pushed or sliced (to the right) suggest that the shaft flex is too firm; high, quick pulls or hooks (to the left) are often a symptom of flex that is too weak.

» **Flexing shaft**
Padraig Harrington demonstrates how the shaft bows away from the toe of the club at the top of the backswing. At impact, this characteristic is reversed.

» **Steel and graphite shafts** Steel shafts for irons weigh 3½–4oz (100–120g); graphite shafts for woods are lighter at around 3½–5oz (100–150g).

Steel shaft

Graphite shaft

Steel or graphite?

Due to the consistently high quality of their manufacturing, steel shafts have dominated the golf market since their introduction in the late 1920s. However, graphite has caught up in the last two decades and is now used almost universally for drivers, where its light weight can be translated into extra distance.

More experienced players tend to prefer steel shafts in irons, claiming they keep the clubhead more stable when contacting the ground on impact, thus improving accuracy and distance control. But the gap is narrowing, and graphite-shafted irons are popular with beginners, who most benefit from the slight distance advantage.

Grips

For hundreds of years, all golf grips were made of genuine leather. In the 1950s, they were widely replaced by more durable, lighter,

WORN GRIPS

Grips are sensitive to the elements and also the heat in the trunk of a car, which makes them deteriorate with age. Unbuffed rubber can be simply wiped clean and dry, while buffed and cord need scrubbing with an abrasive pad and detergent. As a guide, golfers playing 35 times a year should clean their grips every six weeks and fit new grips every year. Worn grips compromise a player's performance.

and cheaper slip-on grips made from molded rubber. Today, golfers can experiment with a variety of designs and materials, all offering slightly different textures, comfort, and sensitivity (*see* below).

The cheap plastic grips found on some beginners' clubs are a false economy; they are prone to slipping and create tension in the hands and arms when the player is gripping too tightly. If you are just starting to play golf and are trying to decide which clubs to buy, it is a much better idea to spend a little more on some decent grips.

While real leather grips are now almost extinct because of their high cost and difficult maintenance, a few models such as Golf Pride's GL grip are still favored by a small band of golf purists.

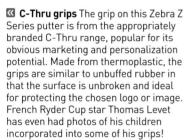

《 C-Thru grips The grip on this Zebra Z Series putter is from the appropriately branded C-Thru range, popular for its obvious marketing and personalization potential. Made from thermoplastic, the grips are similar to unbuffed rubber in that the surface is unbroken and ideal for protecting the chosen logo or image. French Ryder Cup star Thomas Levet has even had photos of his children incorporated into some of his grips!

《 Buffed rubber grips By far the most common grip, and popular among pros as well as amateurs, is a mixture of rubber and synthetics that are buffed with an abrasive substance to roughen the surface. Buffed grips improve their performance over the course of a round of golf by absorbing perspiration to give a more secure feel.

《 Unbuffed rubber grips Whereas buffing leads to a slightly porous surface, the smooth, unbuffed version does not absorb water. This makes it very easy to dry, but can be slippery for those with sweaty hands. These grips can be slightly more expensive than the conventional rubber types and are usually found on premium clubs.

《 Cord grips This type of grip combines rubber with rough, twisted lines of cotton, making for a particularly secure contact that is especially favored by more experienced players. However, the higher price reflects the more intricate process of construction.

Golf balls

While there are tight rules regulating the specifications of golf balls, the market is flooded with models that perform differently according to their construction, cover material, and dimple design. The amount of spin generated by a player's swing is crucial when choosing a ball.

Ball regulations

In order to conform to competition rules, every model of golf ball must pass various stringent tests: it must not be less than 1.68in (4.26cm) in diameter or more than 1.68oz (47.62g) in weight.

The Initial Velocity and Overall Distance tests stipulate that the ball cannot leave the clubface at more than 255ft/sec (78m/sec), or travel more than 320 yards (293m) under the USGA's and R&A's specific test conditions.

Ball construction

Despite the rules, there is plenty of scope for differences in the distance that a ball will travel, and the way it spins and how it feels. These factors of spin and feel should be influential in a player's choice of golf ball. Durability and price will also be a major factor in the decision.

The basic dilemma is that less spin means more distance, but more spin facilitates control around the green. Most importantly, the ball should complement the spin (both backspin and sidespin) that a golfer naturally imparts in their swing. The swing style is a function of the player's speed, hand action, and angle of attack.

Golfers who generate a lot of destructive sidespin—the cause of hooks and slices—should favor a low-spinning, two-piece construction that combines a large, rubberized core with an outer cover made from a hard, durable synthetic material,

Dimpled surface
While many balls share the same basic construction, their varying performance is largely due to differences in their dimpled surfaces, which are essential to lift. Different numbers, shapes, and patterns subtly affect a ball's trajectory and flight—though results vary according to a player's particular swing.

Titleist Pro V1 As well as the standard ball (above), a Pro V1x version is aimed at golfers who generate high ball speeds, spin rates, and launch angles.

Ben Hogan Apex tour This four-piece, multilayer ball comes in both a high-spin, high-feel version (red); and a lower-spinning distance model (black).

Srixon AD333 This modern, two-piece construction is geared for maximum distance, with a Rabalon elastomer cover that is both durable and soft to the touch.

Nike One As played by Tiger Woods, this multilayer solid-core ball has three covers designed for distance, control, and feel.

Durable cover   Large core

《 Two-piece ball cutaway Two-piece balls are defined by a large core for distance, surrounded by a cover usually made from a highly durable synthetic that is resistant to scuffing.

Small core   Midlayers   Thin cover

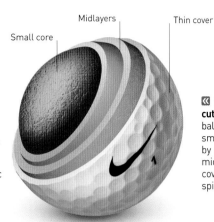

《 Multilayer ball cutaway Multilayer balls feature a much smaller core, surrounded by usually two or three midlayers, and a thinner cover within a higher-spinning construction.

usually Surlyn. While typically marketed as distance balls, the accuracy of two-piece models is usually more valuable than the extra distance.

More experienced players can exploit the higher-spinning properties of multilayer balls. The greater number of layers and the softer cover create more spin, allowing players to deliberately shape shots, and to achieve more control around the greens, especially in dry conditions. The rules allow amateurs—though not pros—to switch between different ball constructions during a round. However, they cannot do this to exploit their performance differences during a hole.

⌃ **On the tee** One of the few generous concessions in the rules of golf allows the golf ball to be replaced on the tee peg if it is accidentally knocked off at address.

TYPES OF TEE

Dating from early in the 20th century, golf's most essential accessory makes tee shots more inviting. Tee peg materials range from plastic and conventional wood to environmentally friendly, biodegradable models, while tee lengths have increased in line with clubheads.

Plastic tee
Many golfers prefer to use plastic tees because they are more durable; wooden tees are prone to snapping. However, drawbacks include a tendency to bend that can compromise their stability.

Graduated tees
Available in either wood or plastic, graduated tees are very useful for teeing the ball up to a consistent, predetermined height. The precise height should suit the sweet spot of the club and the style of swing.

Brush tee
Golfers concerned with the potential scuffing that conventional tee pegs can make on the soles and faces of clubs can opt for an elaborate design where the ball sits on thin columns of soft brushes.

Rubber pyramid tee
Inserting a conventional tee peg into hard or frozen ground at certain times of the year can be almost impossible. This rubber, inverted-cone design that sits directly on the ground is an ingenious solution.

Custom fitting

To play to their full potential, golfers should have their clubs tailored to fit their individual swings rather than buying directly off the shelf. Lie angle, grip thickness, and various shaft features can all affect performance. Today's high-tech launch monitors are transforming custom fitting.

Lie angle

The lie angle is the angle of the shaft relative to the horizontal sole of the iron or putter. Correct fitting ensures that the player returns the clubface parallel to the ground at impact, rather than making contact with the toe (lie too flat) or the heel (club too upright), which often account for slices and hooks, respectively.

Players who carry their hands low at address, or have flatter swing planes, usually need clubs with flatter lies. Players who have upright swings often need more upright lies.

A pro can quickly check this by asking the player to make a few swings and checking the marks on a strip of masking tape applied to the sole of the club.

CLUB-FITTING SYSTEMS

In practice, custom fitting requires a golfer, with the help of a pro, to experiment on the practice ground with a variety of permutations of heads, shafts, and grips to arrive at the best combination for that particular player. Given the large number of demonstration clubs needed to make useful comparisons, some companies have devised novel methods to speed up the process. The Mac Quick-Fit System by Burrows Golf uses a smart-lock connection that allows the custom fitter to mix and match any of the Mac driver's 18 different clubheads and 30 shaft options in just a few seconds. This makes the entire process of finding the best combinations much quicker and easier.

Quick-fit
The smart lock temporarily joins the head and shaft without glue

▼ **Color-coded lies**
Ping was the first brand to offer irons with different lie angles. Their color-coded dots in the rear of their cavity-back irons refer to varying degrees of lie angle either side of "standard."

Coding
Black dot refers to the standard lie angle

Grip thickness

The thickness of the grip can have a dramatic impact on a player's accuracy, and grips should be chosen according to the size of hand and length of fingers. Grips that are too thick will prevent the wrists from closing (turning over) through impact, thereby pushing shots to the right of the target. If a grip is too thin, the wrists will close too much, pulling the ball to the left of the target.

Shaft length

Clubs are normally already fitted with standard-length shafts, but custom fitters estimate that three out of four golfers need a longer or shorter fit, whether just ¼in (50mm), or 1in (2.5cm) or more.

Quite separate to the belief that a longer driver generates more clubhead speed and hence more distance, golfers actually need shaft lengths to match their posture. Tall golfers generally need longer shafts, but this is only a rough guide. An experienced fitter will take both arm length and swing plane into account.

Shaft kick point

As well as flex (*see* p.34), custom fitting gives golfers the chance to compare shafts with different kick points—the point of maximum bend that influences the trajectory of a shot. Golfers needing a higher ball flight will prefer a low kick point, because it increases the effective loft of any given club, and vice versa.

Weight and swingweight

In theory, golfers should have the heaviest clubhead that they can manage (because more mass behind the ball means more distance), providing that it does not slow down their swing speed. As well as advising on absolute weight, custom fitters will also consider swingweight— the way weight is distributed between grip, shaft, and head. This affects how the club feels.

Launch conditions

Computer-based launch monitors that capture a detailed snapshot of a player's swing are transforming both clubfitting and instruction, with their high-speed cameras confirming the

MONITORING YOUR GAME

Custom fitting should not be a one-time event, as a golfer's equipment requirements will change as his game develops. Many young players will need to switch to longer shafts and firmer flexes as they move into their prime, while seniors often change to graphite-shafted irons, flatter lies, and lighter heads as they become older. Meanwhile, tour pros take advantage of the various mobile workshops present at tournaments to tinker with their lofts, lies, grips, and shafts on a weekly—and sometimes daily—basis.

Two-time US Open champion Retief Goosen is a perfectionist with his equipment—sometimes adjusting lofts between rounds, according to the wind.

---

saying that "your swing is as unique as your fingerprint." Even a few swings in a modern clubfitting center are usually enough to estimate a golfer's launch conditions—the ball speed, trajectory, and spin rate generated. This allows players to quickly compare the performance of different clubheads and shafts, and to home in on the most appropriate permutation of weight, loft, and flex for their golf clubs.

Tracking system
High-speed sensors track the movement of the golf ball

>> **Launch monitor** When comparing equipment, amateur golfers can now take advantage of high-tech computers that measure a player's swing speed, launch angle, and spin rate, while predicting the accuracy, carry distance, and roll of every shot.

Instant information
Launch conditions are instantly displayed on-screen after each shot

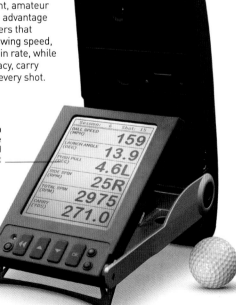

Session:	6	Shot:	15
BALL SPEED (MPH)			159
LAUNCH ANGLE (DEG)			13.9
PUSH PULL (DEG)			4.6L
SIDE SPIN (RPM)			25R
TOTAL SPIN (RPM)			2975
CARRY (YDS)			271.0

<< **Golfers can now** track changes in their swing speed and distance by using launch monitors alongside smartphone applications.

Ventilation holes For comfort in hot conditions

Padded palms Insert for extra durability

⌃ Gloves As well as coming in a range of natural leather and synthetic materials, golf gloves offer various performance features, such as moisture evaporation systems designed for different weather conditions.

Gloves, rain jackets, and shoes

Since golf often involves a four-hour outing in a variety of weather conditions, it is essential to wear comfortable clothing. Cutting-edge technology is increasingly finding its way into a new range of rain jackets, clothes, shoes, and gloves to combat weather extremes.

Choosing gloves

A left-hand glove for right-handed golfers (and vice versa) helps to provide support and comfort for the hand in most contact with the grip, and also reduces tension in the hands and arms to allow the player to swing more freely. Soft cabretta (goat hide) is most comfortable in dry conditions, while rain-resistant, silicone-treated leather and all-weather synthetics are more durable and stop the club from slipping.

Wearing rain jackets

Most models of rain jackets now feature breathable linings, such as Gore-Tex. This forms a barrier of tiny holes to keep out rain droplets, but which are large enough to let sweat vapor escape.

These laminated fabrics are often complemented by waterproof coatings, such as Teflon, that directly repel the rain by creating a slippery surface on the outer material. This creates a double barrier against the elements.

Zippers should be protected by storm flaps, while Velcro or elasticated cuffs are a matter of personal choice. Other features designed especially for golfers include detachable sleeves, low-noise fabrics, stretch inserts for flexibility when swinging, and short front hems to prevent bunching at address.

Choosing shoes

A round of golf involves a lot of walking, so it is essential to wear comfortable shoes that also support your feet during the swing. As well as

» Keeping dry on the golf course As well as full waterproofs, a sturdy golf umbrella with a reinforced fibreglass frame and an "anti-flip" canopy is recommended.

traditional leather, shoes are available in a variety of wet (and warm) weather styles. The more expensive full-grain leather uppers are generally more comfortable, though high-tech synthetics are closing the gap. Wet-weather shoes have waterproof-treated surfaces, as well as breathable linings that carry moisture away from the skin.

Other useful construction features include cushioned heels and footbeds (some using special gel and air inserts), and flexible soles that give with the foot.

Spikes on the sole—seven are enough—are essential for providing grip and encouraging a controlled foot twist during the swing. However, some golf shoes have convenient, spikeless, rubberized soles.

Nike Airspeed Saddle Cushioned soles are ideal for golfers looking for real comfort. Nike developed the idea of air-filled pads that are incorporated directly into the heel and footbed.

FootJoy DryJoy PRO As well as waterproof uppers, internal fabrics that carry away moisture are useful in wet weather. The PRO uses DriLex-covered inner soles that help moisture evaporate.

SYNTHETIC STUDS

Since the development of the green-friendly synthetic spike in the early 1990s, the number of courses that now insist on them in preference to the traditional metal cleat has increased dramatically. Different shapes offer different amounts of grip and traction, while the elaborate quick-lock systems need only a quarter-turn to adjust.

Rubberized
These grooves provide extra grip on the grass

Flexible insert
Allows sole to move naturally with the foot

Gentle spikes
Synthetic studs are now mandatory at most courses

Adidas ClimaCool Summer golf shoes are designed to keep the foot cool in hot conditions. The Adidas ClimaCool uses a system of air vents in the upper, and a perforated footbed.

Nike Tiger Woods Tour High-quality shoes adopt a variety of Moisture Management Systems, and Nike incorporates the pioneering, breathable Gore-Tex lining in many models.

FootJoy Classic Premier Dry The famous Classics have traditionally favored genuine leather, including calfskin uppers, linings, footbeds, and soles—here with a waterproof lining.

Bags and carts

Modern golf bags come in all shapes and sizes to suit players' requirements, with some offering special features such as insulated beverage pockets and cell phone pouches. Hand carts, including powered models, make it much easier to carry a full set of clubs.

Size and weight

Although beginners favor thin pencil bags and pros tend to use large staff bags, most golfers have either a lightweight carry bag, usually with a mechanical stand, or a pull bag that has a more rigid construction in a waterproof PVC outer layer. Personal preferences will dictate the size and style of tops, with 8in (20cm) diameters providing plenty of space for 14 clubs. Meanwhile, dual straps are beneficial because they spread the load across the back when carrying the clubs out on the course.

Dividers and features

Most players use tops that divide at least six ways to help separate the clubs. Today, 14-club dividers in various user-friendly configurations, which allow instant club selection, are increasing in popularity. Individual tube systems offer the best protection for graphite shafts.

Look carefully at the positioning of the carry handles and the size, location, and number of pockets to accomodate cell phones, food, drinks, and jewelry as well as balls, shoes, and rain jackets.

» Carry bags

With the help of durable nylon materials and graphite frames, some modern carry bags now weigh less than 3lb (1.3kg). This lightweight TaylorMade model features five pockets, a six-way top, and a stand that engages automatically when the base touches the ground.

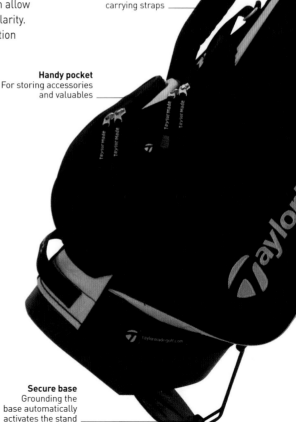

Comfort
Padded carrying straps

Handy pocket
For storing accessories and valuables

Secure base
Grounding the base automatically activates the stand

» Ben Hogan staff bag
The largest golf bags have wide-diameter tops—here 9½in (24cm)—with multiway top dividers to separate the clubs. These run full-length to protect the graphite shafts. Made from durable vinyl, they have at least eight pockets to house every conceivable accessory.

⏩ Ping moon bag This slim "pencil" design only holds a half set. It is ideal for beginners and juniors—or for a quick trip to the driving range.

Tee holder
Positioned for easy access

Lightweight stand
The stand has locking legs for stability

Storage
Pockets to carry extra clothing

⏫ Nike bag Made from rugged nylon, this carry bag has a modern top with a carefully designed club management system. The mechanical stand can prop the bag upright in an instant.

Types of hand carts

Ranging from the simple pull carts to highly sophisticated powered models, hand carts are transforming the enjoyment of the game for all age groups. Hands-free models, controlled by a pocket-sized remote box, are not only an extremely stylish accessory but also prevent the postural problems associated with both carrying and pulling. Golfers should always check weight, noise levels, and battery life before purchasing this kind of cart. It is also essential that the base of the chosen golf bag fits snugly in the cradle of the cart.

⏪ Powered cart
The Powakaddy is a three-wheel model with a rechargeable battery, designed for at least 18 holes. It is radio-controlled by means of a small handset and is an efficient replacement for the traditional caddy!

⏪ Pull cart The Masters Trakka is a good example of a simple lightweight pull cart that is easy to fold, with course-friendly wide wheels for better balance. Always ensure that the bag fits snugly on the base.

Bag holder
This secures the base of the bag firmly to the cart

The Basics of **the Game**

If you understand the fundamentals of golf from the outset, you will have a firm foundation on which to build. Knowing the types of play, grasping how to score, and having an understanding of general etiquette are essential starting points. Once you have this basic knowledge, you can learn the skills required to play the game to a high standard.

Types of play

One of the attractions of golf is the number of different ways in which the game can be played competitively or with friends, allowing numerous team and individual scoring systems. If you are an amateur player, varying the types of golf you play, and competing under different circumstances, is more challenging, not to mention great fun.

Stroke-play format

In stroke play, each golfer marks a scorecard after playing each hole and adds up the total strokes for the round. The lowest score wins. This is the standard format for tour professionals, as most tournaments played around the world exist in 72-hole (four 18-hole games) stroke-play format. It is also how monthly medal competitions are played at golf clubs for amateurs.

Match-play format

This is the original form of golf. It is played by holes and exists either in singles or pairs format. Each hole is a minimatch in itself, contributing to a "running" scoring system. A hole is won by taking the fewest number of strokes. So, if you win the first hole you are "one up." Win the second hole and you are "two up." If you then lose the third,

the match is back to "one up." Holes where the same number of strokes are taken by both sides are said to be "halved" and the match score stays the same.

The outcome of the match is decided when one pairing, or player, is "up" by more holes than there are left to play. For instance, five holes up with four holes to play is described as a victory by 5&4. This match would end on the 14th green.

Foursomes play

This style of play usually exists under the match-play scoring system and is played in pairs, each partner sharing the same ball and playing alternate shots. By agreement one player in each pairing tees off on the odd-numbered holes, the other player tees off on the even-numbered holes.

» **Checking the scorecard** Whichever type of golf you play, you need to know the appropriate scoring system. Here, Nick Faldo's caddie, Fanny Sunesen, keeps track of the score in a stroke-play event.

PLAYER DEFINITIONS

Each term has a bearing on how games are played and how the rules are interpreted. You need to know these terms in order to understand how competition golf is played. There are three definitions that define the status of each person in your playing group.

Competitor and fellow competitor
Competitor describes a person playing in a stroke-play competition—you, for instance, in the next monthly medal competition at your local club. A fellow competitor is the person you play with in your group.

Partner
This term describes a person on the same side as you in a match. For instance, your partner in a fourball betterball or foursomes game.

Opponent
This is the person (or persons) you play against in a match-play competition.

The British Open Championship Huge scoreboards at the 18th hole, where stroke play is played, keep players and spectators informed of the leader's progress out on the course.

Fourball betterball

Fourball betterball is very popular at club level. Like foursomes, it is played in pairs, but each partner plays their own ball and the best score on each hole is the one that counts.

Stableford

An example of a different scoring system, Stableford can be applied to any of the playing formats. The number of shots taken on each hole earns a certain number of points. A bogey is worth one point; a par—two; a birdie—three; an eagle—four; and a double eagle—five points (see p.48). Anything worse than a bogey scores no points. Add up the number of points scored on each hole and the highest total wins.

Bogey format

This game is head-to-head against the course. The match stays "alive" for the full 18 holes to arrive at a final score. Golfers either finish "up," "down," or "even" with the course par (see p.48). The golfer who is "up" by the most holes is the winner.

Greensomes

This is a variation on foursomes. Instead of teeing off on alternate holes, both golfers play each hole and then select the ball that finishes in the best position. They then continue to play alternate shots with that ball.

The dynamic Spanish duo Seve Ballesteros and José Maria Olazabal were one of the most formidable fourball and foursomes partnerships ever to hit a ball in golf's Ryder Cup.

How to score

A golf course consists of 18 holes, made up of par-3s, par-4s, and par-5s. Par is the theoretical "ideal" number of strokes required to play a particular hole. These individual par figures, added together, give the overall par for the course. Typically this is 72—for instance, it might consist of four par-3s, four par-5s, and 10 par-4 holes.

⬆ **Mark your scorecard** Seve Ballesteros marked some low numbers on his scorecard during a great playing career.

Scoring system

The universal golf scoring terms are as follows: a birdie describes a score of one under par for a hole (for example, two strokes on a par-3); an eagle is a score of two under par for a hole; and a double eagle (sometimes referred to as an albatross) is a score of three under par for a hole. At the other end of the scale, a bogey is a score of one over par for a hole; a double-bogey is two over par; a triple-bogey is three over par; and so on.

The handicapping system

Golf's handicap system is a means of allowing players of varying abilities to compete on equal terms. A golfer's handicap is expressed as a number that, broadly speaking, has a direct correlation with a figure known as the Standard Scratch Score (SSS). This reflects the length, the par, and, to a certain extent, the degree of difficulty of the golf course. For instance, a 16-handicap golfer will, on average, complete a round of golf in a score of 16 over the SSS. A 12-handicap player will generally go round in 12 over SSS. So, the lower the number of the handicap, the better the player.

A golfer with a handicap of zero is described as a "scratch" golfer. Better than scratch is described as a plus-handicap. These golfers are among the top amateurs and it has been known for some to reach plus-five or even plus-six, which means that their average score approximates to five or six under SSS for the round. Professional

⏩ **A fair game for all levels** Handicaps do not apply in the pro game, but elsewhere the system is golf's great leveler, enabling players of different abilities to compete on an equal footing.

Number/name of hole
Few courses will have names for every hole, but it is a nice feature on those that do.

Yardage of hole
Simply, the yardage from each set of tee markers to the front of the green.

Par classification
Par indicates the theoretical ideal number of strokes required to complete the hole.

Markers Score	Hole	White Yds	Yellow Yds	Par	Index	Strokes Recieved A	B	Gross Score A	B	Result or Points	Yards	Par	Index
	1. Roon the Ben	337	330	4	13						330	4	14
	2. Bonny Doon	367	357	4	9						357	4	2
	3. Wee Burn	410	398	4	3						398	4	16
	4. Neeps & Tatties	315	298	4	11						298	4	13
	5. Clarsochburn	332	320	4	17						320	4	9
	6. Wallace Way	133	115	3	15						115	3	3
	7. The Pond	298	276	4	7						276	4	11
	8. The Branoch	446	420	5	1						420	5	17
	9. Clan Pass	378	356	4	5						356	4	15
	OUT	3022	2915	36							2865	36	
	10. Roon the Ben	356	337	4	12						337	4	7
	11. Roon the Ben	156	140	3	10						140	3	1
	12. Roon the Ben	512	497	5	4						497	5	5
	13. Roon the Ben	368	352	4	3						352	4	12
	14. Roon the Ben	403	382	4	18						382	4	10
	15. Roon the Ben	387	359	4	6						359	4	4
	16. Roon the Ben	348	332	4	14						332	4	3
	17. Roon the Ben	451	435	5	2						435	5	18
	18. Roon the Ben	234	221	3	16						221	3	6
	IN	3128	2865	36							2865	36	
	OUT	3022	2915	36							2915	36	
	TOTAL	6150	5780	72							5780	72	
	HANDICAP												
	NETT												

S.S.S WHITE 71 YELLOW 68 RED 72   PAR WHITE 71 YELLOW 70 RED 74

Markers Signature _____   Players Signature _____

Competitors' names
Players' names should be entered on the scorecard before the round begins.

Stroke index
This is to determine when shots are given or received in a match-play situation.

Strokes received
Use this to indicate when strokes are received in a bogey competition.

Players' scores
Cards are swapped on the first tee. All players should mark all scores.

◀◀ Stroke-play scorecard Players should mark their scorecard after each hole, once they have moved onto the next tee.

golfers do not have handicaps, as their level of ability means that they should be playing to scratch or below on every occasion.

Calculating allowances

Shots are given on the holes that have a stroke index equal to or less than the total number of shots due. For example, if you are due to receive four shots from your opponent, you will receive these shots on holes with a stroke index of between one and four. If you are to receive eight shots, you will receive these shots on holes with a stroke index of between one and eight.

Singles match play: The low handicap player gives an opponent shots based on three-quarters of the difference in handicap. For example, in a match between a four-handicap golfer (player A) and a 16-handicap golfer (player B), the difference in handicap is 12 and therefore player A will give player B nine shots—that is, three-quarters of the difference between their two handicaps.

Fourball betterball: The lowest handicap player in each fourball gives shots to the other three players in the group, based on three-quarters of the difference in handicap.

Foursomes: The team with the lowest combined handicap gives shots to their opponents based on three-eighths of the difference between the handicaps.

Greensomes: The same scoring system as with foursomes is used in calculating the number of shots given in greensomes.

Stableford: A player receives shots based on three-quarters of their full handicap.

Bogey: The par of the golf course gives a player shots based on three-quarters of their handicap.

▽ Scoring in tournaments
Most tournaments are played using the stroke-play format. The score is recorded at the end of each hole, and the player with the lowest total score wins.

Care of the course

The rules of golf do not make specific provisions for the care of the golf course, but it is an integral part of golf etiquette that players respect the environment in which they play and look after the course to the best of their ability. This ensures that the playing surfaces remain in the best possible condition, for the benefit of everyone.

The putting green

This is the most manicured area of the course, and consequently, the most prone to damage. Pitch marks are the most obvious area of neglect among golfers at club level. On tour you will see every player who walks onto a green first repair the pitch mark, before doing anything else. Repeated often enough, the procedure becomes second nature.

Every golfer should get into the habit of repairing pitch marks using either a wooden tee peg (plastic ones bend too easily on firm putting surfaces) or a tool known as a pitch mark repairer, which can be bought cheaply in any pro shop. Use the fork of the pitch mark repairer or the tee peg to raise the turf around the indentation, then tread it or tap it down with the sole of the putter. It makes a real difference to the quality of the greens. The damage

⏏ **Repairing a pitch mark on the green** This procedure could not be simpler and it helps ensure that the putting green stays free from blemishes, offering a smooth roll for your line of putt.

from a pitch mark left unrepaired lasts up to two weeks, whereas if it is repaired moments after it is made, it mends within 24 hours.

The rules state that a golfer is not allowed to repair shoe spike marks until all the members of that playing group have putted out. However, it is permissible for a golfer to tend to spike marks that are not on the line of play (*see* p.52) and plug marks where old holes once were.

Another integral part of golf's etiquette is to ensure that you do not stand on the line of another golfer's putt. Professional golfers on tour take great pains to avoid this. Amateurs should show the same consideration for their fellow competitors.

Divot damage

When a golfer hits a straight shot down the middle of the fairway, it should be rewarded with a decent lie. Sadly, this is not always the case. Divots which are not replaced leave nasty scars in the fairway, and if a ball lands in one, it can result in an awkward shot. As with the sand in bunkers, though, no one would ever get an unnatural lie if all golfers replaced their divots. Every time you hit a shot that removes a divot, pick it up, then put it back where it came from and give it a good stamp down. The roots of the grass will then bed in and repair the divot naturally in a matter of days.

≫ Taking divots
Dislodging a divot at impact is an inevitable consequence of some golf shots.

There are exceptions. In some parts of the world where different types of grass are used on the fairways, you are not always encouraged to replace divots. Bermuda grass, commonly found on golf courses in the USA, is a good example. A divot will not grow back, even if it is put back in its hole, so the club provides a soil or sand dispenser on every golf buggy, which can be used to fill in divot holes.

This is the procedure that is recommended on teeing grounds all over the world. Many clubs supply a soil-and-seed mix to the side of the teeing ground, especially on the shorter par-3s, and this can be used to fill in divot holes. It helps generate a much more uniform growth on the teeing ground.

Covering your tracks

Bunkers are often a neglected area of the golf course. Admittedly, these are hazards and as such are supposed to present golfers with a degree of difficulty, but the sand should not resemble a beach on a busy day. Once safely out of a bunker, golfers should smooth over the footprints made in the sand with a bunker rake, not forgetting the trough made by the clubhead at impact. Any other footprints should also be raked over. It might seem unfair to have to correct another golfer's error, but this is part of basic golfing etiquette. If all golfers take the trouble to make use of rakes, then everyone stands an equal chance of getting a good lie in the bunker sand.

Always rake bunkers
Once the shot is played and the ball out of the bunker, golfers should always rake the sand and smooth over all footprints.

Essential etiquette

A basic understanding and respect for the golfing etiquette is fundamental to everyone's safety and enjoyment on the course. Codes of conduct and behavior are quickly learnt by newcomers to the game through practice, particularly when they play with experienced golfers who can offer good advice.

Timekeeping and dress

The first priority with any game of golf is to be punctual. Not only is it a matter of politeness to your fellow players, in a competition it is a requirement of the rules. You can be disqualified from a tournament for not teeing off in time, which can be an expensive mistake (*see* p.155). Golfers who are new to the game should also bear the dress code in mind. Jeans are not allowed and most clubs insist that casual tops have a collar. This might seem overly fussy, but in some clubs you will not be allowed to play if these rules are not observed.

Line of sight

The correct place to stand on the tee while others are driving off is behind and slightly to the right of that golfer. Elsewhere on the course, simply try to avoid standing on an extension of the line of play, as that tends to be in the player's-eye view and can break their concentration. You should also refrain from talking or making any distracting noises while others in the group are playing their shots.

Getting hit by a golf ball can be very painful, so make sure you wait for the group in front to be comfortably out of range before you tee off. Being struck by a golf club also has potentially serious consequences, so check the space around you before you make a practice swing: not everyone may be paying attention or aware of what you are doing.

Slow play

On the professional tours, slow play is a serious issue and the punishment is either a fine or penalty shots. At club level, penalties for slow play are often not enforced, but having to continually wait between shots makes the game a far less pleasant experience.

There are many simple measures that golfers can take to ensure that the pace of play is not too leisurely. First and most importantly, always keep up with the group in front. If a gap develops, make an effort to close it. Be aware of the order of play and be ready to hit when it is your turn. Providing you are not the one to play first, it is easy to do some of your preshot preparation while others are playing. For instance, there is no reason why you cannot study your putt while another member of the group is in the process of hitting a putt, although you should try not to disturb the person playing.

When you get near to the hole, leave your bag or cart on the correct side of the green—on the route you will be taking to the next tee. If you are playing in a competition, do not mark

» **Classic golfing attire**
Professional golfers are usually well turned out on the golf course, something that all amateurs should try to emulate.

⏶ **Play at a reasonable pace** Golf is so much more enjoyable if the pace of play is brisk, rather than leisurely. The maxim should be – always keep up with the game in front.

your scorecard on the green of the hole just completed. That is discourteous to anyone in the group who might be waiting to play their shot into the same green.

Lost balls

One of the greatest time wasters in golf is the search for lost balls. There will be occasions in virtually every round where you have to look for a ball, if not for yourself then for someone else in your group. The problem arises when failing to call through the group behind. This should always be done as a basic courtesy as soon as a ball is lost on a busy golf course. Simply stand to the side of the fairway and wave the following group through, inviting them to play their tee shots and pass you down the fairway. Some golfers use up the full five-minute limit permitted under the rules of golf in trying to find a missing ball. Only afterward do they then consider waving through the group behind.

If others in your group have yet to take their shot, then the player whose ball is lost should look for it alone while the rest of the group finish their turn.

Priority games

There is also an etiquette that dictates the priority games on the course. Two-ball matches (which includes foursomes) have priority over threeball or fourball matches. This means that they should be invited to play through at the earliest opportunity. A single player, although quicker than anyone else on the course, unfortunately has no standing at all.

◀ **Stand out of line**
Tiger Woods stands in the correct position, to the right and behind the player, so he is not in their line of sight when teeing off.

Playing **the Game**

Intelligent practice will make a big difference to the quality of your game. Golf is at least as much a game of accuracy and holding your nerve as it is about distance and hitting big shots. Patience will be rewarded with improvement as you gain experience.

Getting started

As with anything worthwhile, you get out of golf only what you put into it. The nature of the game is such that time—or rather a lack of it—is likely to be your toughest opponent when it comes to developing your skills and getting onto the course to put theory into practice. In the long run, the smart thing to do is to find a qualified teaching professional who can provide you with a sound understanding of the game's basics and give you a structured framework to follow.

Proven principles

Golf instruction has come a long way over the last 15 to 20 years. High-speed photography and ever-more sophisticated video analysis has enabled the leading professionals and coaches to identify the specific moves that define a sound, repeating swing. This information has led to a general standardization in teaching methods worldwide, and an increasing number of today's young superstars are swinging the club in the same

⬆ **In safe hands** Once the fundamentals are firmly in place, a good teaching professional will help you to understand the workings of the swing. They will highlight certain key checkpoints, such as the top of the backswing, to enable you to monitor your own progress.

fashion. As a result of this greater understanding, teaching pros have at their fingertips a number of proven principles—the nuts and bolts necessary to play good golf—which they are able to share with golfers of all ages and abilities.

One of the most practical concepts to have emerged in recent years is the idea of visualizing a good swing as a flowing "chain reaction," with one move leading seamlessly to another. The beauty of thinking about your own swing in these terms is that the importance of the setup position—the first link in the chain—is immediately crystal clear.

Fundamentals of golf

The thrust of the message that a good teaching pro will give you is that the one sure way to realize your potential as a golfer is to adhere to the game's first principles— the so-called "fundamentals" of grip, setup, posture, and alignment.

Do not be fooled into believing that the experts in the game are somehow privy to a secret mantra that bypasses these basics. Tour players spend the majority of their time on the practice tee honing the details of their setup position and developing a preshot routine. This enables them to go out and play instinctively on the course.

This ongoing repetition is the key to getting it right, and with the guidance of a good professional, the fundamental lessons will create a blueprint for a solid swing, leaving you with a series of good habits that will keep your game on track.

Practicing at home

Your only physical point of contact with the club is your grip, so a good grip is vital for good golf. For that reason alone, keep a club at home and pick it up from time to time. Familiarize yourself with the sensation of placing your hands correctly on it. As you do so, the instinct to hinge your wrists to get the clubhead swinging gently back and forth—a move known as the "waggle"—will become second nature. Then, as one good move leads on to another, your ability to feel, build, and shape a good swing will develop. Spend just 10 minutes every day standing in front of a mirror and checking the details of your grip, setup, and posture. Monitoring and fine-tuning these essential basics will make a world of difference to your progress as a golfer.

On autopilot A player well tutored in the basics can look forward to a lifetime's enjoyment of golf, knowing that his or her swing is based on proven first principles.

Balancing act If a solid swing is a chain reaction, the finish will be a picture of balance and poise. This is the natural conclusion to a controlled motion in which the hands, arms, and body work together.

Positive practice
When it comes to practicing, the most important thing to remember is that it is the quality not the quantity that counts. Organize your practice time well, and that practice will be more effective. Practice each part of your game, but split the time sensibly. For example, the briefest analysis of the game shows that 70 percent of shots are hit from within 100 yards (90m) of the flag, so do not spend hours practicing shots longer than this.

Follow a disciplined preshot routine on every ball. This bucket should last a good 40 minutes.

Use the yardage posts as targets so that you always have a specific shot in mind.

First lessons

Whatever your capabilities, a solid grounding in golf's so-called "fundamentals" is the one sure way to unlock your potential. These ground rules, detailing grip, posture, and basic swing movements, will provide you with the vital information that you need to go out and enjoy the many challenging facets of the game.

The grip is key

The first and most important lesson on the road to good golf is how to create a good grip. The grip provides the vital hinge that transfers the centrifugal forces from the "core" of your body into a strong swinging motion. A good grip allows your wrists to hinge freely, and the better your wrist action, the better you strike the ball.

Copy the pros

Why is it that the world's best players make the game look so easy? How are they able to generate such terrific clubhead speed and strike the ball so far with seemingly little effort? The answer is that they combine the rotation of their body with a fluid wrist action that "loads" the club with energy in the backswing before it is unleashed on the back of the ball through impact. Strip away the mystique that surrounds the golf swing and you are left with two components: a basic body turn, and a good grip and wrist action.

When you place your hands correctly on the grip, you can hinge your wrists in such a way that you are able to generate maximum clubhead speed through impact—and speed means distance.

Good plane The proof of a good grip is when your hands work together as a cohesive unit. When they do, you will reap the benefit in the speed you are able to generate. Your wrists will also hinge in such a way that you can get the club swinging on a good plane.

PLAY LIKE A PRO

Vijay Singh
You can see here how energy from the core of the body can be transferred, via a good wrist action, into maximum clubhead speed on the ball.

Key to a good swing If you start your swing correctly and employ a sound wrist action, you will find that you are able to get to this key checkpoint in your swing with your wrists hinged up and the club on plane. From here, you can finish your full shoulder turn to complete a good backswing. Then instinct will take over as you unwind through the ball.

"Neutral" clubface
With your wrists hinged, the clubface and back of your left hand should mirror each other—a symmetry that confirms your swing is on the right track

Stand tall
It is important that you maintain your height—and thus your spine angle—as you turn your upper body

Head right
Ease your head to the right to allow your shoulders to turn freely beneath your chin

Body rotation
As the core, or hub, of the swing, your body generates a tremendous series of forces when it rotates. These are conducted through your arms and wrists into the clubhead

Eyes fixed
Your eyes should remain fixed on the back of the ball

Comfortable position
As your body turns, your left arm swings across your chest. It is neither bent nor too rigid, but comfortably extended at this stage in the backswing

A good grip

To unlock the power and the mobility of a good wrist action, you need a grip that allows you to cock and uncock your left wrist fully in the course of making your swing. Problems occur when you place the club too high in the palm of your left hand. Make sure that, as you prepare to make your grip, you lay the club fairly low across your fingers (*see* below).

The "short" left thumb

One of the details of a good grip that is often overlooked concerns the position of the left thumb. Rather than extend your left thumb long down the shaft, make a note to "pinch it short" as you place it on top of the grip. A short left thumb improves the "hinge-ability" of your left wrist, and also helps you to support the club correctly at the top of your swing.

1 Lying low in the fingers The process of making the grip always starts with positioning the left hand. If you hang your left arm down by your side, you will notice that the fingers tend to curl inward naturally. This helps you to establish a good hold. The club falls into the fingers diagonally.

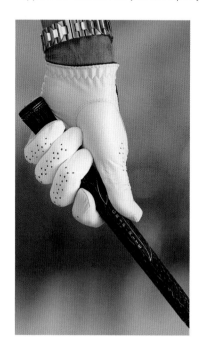

2 Foundation for a secure hold The last three fingers squeeze the butt-end of the grip, which protrudes from the hand by about 1in (2.5cm). This provides the security of the grip. The fingertips just touch the pad at the base of the thumb. This is a good sign that the grip on your club is the correct size.

3 Mirroring the clubface The right hand is introduced to the grip in such a way that the left and right hands complement each other. The palm of the right hand is held square to the clubface with the grip of the club lying diagonally across the fingers.

4 Joined in perfect union When the right hand is closed, the left thumb should disappear under the fleshy pad at the base of the right thumb. The base of the V-shape that is created by the thumb and forefinger of the right hand should point between the chin and right shoulder.

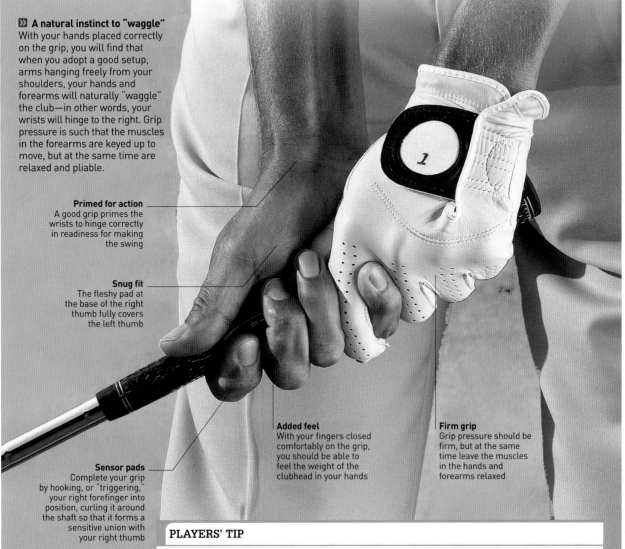

≫ **A natural instinct to "waggle"**
With your hands placed correctly on the grip, you will find that when you adopt a good setup, arms hanging freely from your shoulders, your hands and forearms will naturally "waggle" the club—in other words, your wrists will hinge to the right. Grip pressure is such that the muscles in the forearms are keyed up to move, but at the same time are relaxed and pliable.

Primed for action
A good grip primes the wrists to hinge correctly in readiness for making the swing

Snug fit
The fleshy pad at the base of the right thumb fully covers the left thumb

Sensor pads
Complete your grip by hooking, or "triggering," your right forefinger into position, curling it around the shaft so that it forms a sensitive union with your right thumb

Added feel
With your fingers closed comfortably on the grip, you should be able to feel the weight of the clubhead in your hands

Firm grip
Grip pressure should be firm, but at the same time leave the muscles in the hands and forearms relaxed

PLAYERS' TIP

Comfortable grip

The specific way in which you choose to marry your hands together on the grip is a matter of comfort. There are no hard and fast rules, and it is up to you to experiment to see which grip works best for you. While your hands must always be in a "neutral" hold, that is with palms opposing each other, the way in which you bond them is personal preference. There are two standard alternatives: the overlapping grip, favored by most tour players, in which the right little finger overlaps the left forefinger; and the interlocking grip, used by Tiger Woods among others, in which the two little fingers interlock.

In an overlapping grip, the right little finger sits on the left forefinger or between the first and second fingers.

In an interlocking grip, the right little finger and the left forefinger intertwine to form a compact union.

Good posture

The foundations of a good swing lie in the way in which you set up to the ball—in other words, your posture. Creating and holding the right spine angle are basic to repeating a good turn with the upper body. The angle also helps you to swing the club in balance, which is vital if you are to keep control as you increase your speed through the ball.

Bend from the hips

Of all the angles you create at the setup, the spine angle that is formed as you tip your upper body forward from the hips is the most vital. You get the feeling of being in an "athletic" position as you flex your knees and stick out your rear.

Spine angle
Tilt your upper body forward from the hips to create this distinct spine angle—the axis to the swing

Chin up
Keep your chin up off your chest so your head does not droop but remains aligned with your spine

Arms hanging
Once you have created a good spine angle, simply let your arms hang from your shoulders so your hands are beneath your chin

Simple check
In a good setup position, with your hips at the correct angle, your belt buckle will face down toward the ball

Flexed knees
Keep your knees nicely flexed, braced, and ready to support the turning of your upper body

⌃ Good athletic posture One way to appreciate the sensation of a truly athletic posture is to imagine you are about to dive into a swimming pool. With your knees flexed, you instinctively create this spine angle as you bend from the hips, your weight balanced on the balls of your feet. From here, your arms hang in front of you and you are ready to play.

Tilting the spine

Tilting the axis of your spine slightly away from the target is a critical and yet often overlooked element of a sound setup position. The key is to allow your right side to sink gently as the left side grows a little taller. When you check your position in front of a mirror, look out for this slant across your shoulders. Your torso is now primed to rotate correctly in the swing.

Poise, balance, control

Given that your right hand is placed below your left on the grip, tilting the axis of your spine slightly away from the target is perfectly natural. The right side of your body (shoulder, hip, and forearm) should be in a fairly passive position in relation to the left side. A feeling of "perking up" the left side will help you to achieve this, and leave you ready to make a full turn behind the ball.

Correct line
Make sure the shaft of the club follows the line of your sternum toward your chin

Angled club
The club confirms that your upper body is tilting slightly away from the target

Straight arm
The left arm is comfortable in a straight line with the club

Good setup
In a good setup, the right shoulder is slightly lower than the left

⌃ **The correct angle** A good way to check the position of your upper body is to take hold of a club and place it vertically down your chest so that it tracks your sternum. When you settle into a good posture, make sure that the shaft is angled away from the target, placing your upper body in the perfect position from which to turn correctly.

⌃ **Solid setup** Resting the upper part of each arm snug on the upper part of your chest gives you a sense of "connection" between your arms and upper body. Look out for the distinct triangle formed by your arms and shoulders. All good players show this feature at the setup. In order to create a stable base with your lower body, make sure that the insides of your heels are shoulder-width apart. Check also that your toes are turned out just a little, the left fractionally more than the right.

Swing principles

One of the most important first lessons in golf is that the basic swing principles apply to every shot. For all practical purposes, one swing fits all, and the nature of that swing is determined in the way that you set up to the ball. Whether you are using a 9-iron, a 5-iron, or a driver, bending from your hips and flexing your knees gives you a perfect posture, and helps you to identify the correct distance that you should stand away from the ball at setup. As shown in these two examples below, the angle of your spine serves as the axis about which your body turns during the swing.

Good connection
Upper part of the arms rests lightly on the upper part of the chest

Gentle bend
With knees flexed, bend from the hips until the sole of the club is flush on the ground

Relaxed arms
Forearms hang freely, placing the hands directly beneath the chin

Clubshaft angle
With the clubhead flush on the ground, the shaft falls naturally at the correct angle

Iron setup As you will discover, the shorter the iron you are using, the more you need to bend from the hips to ground the club. With your knees flexed, bend forward from the hips until the sole of the club sits flush on the turf. That will establish the correct distance that you stand from the ball, leaving you ready to make a sound, repeating swing.

Important body angles The angle of the swing depends on the angles created at the setup. With its shorter shaft, the 7-iron sits at a noticeably more upright angle than the driver, and this is reflected in the plane of the swing.

Using a driver

Because the ball is played slightly farther away from the body with the longer-shafted driver, the plane of the swing, as determined by the angle of the clubshaft at the setup, will be a little flatter. As you move the club away from the ball, you will be aware of a real feeling of swinging the club around your body as you turn about the axis of your spine. As always, your right knee and thigh serve as the brace against which you coil up your backswing like a spring.

Standing tall
Stand up a little taller with a driver, your chin up off your chest

◀◀ **Driver setup** The driver may be the longest and most powerful club in the bag, but the setup rules are the same as with the irons. With a good grip, your arms comfortably extended, bend gently from the hips until the clubhead is on the ground. With your weight balanced on the balls of your feet, stand tall with your chin up off your chest. This creates the ideal posture you need for using a driver, gearing you up to make a full and powerful turn of the upper body.

Arm position
Upper arms remain lightly in contact with the upper part of the chest

Free elbows
Elbows are free of the chest, not pushed in

Comfortable grip
Hands are comfortably placed on the grip, the forearms relaxed, ready to create a flowing swing

▲ **Driver backswing** The longer the swing, the more important it is that you swing with a smooth rhythm. That way, the two most important components of the swing—the body turn and the arm swing—"match up" to reward you with a compact and on-line backswing position.

Square aim
Clubhead is squarely placed behind the ball, aiming down the target line

Alignment

Good alignment is vital for consistently accurate shot-making. If either the club or your body are poorly aligned, you will struggle to swing on the correct path and plane. You can avoid that problem by building the habits of good alignment within a preshot routine.

1 **Start behind the ball** Always start your routine behind the ball so that you get a full view of your target line and are able to picture the shot you want to play. Pick out an intermediate target, such as an old divot or bare patch of grass, that lies just a few meters ahead of the ball on your intended line to the target. This provides a useful guide when it comes to positioning the clubface.

2 **Trace the target** From the moment you identify your target line, constantly check and double-check the alignment of both the clubface and your body. Place the leading edge of the club squarely behind the ball, then trace the line from the club all the way to the target and back again before you complete your stance. The key is that your body takes its orders from the position of the clubface, not the other way around.

Visualizing the shot
Study your target to create a vivid image of the shot you intend to play, and keep that shot in mind

Low right shoulder
Think about relaxing your right shoulder so that it is lower than the left. In that way, you prime good posture

Body angle
A good body angle should be in place as you check your target

Trace the line
You should constantly trace the line from the ball to the target as you set up

Feet together
Stand with your feet close together as you aim the club and prepare to finalize your setup position

Parallel lines
Your shoulders must be parallel to the ball-to-target line

Head and spine
The head is a comfortable extension of the spine, not drooped forward

Eyes level
For a true perspective of the shot, make sure that your eye-line remains level as you finalize your position

Good grip
With a good neutral grip, your hands are placed perfectly on the club

Foot check
Imagine a line running across your toes parallel to the ball-to-target line

Square aim
The clubface aims squarely at the intended target

3 **Establish body position**
Spread your feet comfortably for balance and check that your body is square, or parallel, to the ball-to-target line. The best way to understand this is to visualize a railroad track. The ball and the clubface lie on the outer rail, while your body is aligned on the inner rail.

4 **On target** Following a disciplined preshot routine enables you first to engage with the target, and then to react to it all the way to the conclusion of your swing. Good alignment instills the confidence that you need to swing freely through the ball to a balanced finish.

Rhythm and motion

A good golf swing is a combination move. As the body rotates, it serves as the hub of the wheel that swings the arms and the club in unison. Developing the quality of your body motion is the key to repeating a consistent movement and pacing your swing with a free-flowing rhythm.

1 **Create good angles** The most important part of this pivot exercise is to create a good spine angle (see p.64). With your arms crossed, hold a club across your chest. This increases the feeling of your arms and upper body turning together. Keep your chin up as you flex your knees and bend from your hips.

Primed for action
With arms crossed, hold a club across your shoulders, ready to turn your upper body

Slanting shoulders
Clubshaft matches the natural slant of the shoulders

⌃ Balance your weight
Feel the athletic balance in your lower body. Place your weight on the balls of your feet, not back on your heels. Do not be shy of sticking out your rear. Keep reminding yourself to flex your knees and keep your chin up.

Shoulder turn
Left shoulder turns
through 90 degrees

Natural rotation
Head rotates
naturally in tandem
with the shoulders

Straight spine
Spine is vertical, and
your belt buckle
faces the target

2 **Turn your torso** Focus on turning your right shoulder out of the way while, at the same time, resisting the motion of your upper body with the flex in your right knee. In other words, create and feel the resistance of a good body motion. Turn your left shoulder fully under your chin, maintaining the distinct spine angle that you created at the setup.

⏶ **Feel the resistance**
As you rotate your shoulders, you should feel a stubborn resistance in your right knee and thigh. Enjoy this feeling of coiling the muscles in your torso, winding up your upper body like a spring.

3 **Release the spring** Having created resistance and coil in the backswing movement, you can use all that energy. The important thing is to unwind your body from the ground up. A gentle rolling of your ankles back toward the target is all it takes to start the process of unwinding and then rotating your body through to a fully spent finish, your eyes facing the target.

⏶ **The finish** As the left side of your body rotates and clears out of the way, the right side can drive through toward the target. Your knees are comfortably together at the finish, your weight firmly into the left side.

Head-start drill

Once you have the basis of a good swing, developing rhythm and motion sets you firmly on course to improving the quality of your ball striking. There are a number of ways in which you can do this. One of the most popular among tour players is the head-start drill, which you can see demonstrated here. The idea is that you first extend the clubhead a little way beyond the ball. You can then gather and build on its momentum as you let it fall, and use that energy to complete your swing—back and through.

Shoulder control
Turn your shoulders to move the clubhead forward

Straight arms
Your arms are comfortably straight as you get ready to swing

On a tee
Teeing-up the ball 1in (2.5cm) or so helps your confidence because this is not normally done with an iron

Steady head
Keep your head steady as you let the clubhead fall and flow all the way to the top of the backswing

Athletic balance
Knees and lower body are ready to stabilize the swinging motion

1 **Get a head start** To maximize the benefit of this exercise, limit yourself to using no more than a mid-iron. Keep a sensitive grip pressure as you extend the clubhead a little way beyond the ball. Feel the weight of the club on the end of the shaft as you prepare to let it fall, and gather its momentum to flow into a good backswing movement.

2 **Wind up your body** The beauty of this exercise is that it inspires a real sense of harmony between your arm swing and body turn. Giving yourself a running start helps you to develop a rhythm that effectively repeats itself as you wind up your body and swing your arms and club in unison.

3 **Release the speed** In addition to helping with your rhythm, starting the clubhead a little way ahead of the ball gives you a good feeling of where you want to return immediately after impact. As you unwind, the speeding clubhead pulls the arms straight.

PLAYERS' TIP

Swing with extra weight
One of the most damaging swing faults in the game stems from a tendency to over-control the club with the big muscles in your upper body. This is simply not possible when you swing with two clubs held together, which is why this is a good exercise to do. You will be aware of the extra weight in your hands, and will find that the exercise encourages you to develop a true swinging motion, harmonizing the movement of your arms and body.

Your body will respond naturally to the extra weight of the two clubs.

Your balance is improved as you unwind your body to a full finish.

Relaxed finish Hands finish above the tip of the left shoulder, arms relaxed

Club position Clubshaft arrives comfortably behind the head

Full rotation Level belt buckle confirms that the hips have rotated all the way through the shot

Balance Weight is now fully on the left side, counter-balanced on the toe of the right shoe

4 **Finish in style** As your confidence in your swing grows, so will your ability to sweep the ball off the tee peg and wrap up the motion with a full and balanced finish. Always aim to hold your follow-through for a few seconds, your weight supported on the left side.

Swing-building

The process of learning a good swing is made much easier when you have a visual blueprint of the key positions that you are trying to achieve. Use this eight-step sequence to create in your mind a chain reaction, in which one good move leads smoothly to another.

1 **Perfect posture** A good setup primes all of the components of a good swing to work together. The way in which you bend forward from the hips to create the correct spine angle (see p.64) is vital to the consistency of your swing. Flex your knees so that you feel "springy," keeping your weight on the balls of your feet, not back on your heels.

☑ **Ready to move** Bend from your hips, keeping a good flex in your knees. Your arms hang freely from your shoulders, placing your hands beneath your chin. Keyed-up and ready to move, you are also relaxed and poised.

Relaxed arms
Feel the "connection" between the upper arms and the body

In unison
Left arm and the clubshaft fall comfortably in line

Not too tight
A light grip pressure leaves the forearms relaxed, ready to swing

Good balance
Insides of the feet are shoulder-width apart

"Quiet" hands
Relaxed, passive hands maintain a comfortable grip on the club

Resistance
The hips and the legs resist the turning of the upper body

Weight change
The left knee is drawn in gently as the weight "bumps" across to the right side

Low clubhead
The clubhead remains low to the ground for the first part of its journey

2 **First move** For a consistent shape and tempo to your swing, it is important that the first move away from the ball *sees* your hands, arms, stomach, and shoulders all working together. Concentrate on maintaining the triangle formed by your arms and shoulders. Rehearse this in slow motion to get a feel for this "one-piece" move. With your hands essentially passive, the club remains fairly close to the ground, tracing a wide arc as it swings away from the ball.

Natural symmetry Because the ball is played away from the body, there is a naturally pitched angle to the swing. As you move the hands, arms, and body together, the clubhead works inside the ball-to-target line—as symmetry dictates.

5

6

7

8

3 **Halfway position** Having combined the movement of the arms and the upper body to get the swing under way, the next link in the chain sees the wrists hinge to swing the club up into a good halfway position. This wrist action is vital in the process of developing a true swinging motion. By the time the left arm reaches this position, where it is parallel to the ground, the wrists are fully hinged, setting the club on a good plane as the body turns.

☑ **On line and on plane** As your left arm swings across your chest, your right elbow "softens" and folds neatly away. When you check your swing at halfway, your right forearm should be at about the same angle as your spine. From here, you can get into a good position at the top of the backswing.

Right-angle
The clubshaft is at 90 degrees to the angle of the forearms

Neutral position
Clubface remains square to the path of the swing

Control center
The shoulders continue to turn about the axis of the spine—the "hub" at the center of the wheel

"Loaded" up
Wrists are fully hinged as the left arm reaches the horizontal

Resistance
Hips and legs move only in response to the turning of the upper body

Anchored in balance
While the weight is moving across and into the right side, the left foot remains planted

1

2

3

4

Good grip
Hands maintain full control of the club, not slipping in the grip

Safe position
Clubface is in a safe, neutral position, mirroring the back of the left hand

Head rotation
Head rotates away from the target to allow you to make a full turn

Arm swing
A compact, three-quarter arm swing combines with the full turn of the upper body

Secure footing
Left knee points behind the ball, while the left foot remains planted

4 **At the top** From the halfway position, completing a full shoulder turn rewards you with a good position at the top of the backswing. Retaining its flex, your right knee serves as the brace against which you really do enjoy a feeling of stretching and coiling the muscles in your torso. Your left shoulder turns under your chin, while your arms and hands arrive at a compact three-quarter position.

☑ **Free right elbow** When you work on your backswing, make sure that your right elbow is not tucked in too tight to the side of your body. You should allow it the freedom to swing freely, supporting your hands and the club in a good position above the tip of your right shoulder.

5

6

7

8

5 Unwinding the spring

With a gentle rolling of the ankles, the momentum of the swing is reversed and it is vital that your body unwinds from the ground up. As your lower body shifts back toward the target, your arms and hands are able to fall into a natural hitting position. Note that your wrists remain hinged, ready to unleash a final burst of speed on the ball when they finally "snap open" at impact.

☑ **Inside track** As your body unwinds from the ground up, your arms fall into this hitting position. The club is on the desired inside path as it approaches the ball. This is vital for a square contact, which produces a straight shot.

Still head
Head remains very still as the body unwinds and the arms fall into position

Rotating torso
The torso rotates back toward the target, creating the forces that generate speed

Right elbow
As the lower body eases toward the target, the right elbow falls toward the right hip

Hinged wrists
The wrists remain hinged and loaded with energy deep into the downswing

6 Impact As you approach impact, you should be aware of a free-wheeling acceleration of the clubhead as the centrifugal forces generated by the rotation of your body pull your arms and hands through toward the target. This position is a "freeze-frame" within the motion of a chain reaction that maximizes clubhead speed on the ball.

Open shoulders As the body rotates, the shoulders are open to the target line at impact

Square at impact Rotation of the body returns the arms, hands, and the club squarely to impact

Hand speed Wrists unhinge to deliver the final burst of speed, releasing the clubhead into the back of the ball

Natural balance Right heel is pulled up off the ground as the body continues to rotate in the direction of the target

Striking force Flex in the clubshaft reveals the forces that are at work as the hands accelerate

Weight left Most weight is now on the left side as the body clears the way for impact

Open hips and shoulders A view of the impact position down the line reveals just how open the hips and the shoulders are as the clubhead meets the ball. The left side of the body is braced to absorb the hit as the entire right side—knee, hip, shoulder, arm, and hand—"fires" to accelerate the clubhead through the ball.

7 **Committed release** The symmetry that exists in a good swing is evident as your hands and arms are pulled through the ball by the momentum of the clubhead. This release confirms that the energy generated by the rotation of your body has been channeled fully down through the arms and the hands into the clubhead. The crossover of the hands and forearms is vital for planting maximum speed on the ball.

Clearing the way Looking down the line, the full dynamic of the body rotation is clear. The hips, the stomach, and the shoulders unwind and clear the way for the arms and the hands to "throw" the clubhead toward the target in a full, committed release.

Focus
Eyes remain fixed on the back of the ball as the club is released at great speed

Body power
Right side of the body powers through the shot

Arms crossed
Right forearm crosses over the left as the weight and speed of the clubhead pull the arms straight in the release

Hips clear
As the body clears the path for the arms to swing the club all the way through, the hips open up to the target

Muscles pulled
Stomach muscles turn and pull hard as the hub of the swing continues to spin

Heel up
Right heel is pulled up off the ground as the forces pull the arms through toward the target

1

2

3

4

Straight body
Body straightens to face the target, free from harmful stress on the lower back

At the finish
Right shoulder points at the target, hands comfortably placed behind the head

Knees together
Right knee works toward the left one as you arrive at the finish

8 **Follow-through** A committed release of the clubhead provides an irresistible momentum that leads you to a full, balanced finish. Your body rotates all the way through the shot, your chest faces the target, and your hips, eyes, and shoulders are now level. You should be able to hold this balanced position for several seconds, the majority of your weight now supported firmly on the left side of your body, your spine free of tension and relatively straight.

Perfect balance As your body rotates to a full finish, the power of your swing is harnessed in a balanced follow-through position. The momentum of your swing should be such that your stomach and shoulders finish facing left of the target, while your right foot is pulled up onto the toe of the shoe.

5

6

7

8

Driving

South Africa's Ernie Els is the perfect role model for any golfer who wants to develop and improve their driving and fairway play. All the elements that make up his powerful swing are clearly described in this section. Practice your technique and always keep the key points in your mind when you are playing your shots. By doing this, you will learn to swing with an unhurried motion and a good sense of rhythm, so improving your game overall.

Off the tee

Great drivers of the ball share one vital quality: relaxed and unhurried from the setup, they give themselves the time to wind up their backswing fully, storing energy in a powerful coiling motion that sees them turn fully behind the ball. Keep that in mind as you prepare to work on your skills off the tee.

Poised for power
Right shoulder set slightly lower than the left, ready to make a powerful turn

Giving width
Left arm remains straight, providing width in your swing

Turning away
Right shoulder moves back as the upper body begins to turn and wind up the backswing

Low and slow
Clubhead traces a naturally wide arc as it is drawn away smoothly. Do not jerk it back

1 **Creating a launch pad** With your knees flexed, settle your weight 60:40 in favor of the right side and feel the full extension of your arms as they hang from your shoulders. Although you are naturally keyed-up, ready to make a swing, you must also be free of tension, ready to make a smooth first move.

2 **A one-piece move** With your hands, arms, and body working together, you will generate a wide arc as you draw the clubhead away from the ball. Many of the world's leading players speak of taking away the club "low and slow."

Up and over
Hands swing high above the tip of the right shoulder

Totally under control
A full shoulder turn and compact arm swing take the club to a position just short of horizontal

Winding up
Core muscles in the torso wind up as you turn your upper body away from the target

Full turn
To complete your backswing, your left shoulder should be fully under your chin

Flexed knee
Turning your upper body against a flexed right knee makes for a good coil

Ball position
The ball is played opposite the left instep, forward of center, where it can be "collected" as the clubhead begins its ascent

3 **Turn and stretch** With a driver in your hands, you really do want to feel a stretch in the powerful muscles in your torso as you turn your upper body away from the target. Concentrate on getting your upper body fully behind the ball, while your knees and hips provide the stability that enables you to wind up your body like a spring.

PLAYERS' TIP

Teeing up the ball
Exotic lightweight materials used in the construction of the modern driver have caused an explosion in the size of the clubhead, with anything from 25cu.in (410cc) up to a legal limit of 28cu.in (460cc). The sweet spot (see p.23) on these clubs is high up the clubface, so it is important to tee the ball accordingly. At least half of the ball should be visible above the clubface.

Head behind the ball
To deliver maximum power, keep your head behind the ball. Many amateurs make the mistake of lunging forward with their head and shoulders

Full extension
The leading arm remains extended to create width through the hitting area

4 **Keep it smooth** From the top, the emphasis is on making the change of direction as smooth and unhurried as possible so that the club has the opportunity to return to the ball on the correct inside path. When you unwind correctly from the ground up, you will enjoy a sense of lag in the wrists, which enables you to hold on to the angle between the wrists and the clubshaft—a key power source that you want to unleash at impact, but not before.

5 **All together now** Good timing is crucial for powerful driving. All the moving parts in the swing must realign at impact to deliver maximum power and accuracy. You should experience the feeling of your hands, arms, and body working in harmony. As you turn back through, make sure that your left arm remains gently extended so that it can apply full pressure to the back of the ball. Keep your head back behind the ball as you swing your arms through impact and release the club in front of your chest.

Hands swing
Your hands should finish behind your head, the clubshaft resting across your shoulders

Position of back
The momentum of a full driver swing will pull your upper body into a position where your back finishes facing away from the target

Final weight
Your weight should finish on the outside of your front foot

6 **A full release** With the driver, it is very important to hit through the ball, not at it. Commitment through impact is crucial, so always look to create good width and extension through the ball as well as on the backswing. See here how the right side of the body "fires" through impact, and how the right forearm releases over the left to square the face at impact and send the ball on its way.

7 **Finish in balance** Nowhere is a relaxed, balanced, and comfortable finish position more important than with the driver. At the end of your swing, the majority of your weight should be on the outside of your front foot. Your chest should be facing either toward or a little to the left of the target, and your right shoulder, right hip, and knee should all be in line.

Fairway technique

The key to mastering your fairway woods lies in making a swing that enables you to sweep the ball off the fairway. To do that, you must play the ball a little forward in your stance, opposite the inside of the left heel, and learn to swing through it with confidence.

Relaxed right side
With your right side set slightly lower than the left, the shoulders are in the correct position to turn and generate power

Comfortably extended
The arms hang from the shoulders to create this distinct V-shape

Perfectly poised
The hands are above or even fractionally behind the ball as you prepare to sweep the ball off the ground

In line
In a good setup, the left arm and the clubshaft are virtually in line

Stable base
The insides of the heels are shoulder-width apart, providing a stable stance for the swing

Ball position
The ball is in line with your left instep, where it can be collected as the club reaches the bottom of the swing arc

1 All set to go
This self-help exercise will help you to recognize and feel the correct swing path that you are looking to achieve with a fairway wood. When you practice, simply create a trail of tees in the ground following a gentle sweeping arc all the way into the back of the ball. Press them down into the ground so that you can hit shots using them as a visual guide. They will encourage you to deliver the clubhead along the same gentle arc.

2 Swing with confidence
The trail of tees provides you with a distinct path to follow. The clubhead must approach the ball from slightly inside the ball-to-target line before meeting the ball squarely and sweeping it toward the target. In other words, you are aiming to achieve the same shallow sweeping motion through impact with the fairway wood as you do with a driver (see p.86).

Visual guide
The tees help you visualize the correct inside path that your club should follow to the ball

⌃ **Collecting the ball** To maximize your clubhead speed, you are looking to collect the ball at the very bottom of the arc in your swing, known as the "flat-spot."

Speeding through
The momentum of the clubhead pulls the arms straight through impact. This is a sign of committed release

Head behind the ball
To maximize the sense of release, the head stays well behind the ball through impact

3 Sweep the ball To
maximize your speed through the ball, and therefore the distance you hit it, feel as if you are "throwing" your right hand into the back of the ball as you release your stored-up energy through impact. The right hand should overtake the left, and the toe-end of the club should overtake the heel. The rotary motion of the body creates centrifugal forces that are multiplied through the arms and clubshaft for a powerful sweeping motion.

Fairway woods

Built on the foundation of a good posture, the general shape of the swing varies very little between clubs. When using a fairway wood, you should be repeating the same basic movement that you would employ with a driver, with a rhythm that enables you to maintain balance as you sweep the ball toward your target.

Body primed
Upper body is tilted gently away from the target—the left shoulder ready to turn fully behind the ball

Fixing the radius
Elbow relaxed, the left arm is comfortably extended, forming a straight line with the clubshaft

Good suspension
The knees are comfortably flexed, promoting the "athletic" nature of the setup and ready to stabilize the swing

1 **Poised setup** While a fairway wood is slightly shorter in the shaft than a driver, it is still one of the longest clubs in the bag and, as such, its use demands that you create a stable platform upon which to make a full turn of the upper body. With your heels shoulder-width apart, distribute your weight fairly evenly, and play the ball just forward of center.

PLAYERS' TIP

The chain reaction
Making your swing a flowing chain reaction is the key to consistency. Think in terms of "chasing" the clubhead after the ball, as you unwind toward the target. Maintain your width all the way through impact. This will reinforce the shallow sweep that you want, and give you the optimum trajectory of flight.

Short of parallel
The club is in a perfect position, just short of horizontal, the hands extended away from the body

Winding up the spring
Hips and lower body provide both stability and resistance to the turning and coiling of the upper body

Shallow sweep
Head and upper body stay behind the ball as the hands and arms sweep the clubhead through impact

2 **Store the power** A smooth, unhurried rhythm is vital as you turn your upper body away from the target and wind up the muscles in your torso to make a solid backswing loaded with energy. You will have a real feeling of turning against your braced right knee and thigh as you combine a full shoulder turn with a relatively compact hand and arm swing.

3 **"Collect" the ball** Your upper body and head stay behind the ball as your hands and arms swing the clubhead past the chin, collecting the ball and rifling it toward the target. Simply let the ball get in the way as you unwind and sweep it away with a free-wheeling acceleration of the clubhead.

Iron shots

One of the most noticeable features of the professional game is that the players make good ball-striking look effortless. They swing within themselves, and that is what you must remember when you work on your iron play. The emphasis is on your ability to make and consistently repeat a compact swing.

Swing radius
Left arm provides the radius to the swing as the upper body turns

◁ Compact backswing
To improve your ball-striking, work on repeating a compact three-quarter length action. A tip is to keep both feet flat on the ground, because this restricts your hips and improves the rotary motion of your upper body.

1 **Direction control** The irons are direction clubs, not distance clubs, so make your swing at a pace you can comfortably control. You want to be able to feel the weight of the clubhead as you swing it into a compact, three-quarter position, your left arm providing the radius as you turn your upper body.

◁ Sizing it up
Always start your preshot routine behind the ball and absorb the full view of the shot. Think about the factors that are likely to influence the shot, such as the lie of the ball and the direction of the wind, and create a positive image of the desired outcome in your mind.

PLAYERS' TIP

A controlled shot
From the setup, the role of the left arm and left shoulder is clear. The upper body turns away from the target and the wrists hinge the club into the three-quarter "slot" for optimum control at the top of the backswing. Unwinding from the ground up makes the arms and hands fall into a natural hitting position, and the club is released to a full and balanced finish.

Hands first
The hands lead the clubhead through the ball

Good leg action
The right knee works toward the left to stabilize the club at impact

《 **Clubface square at impact**
Use the rotation of your body to return the club squarely to the ball at impact—a virtual mirror-image of the setup position. With your head steady, your right shoulder moves under your chin as your hands release the clubhead at speed.

2 **Perfect timing** A controlled swing produces solid contact as the arms and the hands return the club squarely to the ball. As the upper body turns about the natural axis of the spine, the arms, hands, and club are accelerated by the centrifugal forces emanating from the body, free-wheeling all the way through the ball.

⌃ **Consistent axis** For accurate ball-striking, it is important that you maintain the spine angle determined at setup until the moment of impact. This provides you with a consistent axis about which to turn. Once you have struck the ball, your body naturally straightens up as it unwinds to a tension-free finish.

Pitching and Chipping

When it comes to pitching and chipping, there is no substitute for imagination as you weigh up your options and identify the correct shot to play. Then it is a matter of achieving the correct combination of flight and roll to send the ball close to the hole. The pros spend more time honing these skills than anything else—and so should you.

Pitching the ball

The development of a consistent, solid swing is determined by your ability to control the "core" motion of your body. This applies to a good pitching technique too, as you concentrate on using the loft on the clubface to fly the ball all the way to the hole.

Tuned in to the target
While the body is slightly open to the line of the shot, the club is aimed squarely at the flag

Swinging the club
As the wrists hinge, the club swings up on a good plane. The shaft should bisect the right shoulder when viewed from this angle

Linked together
The movement of the arms and the club is linked to the rotary motion of the upper body for a controlled backswing

1 **Comfortable setup** For pitching, the key to a good setup is that it should promote a synchronized arm-and-body motion that will allow you to control the speed of your delivery through impact. Most notably, your body should be slightly open to the line of the shot—in other words, aligned slightly to the left of target. This preempts a good impact position. Your arms, hands, and the club fall into a compact position over the ball.

2 **Backswing** Control the length and the speed of your swing with the rotation of your body. Your arms and hands should respond to the momentum of your shoulders, your wrists hinging up naturally to set the club on the right plane and inject the necessary rhythm.

Tracking the target
Eyes should follow the flight of the ball toward the flag as the upper body turns through to face the target

In control
Arm swing is closely linked to body motion all the way to a controlled finish

Legs still
Minimal leg action reflects the fact that there is little weight shift involved

3 **Striking the ball** The precise nature of the strike is vital for control. As you unwind, you are looking for a crisp ball-then-turf strike that removes a shallow divot immediately beyond the ball. Play the ball back of center in your stance to help you to achieve the desired angle of delivery.

4 **Follow-through** A good way to maintain your rhythm and tempo is to try to match the length of your backswing to the length of your follow-through. There is little weight shift. From the setup, a controlled body action swings your arms back and forth.

All about control

These three images show you a pitching sequence looking toward the ball instead of toward the target. When you go out to work on your wedge play, remember that you are not trying to make a full swing. Power is not the issue. Control, finesse, and good rhythm are the important watchwords. There are no physical limitations in this area of the game, and this means that everyone can easily learn these techniques.

Relaxed setup
With a relatively narrow and slightly open stance, play the ball just back of center, with your hands in front of the ball

Controlled backswing
Shorter-length backswing is for control not power

Controlled center
Standing open naturally encourages a compact arm-and-body motion as you turn your stomach

Stable lower body
Knees remain flexed to stabilize the turning of the upper body

1 **Sound setup** These shots do not require a full body pivot, so a sound setup involves aiming your feet, knees, and hips slightly open to the target line. Settle your weight roughly 60:40 in favor of the left side to promote the downward swing into the ball that generates backspin. Play the ball in the middle of your feet and flex your knees for stability.

2 **Turning away** A number of the world's top players talk about turning their stomach away from the target to initiate the backswing move. Try this and allow your wrists to hinge naturally in response to the weight of the clubhead. Your arms must swing in harmony with the smooth rotation of your torso.

Still head
For accurate striking, the head remains steady until the ball is on its way

Symmetry
The arms and the upper body maintain the symmetry first established at the setup

Follow-through
The right hand and arm are released into the follow-through

Knees to target
As the body unwinds, the knees move gently toward the target

3 **Creating backswing** As you unwind, make sure you do not try to help the ball up into the air with your hands. Fall into that trap and you will end up with a scooping motion and a poor shot. To create backspin and the right trajectory, put your trust in the loft on the clubface. Swing down into the back of the ball and release it freely toward the target.

PLAYERS' TIP

Controlling distance
When pitching, you are looking to make a compact, controlled swing that enables you to send the ball a very specific distance. A good way to do this is to think of your arms as being on a clockface. Make a backswing to a certain time, then match it up on the clockface with the same length follow-through.

Setup is 6 o'clock with the ball in the middle of the feet.

A 9 o'clock swing sees the hands halfway back.

For a slightly longer shot, a 10 o'clock backswing...

... would be matched with a 2 o'clock follow-through.

The art of chipping

Few shots in golf offer the versatility of the basic chipping stroke. The regular chip shot features a subtle wrist action that promotes a silky flow to what is a very short and controlled swing. This enables you to loft the ball through the air and land it on the green, where it rolls toward the hole like a putt.

1 **Setup position** The basics of good motion are again engineered at the setup. You will very quickly learn to adopt a good position if you use the following as your setup cue: "Ball back, hands forward, weight forward." Place your feet close together and lean gently toward the target. At the same time, your upper arms should rest lightly on the upper part of your chest, promoting good connection.

PLAYERS' TIP

Flatten the tee peg
With a chipping swing, it is easy to "quit" at impact and stub the clubhead into the ground behind the ball. Try this drill in order to make a free swing of the clubhead and accelerate it through the hitting area. Tee up a ball. Then try to ignore the ball and focus on flattening the tee peg into the ground at the point of impact.

Tee up the ball ½in (1cm) off the ground. Set up normally and make a smooth, free swing. When you flatten the tee peg you will make a nice chip. Repeat this swing without the tee.

Triangle shape
Create a long, narrow triangle with your arms and shoulders and keep it intact as you control the stroke with your shoulders

Leaning left
For a good position, lean your upper body toward the target

Hands ahead
Position the ball back in your stance, with your hands forward

Feet together
With your feet fairly close together and aimed a little open, settle the majority of your weight on your left side

Perfectly on track
The clubface remains square to the path of the swing, mirroring the back of the left hand

Staying focused
Head should remain steady, with eyes fixed on the ball until it has been clipped forward

2 **Backswing** Once you are comfortable, turn your stomach to help initiate the backswing motion. Keeping the triangle shape, use your arms and shoulders to swing the club back and forth. Maintain a light grip pressure that allows your wrists to flex just a little as you change direction.

>> **Light touch** The clubhead remains low to the ground as it works back and through. A light grip pressure keeps the hands and arms in touch with the flow of a good swing.

3 **Contact on the ball** For solid contact, your hands must lead the clubhead into the ball. Focus on creating momentum with the rotary motion of your trunk. This will determine the speed at which your arms swing back and through. At the same time, let your wrists hinge in response to the weight of the clubhead.

>> **Down the line** From its position toward the back foot, the ball is "pinched" off the turf with a positive descending blow. With practice, you will develop a feel for the speed of the clubhead and the distance you land the ball with different clubs.

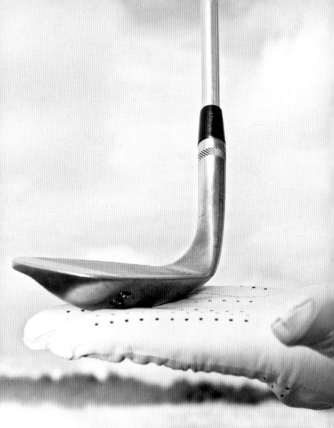

Sand Play

Whether they are protecting a green or lining a fairway, sand bunkers represent some of the most visually striking hazards in golf, and for some players, the most intimidating. The secret to escaping from them unscathed is to make certain key adjustments to your setup. This will enable you to make a confident swing, balanced from start to finish, and achieve the desired contact to hit the ball out of the sand. Then you will have no need to fear these shots.

Using bounce

The greenside bunker shot is unique in golf. Your objective is not to hit the ball, but to skim the clubface through the sand, producing a miniexplosion that propels the ball out of the bunker. The sand iron, characterized by the heavy flange on the sole of the club, is designed to help you do just that. Once again, the setup is the key to success.

Using a sand iron

When it comes to developing a versatile short game (pitches, chips, and putts), nothing is more important than investing in a good sand iron. The heavy flange on the clubface of the sand iron gives the club a playing quality known as "bounce." It acts as a rudder, helping the club to bounce through the sand and "splash" the ball to safety. Good bunker play is all about utilizing this bounce. A close look at the clubhead will help you to appreciate it. Sit the sole of the club squarely on your hand. Then swivel the shaft through your fingers, turning the leading edge to the right to lay the clubface open.

Clubhead
Steel is the standard and most preferred metal for sand iron clubheads

Open face
As the clubface opens, the back edge of the flange increasingly sits lower than the leading edge

⌃ Less loft
The difference between an open and square clubface, shown here, is clear. On a square face, the flange on the sole of the club is not accentuated and the club has less loft. You might typically use a square clubface to play a standard pitch shot from the fairway.

⌃ Increased loft
Turning the clubface to the right, or clockwise, opens it and increases the loft. A greenside bunker shot with a good lie is played with an open clubface. It skims more easily through the sand and maximizes loft.

PLAYERS' TIP

Presetting bounce

The golden rule of greenside bunker play is that you must always preset the open clubface before you complete your grip. To do this, hold the club up in front of your body, and simply swivel the shaft through your fingers, turning the toe-end of the club through to the right. Once you have done this, you are ready to complete your grip and settle down to the shot, safe in the knowledge that you have preset the necessary bounce, and are now free to focus on making a confident swing through the sand.

For a regular greenside bunker shot, turn the clubface about 30 degrees to the right as you look down on it.

Then complete your regular grip. In so doing, you will preset the playing characteristics you need.

⏶ Easing into a good setup

The rules of the game do not allow you to ground the club in a hazard, so, as you settle down to the shot, hover the open clubface about 2in (5cm) behind the ball. Rhythm plays a vital part in a good bunker shot, and easing your knees toward the target will provide you with the feel for your swing.

⏶ Full wrist hinge

Because the sand acts as a buffer and absorbs the speed of the clubhead, you have to be prepared to be quite aggressive with your swing to make the ball pop out just a short distance. It is vital that you cultivate a full wrist hinge in the course of making your backswing, in order to load energy to release through impact.

Greenside shots

Having preset the bounce and finalized a good grip that allows your wrists to hinge freely, the next step is to aim both the club and your body correctly before going on to make a normal swing. This is the key to good sand play—once you are familiar with the specific adjustments to the club and your setup position, you simply make a normal swing.

Final destination
Keep in your mind a positive visual of the ball floating toward the flag on a cushion of sand

Lining up
Aim your shoulders roughly 30 degrees left of the target. They should match the alignment of your toes

Preset wrist action
Hold your hands relatively low at the setup to promote a full wrist hinge in the backswing

Hovering behind the ball
The sand iron hovers behind the ball, the leading edge facing toward your target

1 **Open body line** Once you have completed your grip, aim the leading edge of your sand iron at the flag. Then, to compensate for the fact that you are swinging an open clubface, adjust your body line so that it is open in relation to the target. As you settle down into position, your feet, hips, and shoulders should be roughly 30 degrees open to the line of the shot. Shuffle your feet into the sand to establish a sound base to help you balance.

⌃ **Position at address** For a regular greenside shot, the ball is just forward of center. You hover the clubhead 2–3in (5–8cm) behind the ball, over the point at which you intend to strike the sand. Your hands should be fairly low at address, and your knees noticeably flexed.

Open clubface
A good swing maintains the open clubface ready for impact

Fully loaded
The wrists are loaded with energy, ready to release the clubhead into the sand behind the ball

Body control
As it rotates, the upper body keeps its posture and balance on a constant axis

Suspension unit
Knees and thighs are sensitive to the shot, stabilizing the swing and promoting rhythm

In balance
Legs provide a solid foundation to the swing, maintaining balance

Equal weight
There is hardly any weight shift during the swing

2 **Smooth backswing** When you are comfortable with the adjustments to your setup position, focus on swinging the club along the line of your toes. Although you are only aiming to have the ball travel a short distance, it is important that you play these shots with a relatively long, flowing swing. Resist the temptation to dig down beneath the ball, and focus on combining a full shoulder turn with a free-flowing arm swing.

⌃ **Bunker technique** Good technique in a bunker shot is all about establishing a sound base and making a good upper-body turn while nurturing a full wrist hinge. Many tour players control the speed of their swing with the rotary motion of their stomach as they wind and unwind.

PLAYERS' TIP

How much sand to take

Develop a consistent shot in which you take a shallow cut of sand with the ball. One way to practice this is to draw a box in the sand around the ball. (The rules do not allow you to do this out on the course!) Aim about 2–3in (5–8cm) behind the ball and work on removing a shallow divot of sand from behind and in front of the ball. Lay the clubface open and get a feel for the impact as the club bounces through the sand.

Drawing a box around the ball serves as a guiding visual when you practice.

The club should remove a shallow cut of sand from beneath the ball.

Staying focused
Keep your eyes fixed on a spot a few centimeters behind the ball—the point at which you intend the club to enter the sand

Slicing action
Swinging along the line of your toes promotes a slicing action that splashes both the club and ball up and out of the sand

Open clubface
Maintain an open clubface to allow the clubhead to move freely through the sand

Staying grounded
Keeping the right foot grounded in the sand improves your release

3 Unwind your body From the top of the backswing, unwind your upper body through to the target. This provides the momentum that swings your arms, hands, and the clubhead. Swing along the line of your body and think about releasing your right hand fully to accelerate the clubhead down into the sand. Rhythm is a key factor, and a useful tip is to keep your feet flat in the sand as you accelerate through the sand beneath the ball.

⌃ Accelerate through the sand
It is vital that you commit yourself to a positive release of the clubhead through impact. Do not be afraid to be aggressive. The sand acts as a buffer and absorbs a good deal of the club's energy. You need to make sure that you accelerate the clubhead.

Good technique
The open clubface
is maintained all the
way to the finish

In harmony
The compact nature of the
swing extends to the finish,
with the hands, arms, and club
in total harmony with the body

All the way
For a smooth
acceleration,
it is vital that
you rotate your
body all the way
through the shot

Body speed
Think of your body
as the hub of the
wheel that controls
the speed of your
arms. Experiment
with your turn
speed to adjust how
far you fly the ball

Sensitive knees
Allowing the right knee
to ease through the shot
enhances your feel for
impact and the overall
rhythm of your swing

Good footwork
Momentum of the swing
pulls the right heel up, the
weight now supported on
the left side

4 **Control the speed** Many
players react to their target,
instinctively producing the length
and speed of swing that enables
them to fly the ball the desired
distance. Only with practice will
you develop this feel for greenside
sand shots. You need to work
on generating a consistent rate
of acceleration as you wind and
unwind your body. Think of your
body as the hub of the wheel
that controls the swinging speed
of your arms and hands. Measuring
your swing in this way will reward you
with sound bunker shots.

⌃ **Rhythm from the ground up** Many
of the game's all-time great bunker
players talk about feeling the nature of
the shot in the feet and knees. Easing
your knees toward the target as you
unwind provides a terrific source of
feel and rhythm.

Long sand shots

Often regarded as one of the toughest propositions in golf, a sand shot from about 33–60 yards (30–55m) is a severe test of your ability to control the delivery of the clubhead through impact. The key is to aim to strike the sand about 1in (2.5cm) behind the ball, and regulate distance with the length of your swing.

Eyes down Keep your eyes fixed on where you want the club to make contact with the sand

Body in control The spine angle is maintained all the way to impact—vital for the accuracy of the strike

1 **Secure footing** Set up for this type of shot as you would for a pitch from the fairway—that is, with your body slightly open to the target and weight evenly spread between the feet. "Choking" down on the grip half an inch or so will add to your overall feeling of control of the clubhead. Shuffling your feet into the sand will provide the secure foundation you need to maintain balance.

⌃ **Stable stance** Secure your footing and play the ball in the middle of your stance. Use your knees as shock-absorbers to give you an overall feeling of stability.

2 **Turn and hinge** In common with the workings of a regular pitch shot, this is a swing controlled predominantly by the rotation of the big muscles in your upper body. With the legs passive, there is little or no weight shift to speak of as your shoulders turn and your wrists begin to hinge to set the club up on plane. From here, complete your body turn to produce a solid backswing.

Moment of truth
Square clubface takes a shallow divot of sand from beneath the ball

3 **At the top** From the setup, your spine angle provides the axis for your swing, and retaining it is the key to achieving a solid position at the top of your backswing. Your knees and lower body generally provide all the stability you need to turn effectively. Swing your hands and the club to a position high above the tip of your right shoulder—a useful check that you are on plane.

4 **Eyes fixed on impact** With your objective being to make contact with the sand about 1in (2.5cm) behind the ball, you must keep your eyes fixed on this target as you unwind your swing and release the club through impact. Such is the precise nature of this shot, you must maintain a good spine angle so that you swing on a consistent path and deliver the club with control.

5 **A full finish** In order to create the momentum necessary to displace both the sand and the ball, it is vital that you commit to a full and flowing swing that takes you all the way to a balanced finish. Remember, the speed of your delivery determines the exact distance the ball flies.

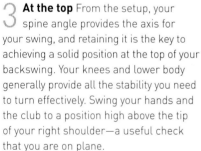

« **Secure footing**
For overall control and accuracy, it is important that you keep your lower body passive as you focus on turning your shoulders to create the backswing.

« **Feel for distance**
Experiment with the length and acceleration of your swing to develop a good feel for shots of different distances.

Putting

While you may not be able to strike the ball as well as the top professionals, there is nothing to stop you from developing a short game and a rock-solid putting stroke that stands comparison with the best players. Putting may not be the most exciting part of the game, but it is where the pros make their scores. To emulate them, all you need is a grounding in the basic principles of putting, and the determination to improve your technique and hone your feel.

Putting basics

The majority of the world's leading golfers put their trust in what is known as a pendulum putting stroke—that is, one that sees the unit of the arms, hands, and putter controlled predominantly by the rocking of the shoulders. Just as in the swing, a good pendulum technique begins with establishing the correct position at setup.

Creating good posture

To establish a setup position that promotes a true pendulum-style motion, first establish a sound stance. Then bend from the hips to create a spine angle that sets the shoulders in a horizontal position, allowing the arms to hang freely.

Lining up
Head and eyes are directly over the ball

Arms and shoulders
Arms hang freely, ready to swing back and forth in response to the rocking of the shoulders

Right hand
Check that the palm of your right hand mirrors the position of the putter-face

Knees flexed
Slight knee-flex provides a stable posture

Anchored
Both feet are planted for a sound base to the stroke

Square-on
Aim the putter-face squarely along the line on which you want to start the ball rolling

≪ Stable posture
Establish a balanced posture with your weight divided equally between both feet. Keep your lower body "quiet" throughout your stroke. Any leg movement can affect your accuracy.

PLAYERS' TIP

Correct setup
Set up with the ball directly beneath your eyes. To check this, set up over a ball and drop a second ball from the bridge of your nose. It should land on top of the other one.

Putting grip

There is an important distinction between the grip you use for the full swing and that which you must learn to adopt for putting. For the full swing, where the emphasis is on the ability to generate clubhead speed, the grip is designed in such a way that the wrists hinge freely in the swing. By contrast, for the shoulder-controlled putting stroke, you create a grip that joins the hands to work as a guiding unit.

The way in which you place the club in your left hand creates the grip for putting. For the full-swing grip, you run the club low in the fingers, thus mobilizing the left wrist. For putting, you are best served with a grip that sees the club run from the tip of your right forefinger to a point high on the heel of the hand. With your fingers closed around the grip, this adjustment locks the putter in place and immobilizes your left wrist.

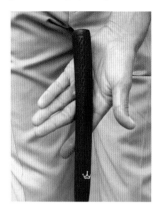

1 **High in the palm** To eliminate wrist action, "lock" the putter in your left hand, laying the grip high through the palm of your hand. This will give you a real feeling of security when you close your hand on the grip.

2 **Palms parallel** For a neutral hold that gives you absolute control over the position of the putter-face, it is important that the palms of your hands face each other as they assume their position on the grip.

3 **Reverse overlap** Drape your left forefinger over the fingers on your right hand to unite your hands. This helps you to have passive hands because your wrists are effectively locked in place.

4 **Secure guiding unit** The back of your left hand and palm of your right should be aligned squarely with the putter-face. Your hands are then ready to respond to the momentum of your shoulders.

SHOULDER-CONTROLLED PUTTING

A good setup creates the framework for a pendulum putting stroke. The arms hang down, creating the control area of the arms and the shoulders.

By gently rocking the shoulders, the unit of the arms and the putter moves in unison into the backswing. The hands remain totally passive.

The shoulder-controlled stroke returns the arms and the putter to the setup position. The head is still as the ball is stroked toward the hole.

The structure of the stroke is maintained into the finish. The eyes are still fixed on the original position of the ball. The legs have been passive throughout.

Pendulum motion

The pendulum-style rocking of the shoulders is the most consistent means of building and repeating a solid putting stroke. This shoulder-controlled method eliminates the uncertainty of wrist action and leaves you free to focus on developing a smooth one-two rhythm and achieving a solid contact at impact.

Steady head
The head is the fulcrum of the pendulum. It must stay very still throughout the whole stroke

Y-shape
A Y-shape is formed by your shoulders, arms, and the club

Passive hands
With a good neutral grip, the two hands are prepared to work as a guiding unit, staying passive throughout the stroke

Still knees
Gently flexed for balance, the knees should remain still to stabilize the body during the stroke

Steady legs
Keep your lower body as steady as possible to anchor the stroke

1 **Feel the connection** This is a great way to develop your feel for a solid, pendulum-style stroke. Trap a club between your upper arms and your chest at the setup, and keep it there throughout the stroke. This forces your arms and shoulders to work as a unit.

⌃ **Primed for action** With the club trapped in position, you are ready to develop a repeating stroke. If you maintain a sense of connection with the club, your arms and shoulders will want to work together, guiding the putter-head back and then through to the hole.

2 **Start to rock** To initiate the stroke, feel as if you are gently rocking your shoulders. The right shoulder works up as the left shoulder goes down. As you do this, you will find that your arms naturally follow suit. If you are doing it correctly, the Y-shape formed by your shoulders, arms, and the shaft of the putter will remain intact. Keep the putter fairly close to the ground as it glides away from the ball.

3 **Keep control** Your through-swing should be a mirror-image of your backswing, as your shoulders and upper body continue to control the movement of your arms, hands, and putter. Keep your hands totally passive through impact and beyond so that you maintain the controlling unit of your forearms and achieve a fluent, even-paced motion.

Shoulder control
As the right shoulder moves up, the left shoulder goes down with the natural symmetry of a true pendulum motion

Flat-footed
Since there is no noticeable weight shift, you can keep your feet flat on the ground at all times

Staying connected
To enjoy total symmetry, keep the club in place across your chest all the way to the finish

Keeping your shape
At the finish, check that your forearms and the putter shaft maintain the Y-shape formed at address

《 Putter moves inside As long as your arms and shoulders continue to work together, the putter will swing slightly to the inside as you draw it away from the ball—the laws of physics dictate that it will. You will notice that the longer the putt, the more the putter-head will work inside the line in response to the turning motion of your shoulders.

《 Putter-face stays square Another benefit of controlling the stroke with your shoulders, assuming your hands and wrists remain passive, is that the putter-face naturally remains square to the path along which it is swinging. When you practice, hold your finish and check that the putter-face has not twisted, but retains its original relationship with your hands and arms.

Longer putts

Your ability to roll the ball close to the hole from long range depends on the consistency of your stroke and your skill at reading the green. From about 7–10 yards (6–9m) of the hole, you must believe you can make the putt. With anything longer you should aim to lay the ball "dead" (so close you cannot miss) for a tap-in.

PLAYERS' TIP

Marking a ball
Once your ball is deemed to be on the putting surface, you are entitled to mark its position with a small disc (a coin or a ball-marker). You can then pick it up and clean it before replacing it in its original position.

A useful tip when you come to replace your ball is to align the maker's name squarely down the line to the hole. That will help you to aim the putter face squarely.

1 **Preparing to putt** From long range, it is common to ask your playing partner to tend the pin, that is to hold the flagstick as you prepare to putt. This helps you to get the best possible feel for the distance you have to roll the ball. Once you have struck the putt, your partner must remove the flagstick and stand aside.

⌃ **Visualize the putt** A positive preshot routine helps you to focus. Study the green from directly behind the ball, and from the side, to get an idea of the subtle slopes that you have to negotiate.

⌃ **Relax at setup** Tension destroys any hope of producing a flowing motion, so make sure that your hands and arms are relaxed at setup.

3 **Feel the pace** For a smooth acceleration that gets the ball rolling and tracking the line to the hole, aim to make your through-swing a little longer than your backswing. This promotes a flowing rhythm and a positive strike. Focus on the tempo of your overall motion to help you glide the putter through the ball.

2 **Judging pace** Your arms and shoulders must work together to produce a truly connected stroke. Keep your hands passive on the grip as you swing the putter-head back and forth. The key to producing the right pace to roll the ball to the hole-side consistently lies in the length of your stroke. The longer the putt, the longer your stroke should be.

⌃ **Smooth stroke**
Controlled by the shoulders, a connected stroke sees the putter-head remain fairly close to the ground as it is drawn smoothly away from the ball.

⌃ **Precise movement**
As you accelerate the putter-head smoothly through impact, your goal is to strike the equator of the ball with a slight upstroke that imparts a pure roll on the ball and helps it hold its line on the way to the hole.

⌃ **Follow-through**
One way to ensure a smooth acceleration is to make your through-swing a little longer than your backswing. Maintain the Y-shape formed by your shoulders, arms, and the putter itself.

Practice

Top tour professionals do not spend hours and hours on the practice ground just for the fun of it. They know that there are no shortcuts to playing good golf. The only way to realize long-term improvement is to set aside the time to go out and practice. Repetition of good habits is the key. Do this in conjunction with lessons from a qualified professional, who will keep your game on the straight and narrow. Your efforts will be rewarded.

Basic exercises

Broken down into its raw component parts, a good swing is a body turn coupled with an arm swing—the latter facilitated by a hand action that effectively provides the hinge between you and the club. Swinging with your feet relatively close together is an excellent way to blend these components with a flowing rhythm.

Turn, hinge, and swing

The beauty of the half-swing exercise is that it encapsulates the key ingredients that you are looking to repeat in a full swing. With your feet fairly close together, the emphasis is on "setting" or hinging your wrists to get the clubhead swinging in harmony with the turning of your body. As your wrists hinge up, the butt-end of the club should point approximately midway between the ball and your feet.

Checkpoint
Clubshaft mirrors its original angle at the setup—a sign of being on plane

⊠ **Swing on plane** The correct plane—the pitched angle of your swing—can be identified with a simple checkpoint. Stick a tee peg in the hole at the top of the grip. The key then is to focus on making a full wrist hinge that gets the club swinging up to a halfway position. Your swing is said to be on plane when the tee points roughly halfway between your feet and the ball.

Still head
A steady head provides a consistent axis about which to turn your body

Arm position
Left arm swings snugly across the chest as the wrists hinge

Level hips
Right hip turns backward on a fairly level plane

Stable legs
Right knee remains flexed, providing the brace against which you turn

⏵ **Angles at setup** Comfort is vital at the setup. Once you have created a good spine angle by tipping forward from the hips, you want to feel that your arms hang freely from your shoulders. Your hands should be firmly on the grip, but at the same time relaxed. The muscles in your hands and forearms should be keyed-up and ready to move, but pliable. To begin with, use a short iron and tee the ball.

☑ **Creating a swinging motion** As you will discover, hitting shots with your feet relatively close together very quickly teaches you that you need to use your hands and arms correctly in order to create a swinging motion. At the same time, you will find that repeating that swing with a good rhythm is the key to hitting solid shots. The crossover of your hands through impact is the most vital thing to get right, because this maximizes your speed.

Natural turn
Head turns naturally as the body rotates to the half-swing finish

Hand positions
Halfway through a swing, you should be able to see your left hand under your right

Finishing point
Symmetry of the half-swing is complete when the club bisects the left shoulder

Compact release
Left elbow is close to your side as you throw your hands toward the target

⌃ **Synchronizing motion** The half-swing exercise will develop your sense of timing as you hinge and then release your hands in tandem with the rotary motion of your body. It will also help you to establish the natural symmetry that exists in a solid swing. Once you have a feel for this action, extending the body turn will reward you with a sound full swing.

PLAYERS' TIP

Train your body
Hooking a club behind your back prepares you to rehearse the pivot motion—the heart of a good swing. From the setup, turn your upper body against the resistance of the right knee to make your backswing, and then unwind to finish with your spine straight.

Rotary motion

Many of the problems experienced in developing and repeating a solid swing can be traced to poor rotary motion of the body—usually the result of a general lack of flexibility. This is why one or two well-chosen golf-specific exercises should play a vital part in your practice. They prepare the muscles that you will need so that they will work effectively in creating a sound swing.

Arched body
Stretch your body as you arch your body from side to side

» **Strengthening the torso** Hold your arms above your head and interlock your fingers. Then stretch to your fullest extent. Arch your body over to one side, holding the full stretch for a couple of seconds. Repeat on the other side. With every repetition you will be stretching the muscles in your torso that dominate your body turn.

Helping hand
A coach can help you practice a fuller shoulder turn in the backswing

Head to the right
Rotate your head gently to the right to ease the turning of your shoulders

Pivot exercise

There are a number of popular variations on the pivot exercise, all of which provide an effective means of developing the core movement of your body—the hub of your swing. As you turn your shoulders back, be aware of the shift in your weight in tandem with the motion.

« **Maintaining good angles** To begin with, hold a club tight across the back of your shoulders and adopt a good posture. Then maintain your spine angle as you rotate your upper body through a full 90 degrees over a steady leg action.

Arms and shoulders

The rotator cuffs in your shoulders play a major part in creating a solid swing. To stretch and loosen these muscles fully, use this arms-and-shoulders exercise in conjunction with the pivot exercise below left. Together, they will prepare you for work on your swing.

Good rotation
You should rotate about a consistent axis—just as you should in the swing

Right turn
As you turn away from the target, use your right arm to pull your shoulders as far as you can to the right—feel the burn

Full stretch
Without moving your feet, turn your torso and hold a fully stretched position. Then switch arms and turn toward the target

◄ Stretching the shoulders Stand up straight and hook your right arm around your left elbow to create this isometric exercise. As you turn your shoulders you should pull with the right arm to really stretch the muscles in your upper arms and torso. Hold the position for a few seconds and then repeat on the other side.

PLAYERS' TIP

Two-club exercise

Having limbered up the muscles in your arms and shoulders, use the two-club exercise to train the shape of your swing. It is one of the best exercises there is. The combined weight of two clubs creates an irresistible momentum that inspires a natural, free-flowing motion. Feel and swing that added weight with a coordinated arm-and-body motion. Let the momentum of the clubs pull you all the way around to a full, balanced finish. This exercise will help to remove any tendency that you may have to overcontrol your swing with the muscles in your upper body.

A full shoulder turn combined with a compact arm swing is the ideal combination for control.

As you unwind, let the weight of the two clubs pull your body around so that you finish facing left of the target.

Nearly horizontal
The compact nature of the arm swing sees the club just short of the horizontal at the top

Sign of power
Look for this 90-degree angle between your right forearm and the club

» **Checking position** This is one of the few exercises in which you can easily check a key position in your swing. If you have the correct angle between your right forearm and the club at the top of your backswing, it confirms that your arm has kept full control of the club.

Your target
When you practice, make this compact backswing position your goal with every club in the bag

Body core
Maintain your spine angle as you turn your stomach and shoulders—your body core

Weight change
Good leg action helps in the winding-up of your body as your weight flows into the right side

Coordinated swing

The chances of repeating a compact, coordinated swing are far greater when you combine a full shoulder turn with a relatively short arm swing. When you practice, pay attention to the position of your right arm at the top. Look for a 90-degree angle between your right forearm and the club. A good exercise is to rehearse your backswing while supporting your right arm with the back of your left hand.

PLAY LIKE A PRO

Adam Scott
The coordination of a solid swing is easy to see here. The full shoulder turn confirms the dynamic rotation of the core, while a compact arm swing maintains control of the club. This is a repeatable position that the world's best players look for, and one golfers should try to copy.

Full control
Right hand and forearm
have full control of the
club at the top of the swing

« Supporting the club
Remember, a good
backswing combines a
full shoulder turn with
a relatively short arm
swing. As you turn, you
want to feel that your
right arm fully supports
the club at the top.

Momentum
From the top of your
swing, you want to feel
that a gentle rolling of
the ankles reverses
your momentum back
toward the target

Right arm only

The role of the right hand and
arm is important not only in terms
of creating the structure of your
backswing but also in generating the
whip in the release through the ball.
Clearly, the right arm does not work
alone in the swing, but if you isolate
it by swinging with just your right
hand on the grip, you will find that
you quickly identify with the way it
first positions the club at the top of
the swing, and then governs your
sense of timing as you release it
on the way back down.

⌃ Cracking the whip
Once you can get your right arm into
this slot at the top of your backswing,
you will be able to generate clubhead
lag and make a loud swish on the way
down. Use this exercise to feel how the
wrist cocks and the right arm folds,
and learn to "crack the whip" for
maximum clubhead speed.

Chipping drills

One of the most common and destructive faults in chipping is caused by a tendency to want to scoop the ball into the air. By contrast, a good chipping action combines a subtle hand and wrist action with a gentle body turn to create a descending blow on the ball.

Arm and club in line
Ease your weight onto your front foot so that your left arm and the clubshaft are in a straight line

Ball back
Think "ball back, hands forward, weight forward" for a good setup position

1 **The setup** To get used to the feel of a good chipping action, lay a club on the ground about 4in (10cm) behind the ball and then take your normal setup. Your goal is to create a stroke that allows you to strike the ball without hitting the club on the ground. Keep your weight on your left side as you gently turn your stomach and cultivate this subtle wrist action.

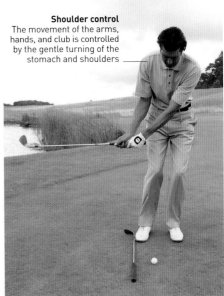

Shoulder control
The movement of the arms, hands, and club is controlled by the gentle turning of the stomach and shoulders

2 **Weight distribution** As you make your backswing with your arms and shoulders, make sure that your weight remains on your front foot. This will encourage the clubhead to rise fairly steeply, setting your wrists in a position from where they can strike down into the ball to deliver the crisp contact that imparts a controlling backswing.

Steady head
For solid and consistent ball-striking, keep your head still throughout the shot

Working as a lever
As the upper body turns, the left arm remains comfortably straight through impact, providing the lever that controls the club

Leaning shaft
To encourage a slightly steeper angle of attack into the ball, the shaft should lean toward the target at impact

Hands ahead of the ball
For a crisp downward strike, the hands lead the club through the ball and are ahead of the ball at impact

3 **Crisp strike** As long as you keep your weight on your left side and trust the loft on the clubface, you will avoid the shaft on the ground on the way down and create the crisp ball-turf strike that you are looking for. Resist the temptation to scoop the ball up and instead, release the club down into the back of the ball. Note that your hands return to a position slightly ahead of the ball at impact. This is exactly as they were primed to do at the setup.

4 **Hold the finish** As your upper body continues to rotate, maintain the relationship between your arms and shoulders all the way to the finish. Do not use wrist action, because this will ruin your shot. If the clubhead stays low to the ground in the follow-through, it shows that you have kept your hands relatively passive throughout.

Putting drills

No matter how good your ball-striking may be, your ability to score depends on the quality of your short game and, in particular, on your skill with the putter. You need to develop a consistent stroke that rewards you with a fine sense of touch for long putts, and the total confidence to knock in the critical shorter putts.

Body control
Hold your finish until the ball is well on its way to the hole

Square to the path
As a result of a pure pendulum stroke, the putter-face remains square to the path along which it is traveling

On target
Released at perfect pace, the ball will follow its line to the target

Shrink your target
Putting to a tee peg will sharpen your focus and boost your confidence

Develop a feel for pace

If you want to be a consistently good putter, you must be able to judge the pace of a putt so that you can send the ball across the green to the hole-side. Develop a feel for the pace of the greens and learn how to have absolute control over your stroke. This will allow you to set the ball rolling at the speed you want. There are a number of drills that you can use to improve this aspect of your putting. One is to stick a tee peg in the practice green and work on clustering balls around it from mid- to long-range. A tee is a much smaller target than a hole, so after this drill, the hole will appear enormous out on the course.

◄◄ **Focus on your tempo** The rhythm of your stroke is a critical factor in developing your feel for the speed at which you release the ball across the green. Try to relax your hands, arms, and shoulders so that you are able to make a flowing swing. This will enable you to strike the ball solidly and consistently.

1 **Brushing the ball** Short putts are all about confidence. The more often you hole a putt, the more confident you will become. This drill can help you develop that confidence. Find a straight putt of about 5ft (1.5m), establish a good setup, and prepare to putt the ball without making a backswing.

2 **Shoulder control** Control the acceleration of your arms, hands, and putter from your shoulders. Feel the ball on the putter-face as you brush it toward the hole. It is vital that your hands remain passive on the grip. Keep your head dead still and visualize the ball running all the way into the hole.

Eyes down
The ball is well on its way to the hole before you turn your head to follow its path

Brush stroke
Imagine you are releasing the ball with the palm of your right hand

Working as a unit
Maintain the relationship between your arms, hands, and putter during the whole stroke

Square to the line
Hold your follow-through, with the putter-face looking squarely at the hole

The desired result
Hit correctly, the ball runs straight for the middle of the cup

3 **Stroking the ball** Think in terms of the palm of your right hand being the putter-face, and simply stroke the ball into the hole. Only as you reach the conclusion of the stroke should you allow your head to come up to follow the line of the putt. As you do so, check to see that the putter-face has remained square to the line. Do this for a couple of minutes and then try to get that same brushing sensation as you work on holing out with your regular stroke.

Right-arm drill

In a good on-line stroke, the palm of the right hand mirrors the putter-face as the ball is struck and the putter released toward the hole. To feel this, set up, then let go of your club. Clasp your right wrist with your left hand and work on repeating a smooth back-and-forth motion. Gently rock your shoulders to set your right arm swinging freely.

Test yourself from all angles

A good practice putting session should include a few minutes fine-tuning your basic technique. Then turn your attention to any one of many challenging drills and exercises. These will help you to improve your feel for distances, and you will soon be producing sound strokes as a matter of course. The compass drill is a good way to test yourself on those important short putts. Place a tee at the four main points of the compass around a hole on the practice green, and putt from each of them in turn.

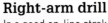

As you work your way around the hole, each putt will feature a different line as you negotiate whatever slopes exist on the green. "Read" each one and identify the exact line you need to take to roll the ball into the hole.

>> Keep on track
To develop the mechanics of your stroke, place two clubs side by side on the green, about 6in (15cm) apart. Position them so that they form a guiding corridor all the way to the hole. This is a great way to improve your general sense of alignment.

ⵣ Feel the way Keep your eyes fixed on the ball, and your body perfectly still. Work your right arm and right shoulder together to get the palm of your hand swinging freely down the line toward the hole.

Putting for real

The right-arm drill will give you the feeling of properly swinging the palm of the hand through toward the hole. With that sensation fresh in your mind, pick up your putter and re-create it when you hit a putt for real. Focus on generating the momentum of the stroke from your shoulders. A simple "one-and-two" movement enables your arms, hands, and putter to swing in unison. Feel the way the palm of your right hand mirrors the putter-face as you stroke the ball toward the hole.

» Perfect pendulum
There is real symmetry to a solid putting stroke. Your feet, knees, hips, and shoulders are all parallel with the line of the putt. Your arms hang freely. The putter becomes an extension of your arms and works back and forth in harmony in a pendulum motion.

Pendulum motion
A gentle rocking of the shoulders gets the hands, arms, and putter swinging in unison

Good posture
The spine angle is retained throughout—vital for consistency of the stroke

Tracking the target
The palm of the right hand mirrors the putter-face—square to the line

Passive hands
The two hands work as one, passive on the grip, muscles relaxed

Safely on line
The ball tracks the line to the middle of the hole

The competitive instinct

Working one-on-one with a practice buddy is the best way to sharpen up your short game. It introduces an element of competition and so tests your skills under pressure. For a balanced practice session, split your time between short-range and long-range putts. Use the crossover drill between two tee pegs that are relatively close together to test your nerve on those putts you hope to make, then move farther apart to place the emphasis more on your feel for distance. Using just one ball each further replicates the reality of the competition—after all, you only get one chance on the course!

Anything you can do to introduce an element of pressure will only benefit the time that you spend practicing. Setting yourself a target and then trying to beat it is one of the most effective techniques there is to sharpen your feel.

Crossover drill To sharpen your touch, take up your position with a partner between two tees stuck into the practice green. Using just one ball each, this drill makes for a good game that can help you get into the habit of stroking a positive and competitive putt. By scoring a point every time you hit a tee, you will naturally be aggressive as you get into competition mode. Make sure that you concentrate on following the ball all the way to the tee. Use that feedback to fine-tune each subsequent attempt you make.

Rock solid
Hands, arms, and shoulders work together for a repeating stroke

Still at the finish
Body, arms, and the putter should be held perfectly still at the finish

Putter on line
For a true roll on the ball, you must swing and release the putter down the line

Feedback
Study the behavior of the ball to fine-tune your reading of the line

The ladder drill

Another good practice drill that tests your stroke under pressure is this ladder drill. From a hole, lay out a line of three or four balls at intervals of about 2ft (60cm). Starting with the one closest to the hole, try to hole out all the balls in the line. If you miss one, start again at the beginning. If this is easy, see how many times you can complete the line before you miss a putt. Increase your target each time you do the drill.

Control zone
Arms and shoulders work together to repeat a solid pendulum-type stroke

Sure touch
Hands remain passive on the grip as you control the stroke with the gentle rocking of your shoulders

Into the hole
Give your full attention to making a good stroke. Visualize the ball running into the middle of the hole

Pitch-mark repair

There is nothing worse than walking onto a green to putt, and finding that it is covered with old pitch marks. Take a moment to repair not only your own pitch marks but also any others that you happen to find. Studies have shown that a freshly repaired pitch mark will recover fully within 24 hours. Those that are ignored can scar a green for several weeks.

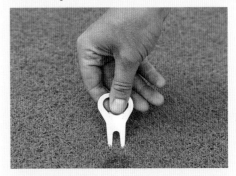

To repair a pitch mark, push the repair tool or a long tee peg into the green behind the indentation. Make sure that you get it beneath the deepest part of the pitch mark.

Press down on the end of the repair tool to lift the turf and bring it back to the surface. Work around the pitch mark until you are satisfied it is ready to be smoothed down.

Finally, use the base of your putter to tap down the repaired pitch mark. This is within the rules of the game, and will leave the surface of the green virtually unblemished.

Fault fixing

One of the difficulties in learning to play golf is that what you think you are doing and what you actually are doing are two very different things! You can ask a professional to help you identify your faults. Here are some typical problems to look out for and some suggestions for how you can go about correcting them.

Sand play—stiff wrists, no flow in the backswing

Fault: Arms and wrists very stiff, rendering the entire movement extremely wooden.

Cause: A mind-set that is determined to scoop the ball out of the sand.

Fix: Good bunker play requires a full wrist hinge that gets the club swinging. Loading the wrists stores the energy in the clubhead that you need to release down into the sand.

Fault

No sense of swing, the hands and arms are ram-rod straight as the club is worked away.

Fix

From the setup, the wrists must be encouraged to hinge fully; crank the wrists back.

Sand play—dipping and falling onto the back foot

Fault: In an attempt to get the clubhead under the ball, the player dips and falls onto the back foot through the impact area.

Cause: A poor concept of correct greenside bunker technique; over anxiety to add loft to the clubface.

Fix: Trust the design of the sand iron and develop the confidence to rotate your body as you hit down and through the sand.

Fault

Overriding anxiety to get the club under the ball sees the right side dip through impact.

Fix

The body rotates through to the target; the club is released fully, down and through the sand.

Chipping—overactive hands and wrists

Fault: Flicking at the ball with the hands and wrists—no consistency of strike.

Cause: A failure to appreciate that a good chipping action involves the hands, arms, and upper body working together.

Fix: Take the wrists out of the equation and develop a body-controlled method that delivers the clubhead on a consistent downward path for a ball-turf strike.

Fault

Overactive hands and wrists flick the clubhead at the ball, making it impossible to judge flight or speed.

Fix

Hands, arms, and upper body work in harmony to produce a repeating stroke for consistent results.

Chipping—poor setup

Fault: The player sets up as if for a full swing. This does not reflect the delicate nature of the shot that is needed from around the edge of the green.

Cause: Poor concept of the mechanics behind the basic chipping action.

Fix: The key is to work on perfecting a setup that primes a good chipping action: i.e., ball back, hands forward, weight forward.

Fault

Body is too square to the target, stance too wide, and weight is evenly spread between the feet.

Fix

With a narrow, slightly open stance, the ball is played back opposite the right toe and the hands are forward.

Putting—standing too tall

Fault: No attempt to bend from the hips. The body is too straight at the setup, eyes too far inside the ball.

Cause: No understanding of the nature of a true pendulum-style stroke.

Fix: Bend from the hips to tilt the upper body forward and allow the arms to hang in a good position. Your eyes should be directly over the ball for a clear picture of the line of the putt.

Fault

Standing too tall at the setup, so feel for the putt is lost; the eyes are looking beyond the ball.

Fix

Bend from the hips to get the shoulders level; the eyes should be directly over the ball.

Full swings—no dynamism at the setup

Fault: Arms and body appear wooden. Lack of effective spine angle at the hips. Legs far too straight.

Cause: Generally poor understanding of the role of a good posture in terms of preparing the body to move correctly.

Fix: An injection of athleticism is required. Just as when a goalkeeper faces a penalty, a good posture leaves you poised.

Fault

General posture is much too straight, with no discernible angle in the hips or at the wrists.

Fix

Bend your knees and stick out your rear to create a good spine angle; feel springy on your feet.

Full swings—poor first move away from the ball

Fault: The clubhead is lifted abruptly with a predominantly hands-and-arms movement. There is little or no rotary motion of the upper body.

Cause: A tendency to want to hit at the ball with the hands; no sense of body movement.

Fix: Rotate the triangle formed by the hands and arms in tandem with the rotation of the torso.

Fault

No hint of a swinging motion as the club is quite literally picked up with the hands, while elbows splay out.

Fix

Arms and shoulders work together as a guiding unit; clubhead remains low to the ground as it swings away.

Full swings—no width at the top of the backswing

Fault: Arms collapse into a weak position, with no coiling motion of the body and therefore no stored energy.

Cause: Swing is made entirely with the hands and arms, with no attempt to wind up the big muscles in the upper body.

Fix: Arm swing has to be combined with the coiling of the upper body for a dynamic position.

Fault

No attempt to swing the clubhead; instead, the hands are simply lifted to a weak position.

Fix

A good body action provides the essential dynamic that inspires the arms and hands to swing correctly.

Full swings—over the top start to the downswing

Fault: Club approaches the ball on an outside path.

Cause: Temptation to "muscle" the ball with the upper body, which leads to the right shoulder working out and around instead of down and under.

Fix: A good downswing unwinds from the ground up as the body settles into a good hitting position, the hands and arms swinging along the inside path.

Fault

Overuse of the shoulders at the start of the downswing forces the club outside the play line.

Fix

Unwinding from the ground up drops the arms, hands, and club into the perfect hitting position.

Full swings—no clubhead speed in the release

Fault: Club decelerates through impact, causing massive loss of distance.

Cause: Lack of effective body rotation—and thus no core speed with which to spin the arms and the hands through impact.

Fix: Back to basics: you must understand that the rotary motion of the body is the engine that creates the centrifugal forces that drive a good swing.

Fault

Without a dynamic body action, there is no energy in the clubhead to pull the hands through impact.

Fix

As the body unwinds toward the target, the arms and the hands are catapulted through at great speed.

Full swings—falling off the shot in the finish

Fault: Totally illogical conclusion to the swing—weight falls on the back foot, total loss of balance.

Cause: Generally accredited to a desire to want to lift or scoop the ball up into the air.

Fix: Only with a correct body action can you hope to swing the clubhead and finish in style. Learn to trust the loft on the club to produce the ball-flight.

Fault

Attempting to scoop up the ball results in you falling off the shot, the weight finishing on the back foot.

Fix

A classic follow-through sees the right shoulder point to the target, weight on the left side, body straight.

Smart Golf

The world's leading players are blessed with truly awesome ball-striking skills, but arguably the largest difference between them and the average player is the quality of their strategy and course-management skills. If you want to improve your game, you need to learn how to play "Smart Golf." You will be surprised what an effect this has on your average scores.

Practice shots All professional golfers hit practice balls before a round. As well as gearing up their golf muscles for a game, it allows them to work on the rhythm of the swing.

Playing the yardage game

Learning how far you can hit with each kind of club is the first step toward being able to manage your golf game. No longer is club selection just an educated guess. There is an exact yardage attached to every club, and this allows you to swing each one with conviction.

Range finder

The process of determining how far each club sends the ball is simple. Take a bucket of balls to the practice range and warm up to get the golfing muscles working properly. Then, start with your most lofted club, the sand wedge, and hit 20 balls with a controlled, balanced swing. Pace out the distance to the center of the main cluster of balls, ignoring the longest three shots and the shortest three. That figure is the typical yardage for you with that club, given normal conditions and a regular swing. Write it down. Repeat the process with your next most lofted club, the pitching wedge, and every subsequent club in your bag.

This exercise can be tedious, but you can spread it out over a period of a few weeks, checking two clubs per session. This will make it a less onerous and time-consuming task. You only have to do it once, or perhaps every now and then to keep pace with any improvements you make in your game. And it gives you valuable information that will help you improve your game.

◀◀ **Yardage chart** Although they vary from one course to the next, yardage charts provide the same basic information and measurements.

⏶ **Checking out the length of the hole** If there are particular hazards that are definite no-go areas, use a yardage chart to devise a strategy whereby you hit shots to safe areas. This minimizes the likelihood of you finding trouble and keeps those big numbers off the scorecard.

Using yardage charts

A yardage chart is a valuable tool that will help you manage your game better. Even if you play on the same golf course most of the time, it is still a worthwhile playing companion. It has an illustration of each hole on the course seen from above, with exact yardages from every set of teeing areas. There are a series of measurements that indicate how far it is to each particular section of the fairway. This is extremely useful information because, now that you know how far you can hit your tee shots, you can make a quick calculation, then drive the ball accurately to lay up short of hazards—perhaps a clutch of deep bunkers or a ditch bisecting the fairway.

A yardage chart also provides measurements into the center of the green from various significant landmarks down the length of the fairway. So, wherever you are, it is possible to work out the yardage of any approach shot. Once again, this is where a knowledge of how far you hit with each club proves invaluable because it will facilitate accurate club selection—this is bound to benefit your execution of a shot. If you are confident you are using the right club, it is far less likely that doubts will creep in mid-swing—a common problem that ruins many well-intentioned shots.

The personal touch

The ultimate numbers game strategy is to buy a yardage chart for the course on which you play most of your golf, then personalize it with additional information that is especially relevant to your game. For example, if you have a particular favorite length of shot—say the 100-yard (90-m) pitch—mark on your chart where, on any of the holes, you can best utilize that talent to your advantage. Tour professionals do this all the time. If a par-5 is out of reach in two shots, they will often not attempt to get close to the green. Instead, they lay up short in an area where they feel comfortable and will be able to use their best shot.

You may find that a yardage chart does not have as many specific landmarks and measurements as you would like, so add your own. Every little bit helps, and these professional touches will help you become a more complete golfer.

How to play the percentages

A popular adage in the professional ranks is that "a great round of golf is as much about the bad shots you do not hit, as about the good shots you do." There is no better way of summing up the merits of smart course management. If you can minimize basic errors and learn to play to your strengths as much as possible, there will be far fewer big numbers on your scorecard at the end of the round.

Position, not power

The great Australian golfer Peter Thomson won the Open Championship four times in five years toward the end of the 1950s. Surprisingly, he hardly laid a hand on his driver. He placed far more importance on position than power, so he drove with a 2-wood, which had slightly more loft on the clubface. It did not send the ball as far as a driver, but it was easier to hit straight, and that was all that mattered. Thomson hated missing fairways and felt that the key priority of any tee shot was to get the ball in play. When he achieved that, it made every subsequent shot easier. His extraordinary results speak volumes for the merits of such a strategy.

» **Course management**
In the pro game, all caddies, including Adam Scott's caddie, Steve Williams, help their players with club selection, wind direction, and general course management.

⌃ Judging long putts Always ask your playing partner to attend the flag if you cannot see the hole clearly from long range. And grip lightly—it will enhance your sense of feel.

Most amateurs take the opposite view and think of the driver as a club for distance alone. This is a dangerous strategy because it encourages a hard hit and a reckless swing. Some drives will go straight, and a long way as well. But those that do not can lead to disaster. Think of the driver as a placement club. If you struggle to hit fairways on a consistent basis, switch down to a 3-wood or even a 5-wood. The extra loft on the clubface minimizes sidespin at the point of impact, producing a straighter shot. You will enjoy many more straightforward approach shots from the short grass instead of the rough. The end result will be more birdies and fewer pars having to be rescued with a chip and a putt.

Safety first

When you find yourself in trouble, do not just throw caution to the wind. Averaged out over the course of a year's golf, the simple chip-out sideways onto the fairway will almost certainly yield a lower score than an aggressive pop at the green. It only ever wastes a maximum of one shot and then you are back in the center of the fairway. A failed hero shot can cost you several shots to par. To use golfing parlance, "take your medicine" if you hit a shot into trouble.

Length, not line

Most golfers who bemoan the quality of their putting tend to complain mostly about the number of shortish putts they miss. They fail to nail the true culprit: a poor approach putt characterized by a total lack of judgement of pace. The ball either goes past the hole or finishes way short. That places too much pressure on the second putt. Unless they are as good as Tiger Woods, they are bound to miss more than they make.

For medium- and long-range shots, you should focus mainly on length, not line. A useful exercise is to make your practice strokes while looking at the hole, and try to develop a feel for the length of swing required to send the ball the ideal distance. Then replicate that stroke for real and simply let the ball get in the way of the putterhead. If you judge the speed correctly, you'll hardly ever be more than a yard away, because line is not a major problem on all but the most severely sloping putts. The result is a stress-free tap-in, which will put you in a good frame of mind for the next hole.

PLAYERS' TIP

Find the safest route back
You rarely see a top-class professional golfer hit two destructive shots in succession. They have a sixth sense—call it self-preservation—that stops them from compounding one error with another. In reality, this comes down to little more than an acute appreciation of the law of averages. Having hit a shot into trouble, they will invariably look for the safest route back to the fairway. Hero recovery shots might be crowd-pleasers, but too often they can cost a pro golfer a lot of money!

US tour professional Christie Kerr shows great finesse and good sense as she plays a sound recovery shot from deep rough during the Women's British Open at Sunningdale.

Perfect strategies

In order to master the many and varied challenges presented by par-3s, par-4s, and par-5s, you need to be versatile in your shot selection and overall strategy. Plan ahead and try to dismantle a hole's defenses with a cunning and safe approach. Your game will suffer if you go for glory and your ambition exceeds your execution.

⌃ **Good approach shot** Simon Kahn demonstrates on this short-iron shot the kind of comfortable, controlled swing that yields birdie putts on par-3s.

Par-3

One of the biggest dangers on a par-3 is over-ambition. The fact that the flag is accessible with one shot gives it an irresistible attraction. Many golfers will aim at the flag, ignoring potential dangers and allowing virtually no margin for error. A smart strategy on par-3s is to aim at the center of the green, regardless of the flag location. You then have the safety of the putting surface on either side of your intended flight. Even the best players in the world sometimes ignore the pin and play safe by shooting for the middle of the green.

It is not uncommon for the green on a par-3 to be 30 or 40 paces long. For the average player, that could mean the difference of four clubs—in other words, using a 5-iron instead of a 9-iron. It is easy to become fixated on the yardage on the tee marker, but in most cases that merely gives the distance to the front or the center of the green. Be conscious of the location of the flag and factor that into your calculations.

Par-4

Short par-4s are golf course architects' classic traps. An innocuous yardage draws the golfer into an aggressive strategy with the promise of a straightforward chip-putt birdie. That is exactly the architect's intention—hence the proliferation of hazards around an often small green, put there to punish the impetuous player who hits a wayward drive. The message is clear. Use a club off the tee that will leave you where you feel most confident of playing an accurate approach shot. On long par-4s some golfers seem to throw caution to the wind, pushing for distance. But the golfer who swings harder tends to hit wilder. The hoped-for par turns into a double-bogey.

The handicapping system allows golfers to drop a certain number of shots to par in each round of golf. Long par-4s are the best holes for this. Play conservatively, and even the toughest par-4 can be completed in five strokes. An added bonus is that you may even achieve par, and a nightmare number is highly unlikely.

Par-5

In order to master par-5s, you need guile, good course management, and clever positional play. Resist the temptation to hit the drive as hard as possible. This creates tension in your hands, arms, and shoulders. Grip the club lightly and maintain a good tempo in your swing. Focus on a specific target and do not become preoccupied with distance. Treat your drive on a par-5 in the same way as a tennis player would treat a second serve. Above all, get the ball in!

Break down par-5s into manageable parts. Your first two shots are simply placement shots, getting you into position for an easy approach shot to the green. Play shots that offer the greatest margin

⌃ **Sensible play** Ryder Cup star Thomas Bjorn laid up well short of the water to play this shot. This is a smart strategy on hazard-strewn par-5s that are out of reach in two shots.

for error. If there are bunkers at 240 yards (220m), hit a club off the tee that you know will send the ball a maximum of 210–220 yards (190–200m). Do not cut it too fine.

Once the drive is safely in play, think ahead. One of the biggest mistakes made on par-5s is trying to get the second shot as close to the green as possible. The theory is that the closer the ball is to the green, the easier the next shot will be, but often this is not the case. A simple pitch from 80 yards (73m) might be easier than a short but awkward chip over a bunker, and therefore more likely to yield a makeable birdie putt.

Position not power Grace Park, one of the LPGA Tour's leading stars, recognizes that it is not always worth trying to overpower a short par-4. Position not power is a wise philosophy.

Playing under pressure

It is easy to assume that the world's best players are immune to pressure and totally impervious to the effects of nerves. They stand on a tee surrounded by hundreds of people—and watched by millions more on television—and hit great shots. But they do feel pressure; they just know how to deal with it.

⌃ **Get a grip** The starting point for good golf under pressure is a soft hold on the club.

Conquering the nerves

The likes of Ernie Els, Tiger Woods, and Vijay Singh feel pressure just like the rest of the golfing population. They are on first-name terms with every nerve in their body. But what separates them from the pack and makes them great is the way they handle the pressure. It is an art and, fortunately, one that to a large degree can be learned.

There is, of course, no substitute for experience. As an old sporting adage goes, you have to lose a few championships before you can learn how to win one. There is an element of truth in this, but there are ways in which you can accelerate the learning process. You must learn how to conquer your nerves and play good golf under pressure, and this is within everyone's capabilities.

Preparation is key

Being well prepared for the challenge ahead will put your mind at rest and give you a positive mental attitude. First of all, make sure you have got everything you need. At the top of your list should be a bottle of water. Drink plenty on the way around, little sips at a time. This will prevent dehydration, which affects mental and physical function.

Hunger will also stop you from playing your best golf under pressure, so take snacks onto the course. Bananas are one of the best foods, because they release energy slowly into your system. Chocolate is better than nothing, but it tends to give you a rush, followed by a lull. Other items that you should pack, depending on the weather, are a hat, sunblock, a spare golf glove, a waterproof jacket, and an umbrella.

The second phase of good preparation is warming-up. It will help your body and state of mind. Do some stretches to loosen your muscles (see pp.124–5), then make some swings. Do not work on the technical aspects. Concentrate on making solid contact with the ball and establishing a smooth rhythm to take onto the course.

Sticking to a routine

The most important discipline in competitions is to take one shot at a time. Concentrate on each shot and do not dwell on past mistakes or worry about future hurdles. Have a preset routine and stick to it, especially with putts. Every putt counts as a shot,

◀ **Consistent putting routine** US golfer Davis Love is one of the top golf earners of all time. He has a methodical approach to his putting and uses the same routine every time.

so treat each one the same. It is tempting to linger longer if it is the last putt, on the last green, to win a competition, but this will only increase the pressure on you.

Switching off

Finally, take time during a round of golf to switch off mentally—"Smell the flowers," as the great Walter Hagen once said. It is impossible to concentrate intensely for four hours, and foolhardy to attempt to do so. Talk to your playing partners between shots, look around at the scenery, let your mind wander. Then, as you approach your ball, mentally "flick a switch" and turn your attention to the shot. The next couple of minutes will require maximum focus, which you will be more likely to achieve if you have previously given yourself time off.

WALTER HAGEN

Enjoy the game
Only Jack Nicklaus and Tiger Woods won more Major championships than Walter Hagen, but none were won with more style than those of this showy and colorful American. Hagen played golf with a *joie de vivre* that endeared him to crowds all over the world. He greeted even his bad shots with nothing more than a casual shrug. Hagen said you had to take time to smell the flowers once in a while. This approach was perhaps his way of dealing with pressure. It certainly worked.

Walter Hagen did not possess the prettiest swing in golf, but it was highly effective. He was a formidable golfer and, in match play especially, almost unbeatable.

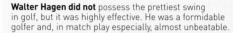

❮❮ Pressure drive
The pressure does not come any greater than on the final hole at Augusta National (*see* pp.222–3). The leading players must thread their tee shots down a narrow fairway edged with trees and bunkers.

Analyzing parts of your game

In the world of golf, there is virtually no limit to the number of performance-related statistics—fairways hit, driving distances, greens hit in regulation, putts per round, sand-saves, and more. Every golfer should collect their own statistics and use them to analyze each part of their game. This is the first step to becoming a better player.

⊠ **Driving force** Sweden's Annika Sorenstam is one of the greatest women golfers of all time, and certainly the dominant force of the late 1990s and early 2000s. She is renowned for her long, accurate driving.

Your performance

Unlike in most other ball sports, a golfer is the only influence on a ball, if you ignore the occasional bad bounce and freak gust of wind. No one else smashes the ball back, commits a foul at the point of contact, or lays a snooker behind another ball. A missed fairway is a missed fairway, and a putt either goes in the hole or it does not. Only the golfer can be responsible for improving scores. Keep a note of your performance in every round so that you can identify which parts of your game need the most work.

Tee shots

In the professional game, statistics are recorded for both the distance and the accuracy of tee shots. Measuring the average distance of your drives is a very involved process. Concentrate on the accuracy part, which is easier to quantify and more important. Add up the number of drives you played on par-4s and par-5s, and whether you hit or missed the fairway. Then calculate the percentage of fairways you hit. For example, if you found 9 out of 14 fairways, that is 64 percent of fairways hit (9÷14 x 100).

The best golfers hit roughly 80 percent of the fairways they look at, which is exceptional. For the club golfer, a figure of about 70 percent is excellent; 60 percent is good; 50 percent is adequate; anything in the 40s or less is poor. Use your own statistics to help you judge what action you need to take.

Greens in regulation

The term "greens in regulation" describes the ideal number of shots required to get from the tee to the green. On a par-3 it is one shot; on a par-4 it is two shots; and on a par-5 it is three shots. If a green is hit in fewer than the required number of shots, it is still a "green hit in regulation." The most accurate golfers hit about 80 percent of greens in

Hole	●	○	○	Stroke	●	Par	Stroke	Scores
1	398	382	360	8		4	14	
2	412	387	364	4		4	10	
3	194	170	149	18		3	15	
4	384	361	338	14		4	17	
5	541	516	491	12		5	4	
6	454	422	402	2		4	6	
7	187	159	141	10		3	13	
8	563	536	503	16		5	7	
9	448	421	401	6		4	2	
OUT	3581	3354	3149			36		
10	426	408	380	3		4	8	
11	208	175	157	13		3	16	
12	531	502	468	11		5	9	
13	338	311	280	9		4	18	
14	443	424	408	1		4	3	
15	548	523	496	17		5	12	
16	465	440	406	7		4	1	
17	225	210	191	15		3	11	
18	443	424	398	5		4	5	
IN	3627	3417	3184			36		
OUT	3581	3354	3149			36		
TOT	7208	6771	6333			72		

⊠ **Scorecard** A scorecard will tell you how many shots you took at each hole. But this is only part of the story. There are many other statistics that reveal useful information about your performance.

>> **Sand skills** Nick Faldo was once labeled a mechanical player, but few golfers have shown such great skill and finesse around the greens, and his sand play is no exception.

regulation—in other words, nearly 15 out of 18 greens. For a typical handicap golfer, the same standards apply as for hitting the fairway.

Putts per round

For the average player, statistics for putting are best analyzed in terms of the number of putts taken per round. A world-class golfer will average about 27 putts per round. Amateurs who average 30–33 putts per round should be very pleased with themselves. An average of 36, the equivalent of two putts on every green, is merely adequate. A higher average than this is poor.

Par-saves

Whenever a golfer fails to hit a green in regulation, it is time for a chip-and-putt-save or a sand-save—in other words, a shot from off the green followed by a single putt. The importance of this aspect of the game cannot be overstated. If you increase your percentage of par-saves from around the greens, it will have a dramatic effect on your scores.

It is easy to work out if this part of your game needs lots of attention. A 70–80 percent success rate with chip shots and bunker shots is exceptional; 55–65 percent is good; 45–55 percent is only average; less than 40 percent is poor.

▲ **Putting scores** France's Raphael Jacquelin is a stylish player and, like all tournament winners, he makes his good scores by holing plenty of putts on the greens.

The Rules **of Golf**

There are few sports with rules as complex, inflexible, and as reliant
on honesty and integrity as golf. What might seem like minor infractions
can impact heavily on a match if you are penalized by one or two strokes.
It is important to follow the etiquette as well as the formal rules in order to
uphold the spirit of the game, and to be considerate toward other players.

Key rules

The first official set of golf rules was established in 1744 by the Royal Company of Edinburgh Golfers, recognized as the oldest golf club in the world. Given the complexities of the game, it is extraordinary that this pioneering document contained only 13 rudimentary codes of conduct, and not surprising that it was later extended to 22 more complex rules.

The modern rule book

Some diehard traditionalists believe that golf needs only one rule: play the ball as it lies and do not touch it from the moment you place it on the tee to the time you bend down and pick it out of the cup. However, today's rule book has evolved into a vast tome by comparison with that early premise. There is now a myriad of golf rules, covering almost any scenario.

Since most amateur golfers do not study the rule book in great detail, they remain ignorant of what they can and cannot do, and put themselves at risk of receiving penalty points during competitions. The rules of golf are at the heart of the game, and without a proper appreciation of them, any player will be at a disadvantage.

Such problems are solved by explaining clearly and succinctly the key rules of golf, and outlining those situations that might typically be encountered when playing a round of golf. As any golfer who has been playing for some time will tell you, the rules of golf exist to help the player, and a useful grounding in this important subject will benefit and enhance your enjoyment of the game. However, do not worry about having to remember every intricacy and exception, since most golfers learn from experience, rather than from studying rule books.

Rules in competition

The typical amateur golfer is more in need of a working knowledge of the rules than a professional golfer, who will have rules officials

and match referees on call at any time during a tournament. Rules queries are unlikely to be raised during an amateur competition, so it is important that the players themselves ensure that the game is played fairly. Only at the very highest amateur level is it likely that a rules official would be present at a tournament.

On the touring circuit, should any scenarios arise that require clarification of the rules, there is always an expert on hand to step in and help. Given that their livelihoods are on the line, it is not surprising that leading tour professionals have become very reliant on referees to ensure that there is no breach of the rules. They know all too well that eagle-eyed television viewers have in the past called in to report rules infringements they have spotted; in some instances players have been disqualified as a result.

Penalty strokes

A "penalty stroke" is an extra stroke that is added to the score of a player or side for the infringement of certain rules. For example, if

you pick up your ball in deep rough without first informing your playing partner, you will incur a one-stroke penalty. A more severe penalty of two strokes applies if you arrive late for your teeing-off time in a competition; in a match-play event, the penalty is the loss of an entire hole (see p.52). Finally, the even worse penalty of disqualification may be served if a player arrives more than five minutes late for the tee-off in a competition.

◁ Keeping your score
Every player, from former World No.1 and double Open champion Greg Norman to the humble beginner, is responsible for checking their own score.

◁ St. Andrews Golf Club, Scotland
The Royal & Ancient Golf Club (R&A) of St. Andrews jointly presides over the official Rules of Golf with the United States Golf Association (USGA).

Practice guidelines

Tour professionals are lucky to have wonderful facilities where they can practice every part of their game. However, not all golf courses have a practice ground, so you will have to be resourceful if you want to loosen up and hit a few balls before a round. Practicing on the course before or during a game may be a breach of the rules.

⌃ **Chipping practice**
Tour pros will practice
their short game just
as much as their
long game.

Stroke play

The rules relating to any type of practice before a round in a stroke-play event (see p.46) are very strict. You are not allowed to practice on the course before you begin your game, which means not even an innocent and seemingly innocuous chip or putt on one of the 18 actual greens. You cannot practice on the golf course between rounds in a 36-hole competition, either, even if the rounds are to be played on consecutive days. At amateur level, if you are playing in a competition which only consists of one round, you are allowed to practice a putt once you have holed out (putted the ball in the hole) on that green. Make sure you are not unduly holding up play, though, as this can lead to a two-stroke penalty.

» **Striving for
perfection** At any
point during the day
at a professional
tournament, the practice
range is busy with
players perfecting
their techniques.

Putting practice One of the best ways to sharpen your skills on the greens is to have a putting competition with another golfer. The competitive aspect makes all the difference.

Match play

In match play (see p.46) the rules are far more relaxed, to the point of being virtually nonexistent. You can hit a few chips and putts before you begin your game, providing you do not get in anyone's way, and you can even play a few holes if you wish. Once on the course, you are allowed to practice a putt, or even a chip, on or around the green of the hole you have just finished playing. However, be mindful of the group playing behind: if they are waiting to hit their approach shots, it is poor golf etiquette to practice a putt. It also constitutes unduly delaying play, for which you can be penalized, usually with the automatic loss of the next hole.

Do not take these rules regarding practice lightly. Even the most innocent of actions on your part—such as having a swipe at an old ball lying in the rough—can lead to penalty points if someone spots you and feels it might benefit your game. It is better to be safe than sorry.

The *Decisions on the Rules of Golf* is an official R&A and USGA publication designed to assist in resolving both simple and complicated rules problems. It includes an incident in which a player played a solitary practice stroke from a tee that was not even being used in that day's stroke-play competition, into an area of the golf course that was designated out of bounds. Even though the shot bore no relationship whatsoever to any shot he would face during his upcoming round, he was subject to disqualification for a breach of the rules on practice. This is an example of how strict the application of the rules can be.

Once on the golf course, the rules are just as strict. A player should refrain from indulging in practice putting, perhaps on the tee or in the middle of the fairway, to kill time between shots. Even though this is not the same as practicing on an actual green, it still counts as a breach of the rules on practice. If that player was to strike even a single putt, the penalty would be two shots in stroke play or the loss of a hole in match play.

Consulting caddies

A player is allowed to send their caddie onto the golf course just before the start of a competition to test the speed of the greens, to identify potentially dangerous pin positions, difficult or awkward undulations in the green, and tricky breaks. The rules state that a player is responsible for the actions of their caddie only during the round itself, so there is a potentially useful advantage to be gained by letting a caddie go out on the course beforehand.

Taking advice from another player Even the greatest golfers benefit from objective advice about the most important part of the game—their golf swing. Here, the legendary South African golfer Gary Player offers Ernie Els some tips.

Help and advice

Giving or receiving advice, no matter how well-meaning, is against the rules. A well-intentioned remark or friendly piece of advice from anyone else can lead to penalty strokes and even disqualification. Advice is defined as "any counsel or suggestion that might influence another player in their choice of club or shot."

Do not ask for advice

If you are heard asking for advice on which club to use, for example, this will result in a two-stroke penalty. However, you can look into someone's golf bag to find out which club they have selected. If your opponent decides they do not want you to find out and covers up the opening of their golf bag, you are not allowed to look in. Once a hole has been completed, you can discuss which clubs were used without any fear of being penalized.

Do not offer advice

Giving technical advice to a fellow competitor results in a two-stroke penalty against you, not against the player who might benefit from receiving the advice. This might occur if you are playing in a competition with a friend. Even if you know where they are going wrong and how they could improve their game, keep quiet, or you will be the player who receives the penalty strokes.

» Beware of advice during competitive play
No matter how helpful the advice might seem at the time, think carefully before accepting the assistance of any other player. You might be infringing the rules.

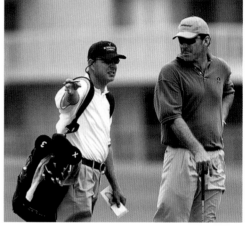

▲ **Listen to your caddie** A good caddie is worth his weight in gold—quite literally in some cases, such is the extraordinary earning power of the top players.

Be aware of exceptions

There are exceptions to the rules on help and advice that relate to matters described as "public information." For example, you are allowed to ask your opponent the length of a hole, or if you are playing an away match on an unfamiliar course, you could ask your fellow players how far the fairway bunker is from the tee. The best way to remember the distinction between advice and public information in golf is to think of the latter as permanent objects. That way you are sure to be on safe ground.

Take counsel wisely

In a team game you have to be careful who you listen to and, if you are a supporter, who you advise. Unfortunately, a little good will can go a long way toward losing a match. For instance, it might be quite common during a club match for several members of each team to support the last few games out on the course. However, only your caddie, your team captain, or in the case of a foursomes match, your playing partner is allowed

to advise you about a particular shot or club selection. If anyone other than those people gives you advice, you immediately lose that hole.

Be informed and honest

The rules relating to information state that all parties involved in a match should be aware of the number of strokes and penalty strokes taken. For instance, in a match-play competition, if halfway through a hole your opponent asks you how many shots you have taken, you have to give an honest answer. You must also inform your fellow competitors or your opponent as soon as possible of any penalty strokes that you have taken during a hole. This reinforces the ideal that the game of golf is played very much in a self-governing—and therefore honest—spirit.

To the vast majority of golfers who have been playing for a while, these considerations have become almost second nature and no longer have to be mentioned. Beginners to the game will quickly learn that the nature of golf has a lot to do with the spirit in which the game is played and therefore will reflect the character of those who play it. Conversely, this honest spirit also serves as a major disincentive to anyone who might want to engage in a spot of excessive gamesmanship.

RULE BREAKER

Do not advise another player
Tom Watson was playing in the final round of the prestigious Tournament of Champions at La Costa Country Club in Carlsbad, California, in 1980 when he made the mistake of telling his fellow competitor Lee Trevino about a swing flaw he had spotted. A TV commentator overheard the conversation and mentioned it, as an example of Watson's good nature. But viewers phoned in to point out this breach of the rules and Watson was duly penalized two strokes. Luckily for him, he had a three-shot lead and still won the tournament.

No one could question five-time Open champion Tom Watson's integrity and good nature, although these qualities cost him a two-stroke penalty in one tournament.

‹‹ Shot consultation
Some players consult their caddie on every conceivable aspect of the shot in hand. Others prefer to shoulder this burden of responsibility alone.

The teeing ground

Infringing the rules as you tee off guarantees a dropped shot, or possibly several. This would be the worst possible start to your game and could put you off for the entire round. Before you tee off, familiarize yourself with the teeing area and make sure you are carrying no more than 14 clubs in your golf bag, the maximum number allowed.

Teeing area

The rules state that you are allowed to tee the ball a maximum of two club-lengths behind the tee markers. This can have several benefits. Most golfers automatically tee up between the two tee markers, which can cause wear and tear, divot holes, and bare patches in this area. Take a few extra steps away from the target and you will almost certainly find the turf in better condition, which can give you a psychological lift as well as a more secure footing.

You can stand outside the margins of the two tee markers, provided the ball is teed between them. Indeed, using the full width of the teeing area has strategic benefits, because you can tailor your angle of attack to suit the character of a particular hole. For example, if there is a bunker down the right side of the fairway, teeing up on the extreme right-hand side of the teeing area allows you to effectively aim away from danger. This is known as the percentage play. You are increasing your margin of error.

▶▶ **Teeing off in a major tournament** Golfing pros take their time in assessing the teeing area, and will choose the most beneficial position in relation to the hole.

⬆ **Teeing up your ball** There are no stipulations in the rules about how high or low the individual player chooses to tee up their ball.

The correct tee

Tee markers are there to denote exactly where within the teeing area you are allowed to tee off. These markers are color coded to help avoid confusion. There will often be three sets of men's tees—championship (often blue or gold), medal (typically white), and everyday play (yellow). The most forward of the tee markers will almost always be red, and indicates the women's teeing area.

When visiting an unfamiliar course, or entering a competition for the first time, it is always prudent to ask in the pro shop which tees are "in play" for the day to try and avoid playing from the incorrect markers.

Playing a shot from the wrong tee is an easy mistake to make. In a tournament, there may be different-colored tee markers (see above), but the tees at the front of the area may not be the competition tees. If you play off the front tees by mistake, the rules vary depending on the type of game you are playing and, to a certain extent, the attitude of your opponent. In match play, if you drive off from the wrong tee markers, your opponent has every right to ask you to play the stroke again. Although no penalty is incurred, you will feel hard done by if you have just hit a cracking drive down the middle of the fairway. However, if you have made a poor shot, your opponent is unlikely to let you play the shot again.

In stroke play, if you play from the wrong tee, you immediately incur a two-stroke penalty and have to play "three off the tee"—that is, you incur an immediate penalty stroke and are required to tee off again, this shot counting as your third. This is the case even if you have already placed yourself at a disadvantage by playing off tee markers that are farther back than those you should have been using.

Teeing off

One classic mistake perpetrated on the teeing ground is accidentally nudging the ball off its tee as you address it. Ignore anyone who says "one," because not only is that joke several centuries old, it is not true. The ball is not yet officially in play. Simply put the ball back on the tee and continue as normal, with no penalty.

If a golfer in the process of attempting to hit the ball misses it, then this attempt still counts as one stroke. It is known as an "air shot." Also, if an attempt to strike the ball off the tee results in a feeble, glancing hit, the end result of which is that the ball does not leave the teeing ground, the golfer is not allowed to re-tee the ball. Even though the ball is technically still on the tee (situated in the teeing area, even though not physically on a tee), it must be played "as it lies." To avoid these pitfalls, make sure you take your time in choosing where to tee up your ball, and do not make a stroke until you are completely satisfied with your position.

◀◀ **Position and demarcation of women's tees** The tees for female players are usually positioned at the front of the teeing area and denoted by red markers. Here, South Korea's Inbee Park tees off.

The order of play

It would be chaotic if hitting shots on a golf course was a free-for-all. This is why the rules include specific procedures relating to the order of play. These procedures should be observed at all times, for safety reasons, as part of basic golf etiquette, and because failure to do so can result in penalties for the player.

Having the honor

The player or side entitled to play first from the teeing ground is said to "have the honor." In a match-play competition, the player or pairing on the top half of the draw usually has the honor on the first tee. Failing that, it is decided by the flip of a coin. Thereafter, the winner of each hole tees off first on the next. In the event of a halved hole—that is, one on which the scores of the individual players or pairings are the same— the honor is retained by the pair or player who teed off first on the previous hole. In a handicap competition when strokes are being given or received, it is the net score that counts toward the honor. If your handicap exceeds that of your opponent, you may be given an extra stroke for certain holes. If you both took four strokes, because you have a "free" stroke, you have the honor, as you would have holed out in three.

If you tee off when your opponents have the honor, they have the right to ask you to play the stroke again. Once you have all played off

the tee, the player farthest from the flag hits first. Again, if you play out of turn, your opponent may ask you to cancel that stroke and replay it. In a stroke-play event, the honor of the first tee is determined either by the draw sheet or handicap order, lowest first. As with match play, the honor on each subsequent tee is then earned by the player with the lowest score on the previous hole. Unlike match play, there is no penalty for playing out of turn off the tee, but it is very poor etiquette to do so.

Foursomes matches

In a foursomes match, in which a pair play alternate shots with the same ball, the key principle is that penalty shots do not affect the order of play. For example, if your partner slashes a drive into the out of bounds area and has to play "three off the tee" (see p.161), it is you, not your partner, who must play three off the tee because you have to alternate your shots in the pairing. Remember, the rule is that penalty strokes do not affect the order of play.

⌂ Conceding putts: part of the spirit of the game Jack Nicklaus gives Tony Jacklin a 2-ft (60-cm) putt on the final green during their 1969 Ryder Cup singles match, one of the most famous concessions in the history of golf.

⏩ Etiquette during holing out As a golfer holes out at St. Andrews in the late afternoon sun, fellow competitors stand away from the line-of-sight, awaiting their turn.

Putting out

Once all the balls are on the putting green, the golfer farthest from the hole plays first. In stroke play, however, you have the right to putt out (or hole out) before your fellow competitors, particularly if you have putted and your ball is teetering near the edge of the hole. However, it is always polite to ask first. Technically speaking, your fellow competitor can make an objection,

◀ **Etiquette on the putting green** The golfer farthest from the hole usually putts first. In the event that one ball is obstructing another, the golfer whose ball is causing the obstruction should lift and mark their ball until it is their turn to play.

but it is unlikely that they will do so, and even if that does happen, you are well within your rights to hole out. Just make sure you follow normal etiquette and do not step on your fellow competitor's line before their putt (see p.50).

In match play, you do not have the right to putt out unless your ball is the farthest from the hole. If you putt out of turn, your opponent has the right to ask you to cancel that stroke and play it again. In match play, if you roll your approach putt close enough to the hole, there is every chance that the hole will be conceded, without your opponent taking their putt.

◀ **Taking turns in a foursomes match** In the Ryder Cup, the world's best golfers pair up in the foursomes, taking it in turns with their shots, and providing the chance to discuss tactics. Here, Stewart Cink and Jim Furyk line up a putt.

Taking a stance and playing the ball

One of golf's fundamental rules is that you should play the ball as it lies—in other words, in the same position where it landed. There are serious implications if you attempt to improve your lie or the area of your intended swing through the ball in any way.

⌃ **Ball identification**
The rules allow you to bend back grass in heavy rough in order to identify your ball.

Improving your lie

On the teeing ground you are allowed to step down imperfections around your ball or even pull out strands of grass, but you cannot do this anywhere else on the course. Improving the area of your intended swing is where a lot of amateurs unwittingly break the rules. The classic example is when a ball comes to rest in or near a bush or other such obstruction. If you clumsily force your way through the undergrowth to get in a position to play the shot, leaving a trail of bent and broken branches and leaves in your wake, it is a breach of the rules. Nor are you allowed to force branches away with your hands or stamp down on them to prevent them from impeding

your shot. The rules do permit you to carefully ease yourself into a position to play the shot. This is known as "fairly taking your stance," and it simply means doing what is reasonably necessary to get into a position to make a swing at the ball.

Check the ball

Before you play a ball, you must first make sure that it is yours to avoid picking up penalty strokes. When your ball is sitting in the middle of the fairway, there is unlikely to be any doubt that it is yours. However, elsewhere on the course, in situations where the manufacturer's logo might not be quite so apparent, a quick inspection of the ball is always prudent.

The rules state that you can touch or bend long grass in heavy rough, but only enough to identify your ball. You must do this without improving your lie or the area of intended swing. In a really terrible lie, where the ball is buried, you are allowed to lift the ball to confirm that it is yours, but you must first mark its position with a tee peg so that it can be returned to its original lie. You must tell your fellow competitor or opponent what you are about to do so that they can observe the whole procedure. Failure to comply with these rules carries a one-stroke penalty or loss of hole in match play.

If your ball is firmly plugged in a bunker, you can brush aside sand to confirm it is there. There is a degree of leniency here, however, because even if you play the bunker shot and then discover it is not your ball, there is no penalty for playing a wrong ball in a hazard. You must not continue playing with that ball, but instead return to the bunker and try to find your ball.

If by some dire stroke of misfortune your ball becomes lodged up a tree, you are allowed to shake the branches or even throw a club at it in an attempt to bring it back down. The latter

⏩ **Playing away from obstructions** If you are unlucky enough to have to take a shot from behind a tree, you might need to improvise. Golf sometimes requires imagination as well as skill.

course of action is not recommended, though, as you may find yourself missing a golf club as well as a golf ball!

Exception to the rule

The only time you are not required to play the ball exactly as it lies is when "winter rules" come into effect. If the golf course is wet and muddy, the committee of a course may permit you to lift, clean, and place your ball, but only on closely mown areas, not in the rough. You should first mark the position of the ball with a tee peg, and then place the ball no farther than 6in (15cm) from that spot and no closer to the hole. This procedure is sometimes known as a "preferred lie." It usually includes a rule whereby, in the rough, you are allowed to "unplug" balls that land and bury in their own pitch mark. However, it is against the rules to clean the ball.

RULE BREAKER

Do not build your stance
You are not allowed to "build" a stance—that is, use anything to help you gain a more comfortable position at address. For example, if your ball is halfway up a slope, you cannot stand on anything to even up your stance. In a US Tour event in the late 1980s, former Masters' champion Craig Stadler landed himself in trouble when he knelt on a towel to stop his trousers getting wet while attempting a shot. There was no real advantage, but he was penalized two strokes.

An action as seemingly innocuous as kneeling on a towel to play a shot in wet conditions cost former Masters' champion Craig Stadler a two-stroke penalty.

◄◄ **Playing a shot from an awkward stance**
Years of experience and a not inconsiderable degree of skill enable US tour pro Fred Funk to make this tricky recovery shot from the bottom of a slope look easy.

Playing the ball

The act of striking the ball is what the game of golf is all about. The aim is to make as few strikes as possible during a round, so you need to make sure the strikes you play do not come with a penalty stroke attached.

The official definition states that a strike (or stroke) "must feature the forward momentum of the club made with the intention of striking and moving the ball." This immediately prohibits any kind of scooping action. So, for instance, if a ball comes to rest close to a fence, while there may be room to place the clubhead behind the ball, there is no way of physically making a backswing. And without a backswing, there can be no strike.

⏏ **Moving loose impediments** This golfer rightly shows great care in removing a loose impediment from around his ball.

Loose impediments

Natural objects—such as leaves, twigs, and pine cones—lying loose on any part of the golf course are called loose impediments. There are a variety of rules relating to these items, and they can make all the difference to the success—or otherwise—of your golf shot.

Lying loose

The difference between a loose impediment and a loose obstruction (see p.168) is that a loose impediment is a natural object, while a loose obstruction is artificial. A loose impediment must not be growing or solidly embedded in the ground. If you are in any doubt, do not attempt to remove the object.

On the fairway

The rules and "relief" procedures vary depending on where you are on the course. If you are on the fairway or in the rough, you are allowed to move loose impediments from around your ball, but a delicate touch is required. If the ball moves while

removing a loose impediment, you are penalized one stroke. The ball must then be placed back on its original spot before you play your shot. If the ball and the loose impediment look too close to one another for comfort, play the ball as it lies.

On the green

Different rules apply on the putting green. You can still move loose impediments from around your ball, but if the ball moves in the process, there is no penalty, as long as you place the ball back on its original spot immediately.

There is one anomaly worth pointing out: sand on the putting surface counts as a loose impediment, so you can brush it away from your ball or the line

» **Course maintenance** Generally, only the best courses in the world receive this kind of treatment, helping to ensure that fallen leaves are not too much of a hindrance.

of your putt. However, sand off the green is not classed as a loose impediment. So even if you are putting from the apron of the green—the manicured edge that separates the fairway from the green—you cannot brush sand from around your ball or from the line of your putt between your ball and the putting surface.

It is these subtle distinctions that make the rules of golf such a tricky subject to get to know and fully understand.

In a hazard

If you are in a hazard, such as a bunker, the rules state that you cannot remove loose impediments. So, for example, twigs and leaves around your ball cannot be touched or moved, even if they are in the way.

⚛ **Getting out of trouble** Sometimes it is not practical, or even permissible, to move all loose impediments from the area around the ball. John Daly resorts to the aggressive approach.

The only exception to this rule relates to stones. Although these are natural objects and therefore count as loose impediments, safety issues have led to an amendment of the rules. At most clubs there is a local rule stating that stones can be removed from bunkers before playing your shot. You can check all local rules very easily, as they are usually printed on the back of the scorecard, or can be found on the noticeboard in the clubhouse.

TYPES OF LOOSE IMPEDIMENT

It is not enough to be able to recognize a loose impediment when you see one. It is essential to know the correct course of action to take, depending on which part of the course you are playing.

Leaves
You are allowed to clear leaves out of the way on the green, the tee, the fairway, or in the rough, as long as the ball does not move. However, you must not clear them in bunkers.

Pinecones
Your shot may be seriously affected if a pinecone comes between clubface and ball at impact. The same rules apply here as with leaves, even though cones are more of an impediment.

Gravel
If gravel is part of a road that is an integral part of the golf course, you may not be allowed to move it from around your ball. Check the local rules at the course you are playing.

⚛ **Clearing the putting line** The rules permit you to remove loose impediments that obstruct the line of your putt on any part of the green. Here, Jack Nicklaus brushes away fallen leaves.

Obstructions

There are two different types of obstructions, movable and immovable, both of which are artificial objects. As soon as you think in these terms, it becomes a lot easier to recognize one on the golf course. Obstructions differ from loose impediments (*see* p.166) primarily because some of them are not "loose." They also tend to be larger.

Movable items

Bunker rakes, garbage cans, and empty drink cans are all examples of movable obstructions. If your ball lands near a movable obstruction that will interfere with either your stance or the area of your intended swing, you are entitled to "relief," which means you can take action to be able to play the ball. The rules state that you can carefully remove the obstruction, put it out of harm's way, and continue with your next shot. If you think the ball might move in the process of taking away the obstruction, mark its position with a tee peg first. Then if the ball does move, you can simply return it to its original spot, which is what the rules state you must do before playing your next shot.

If your ball has come to rest actually in or on top of the obstruction, the same rule applies. First, mark the location of the ball and lift it away. You are also allowed to clean the ball while it is lifted. You should then move the obstruction and drop the ball as close as possible to where it would originally have come to rest. In a bunker, the rules allow you to place the ball, being careful to restore it to its original lie.

⊠ A golf ball lands on an obstruction A ball might well land on a spectator's belongings. In this instance, the ball would be located in the coat, marked, and then the coat removed. The ball would be placed as close as possible to its original location.

Immovable items

Artificial objects that are either much too heavy to pick up, or are fixed and therefore impossible to move, are called immovable obstructions. Typical examples of these are pop-up sprinkler heads located by the side of a green or embedded in the ground on a fairway, concrete tee markers, or an item of greenkeeper's equipment, such as a large riding mower.

You are only entitled to relief from an immovable obstruction if it interferes with either your stance or the area of your intended swing. The procedure

RULE BREAKER

Immovable or movable?
In a PGA tournament during the 1999 season, a boulder was obstructing Tiger Woods' swing and he duly enlisted the help of several members of the gallery to move it. Many observers thought that this was not in the spirit of the game, and telephoned the tournament office to say so. However, according to the rules, Woods was well within his rights. An obstruction can be classified as movable, even if it does require several strong pairs of hands to push it out of the way!

Despite the fact that it took a small crowd to move it, this boulder was deemed to be a movable obstruction. This famous incident occurred in the US in 1999.

for taking relief is straightforward. First of all, establish the nearest point where the item ceases to become an obstruction and then mark it with a tee peg. Measure up to two club-lengths from that tee peg, ensuring that you will be no closer the hole, and mark this spot with another tee peg. You are then free to pick up the ball and drop it in the area between the two tee pegs. If the ball rolls back into a position where it is affected by the obstruction, you can simply pick it up and drop it again.

Dropping the ball

When dropping the ball, stand erect and hold it at shoulder height with your arm straight out. Then release it (see p.176). If it hits anyone or any piece of equipment, such as your golf bag, simply pick it up and re-drop it.

Remember that the re-drop is not a never-ending process. If a golfer is taking relief—getting in a position to make a stroke—from an immovable obstruction, and this scenario is unfolding on sloping ground, there is every

chance that the ball will roll away into an incorrect spot every time it is dropped by the unlucky player. To avoid such an eventuality, the rules state that you may place the ball in the correct position after the second drop. Indeed, this procedure is commonly applied to a variety of situations when a free drop or a penalty drop is involved.

⌃ Immovable objects A modern-day fairway sprinkler head is a typical example of an immovable obstruction.

《 Measuring relief from an obstruction To gain relief from an unplayable lie, the golfer must measure up to two club-lengths from the spot where the ball has come to rest.

《 Putting down a marker If a ruling involves lifting the golf ball, then it is wise to mark its exact location. Here, Robert Allenby is seeking relief from power cables. A rules official is present to offer guidance.

Out of bounds and lost ball

No golfer relishes the prospect of a ball that is lost or out of bounds, but, sadly, this situation happens to everyone at some time. Make sure you know the correct procedures to avoid incurring a rules infringement on top of the offending shot, as this can be very costly indeed.

⌃ **Reaching the limits** The white stakes indicate an out of bounds area at the Suez hole on the Royal St. George's course.

Out of bounds

If your ball lands in the out of bounds area, it is "dead." This means that you can only retrieve it, not play it. The area is usually marked with white stakes. Check the information on the back of your scorecard if you are not sure whether an area is out of bounds.

You should also bear in mind that out of bounds does not necessarily mean the boundary of the course. Some holes feature what is known as "internal out of bounds" on an adjacent fairway. This measure is often introduced as a local rule to prevent golfers gaining some kind of strategic advantage from taking an alternative route up the fairway of another, adjacent hole.

If you suspect that your ball may have landed in the out of bounds area, play a provisional ball from exactly the same spot, but make sure you state your intentions clearly to the other members of your group. If you say nothing, the

⏩ **Searching for a lost ball** Try to help other golfers in your group whenever a ball is lost because the rules allow only five minutes to locate it. Having several pairs of eyes improves the likelihood of the ball's being found and keeps play moving.

⌃ Hitting out of bounds In the first round of the 2003 Open, World No.1 Tiger Woods endured the ignominy of losing a ball on the first hole in front of thousands of spectators.

mere act of playing a second ball renders the original ball lost, even if it is subsequently found "in bounds." If your original ball is, in fact, out of bounds, you incur a stroke-and-distance penalty. Not only are you penalized an extra stroke, you also have to return to the site of the shot before. If it was your tee shot that went out of bounds, your provisional stroke becomes your third shot. That ball is now "in play" and your next shot is your fourth.

Lost ball

If you think your ball is lost in trees, bushes, or thick undergrowth, you should play a provisional ball. You then have just five minutes in which to find your original ball. Always lend a hand if one of your fellow competitors or your opponent is searching for a ball. It is a depressing enough task looking for hidden balls, but especially so if the search is a solitary pursuit. Tread carefully in long rough, however, because if you accidentally cause your ball to move while searching for it, you will be penalized one stroke. This is also the case if your caddie or partner is the culprit. If such an accident should happen, return the ball as close as possible

to its original spot before you play your next stroke. However, there is no penalty if your fellow competitor or opponent accidently steps on, or kicks, your ball.

If you cannot find your ball within the allotted five minutes, you must declare it officially lost and turn your attention to your provisional ball, again incurring a "stroke-and-distance" penalty. This is where the foresight of playing a provisional ball pays dividends. If you choose not to do so, you have to walk all the way back to the spot where you struck the offending shot—tedious for you and for other golfers in the groups behind you who are waiting to play. This is one of the many causes of the slow play that is such a problem at clubs all over the world. Some golfers are simply not aware of the correct course of action to take when something goes wrong, so the ensuing chaos tends to drag the episode out for much longer than is strictly necessary.

Do not be too hasty to reload and hit another ball in an effort to cancel out the memories of your previous attempt. You should wait for the other members of your group to play their shots before taking your turn. Try to use these precious few minutes to gather your thoughts and forget about what has just happened with your previous stroke. It is worth remembering the old adage: the next shot is the only shot in golf that matters.

The only time you do not need to play a provisional ball is when your tee shot plummets into a water hazard. There are various procedures for dealing with such an unlucky eventuality (see pp.172–3).

RULE BREAKER

Hitting a ball out of bounds
Chasing eventual winner Greg Norman down the stretch in the 1993 Open at Royal St. George's, England, Bernhard Langer reached the infamous Suez hole, No. 14. All week his strategy had been to hit an iron off the tee for safety. However, this time he opted for the driver. Seconds later, he sliced the ball over the out-of-bounds fence and, with that single destructive blow, his hopes were dashed.

Club selection can make all the difference. Bernhard Langer chose a driver on this hole—and finished out of bounds.

Water hazards

A water hazard is any sea, lake, pond, river, ditch, surface drainage ditch, or other open watercourse (whether or not it contains water). Your ball can be in a water hazard without actually lying in the water. There are two types of water hazard: the "lateral water hazard," which is marked by red stakes or a painted red line, and the "water hazard," marked by yellow stakes or a painted yellow line.

In the water?

The rules of golf state that there has to be "reasonable evidence" to establish whether or not a ball has actually landed in a water hazard.

If every member of your group sees your ball splash down into a lake, it is "reasonable" to assume that your ball is in the water hazard. Also, if you hit a ball and do not see it land, but the water hazard is surrounded by closely mown grass, again, it is safe to assume that the ball is in the water.

If you hit a shot into a semi-blind area, where, as well as a water hazard, there are several places your ball might be—such as heavy rough and trees—it is impossible for there to be reasonable evidence. So if you cannot find the ball, you must treat it as lost and then proceed under that rule.

Playing your shot

You have three options if your ball has landed in a water hazard. First, you can play it as it lies with no penalty, but playing a shot out of water is difficult and messy. The only time you should try this is if the ball is lying in the grassy area surrounding the water, within the margins of the hazard itself. You cannot ground the club at address when doing this, nor can you take a practice swing where the clubhead makes contact with the grass in the hazard.

>> **The ultimate hazard**
Jean van de Velde had a three-stroke lead in the 1999 Open Championship, until a visit to a water hazard led to a catastrophic final hole.

◄ The ultimate splash shot Only the brave, skilled, or foolhardy would attempt a shot such as this. The chances of success are slim, but a guaranteed result is a thorough soaking!

The second option is to drop a ball behind the water hazard, adding a one-stroke penalty. You must keep the point where the ball first crossed the margin of the hazard directly between the hole and the spot on which you drop the ball.

The third option is to go back to the spot where you played the offending shot, known as a stroke-and-distance penalty. You must add a stroke to your score, and forfeit the distance gained as well.

Lateral water hazard

The lateral water hazard is slightly different to an ordinary water hazard in terms of the options available. It was introduced by the rule-makers to deal with situations where it is simply not practical to proceed under any of the three recommended relief options. The two extra options available are: to drop the ball within two club-lengths of the point where the ball

last crossed the margin of the water hazard; or to drop the ball at a point on the opposite side of the hazard, again within two club-lengths.

In both instances, you will still incur a one-stroke penalty. However, do not forget that you can still select one of the other three options that have been explained earlier.

◄ Retrieving your ball Rescuing a ball from the murky depths will not always be feasible, but given the cost of golf balls, it is usually worth a try. Sadly, there is still a penalty stroke attached!

⌂ Bunker dilemmas
Assessing the relief
option in a bunker is not
always straightforward,
especially in waterlogged
conditions. This player
is receiving help from
the rules official.

In the bunker

Unlike water hazards, there is at least a chance of recovering a ball from a
bunker without incurring a penalty. Experience and practice will improve
your chances, but remember that things can easily go horribly wrong in sand.
So before you even attempt to play a stroke, ensure you know the rules that
apply to bunker play.

Playing from the bunker

It is against the rules to let the clubhead touch
the sand in the bunker at address or during the
course of your backswing.

If you do this, you will be penalized one shot
immediately. So, when attempting the shot, make
sure you suspend the clubhead at a safe distance
above the surface of the sand.

If a bunker is completely waterlogged and your
ball lands in it, you have got three options. First,
you can play it as it lies—which means you are
guaranteed to get a good soaking in the process!
Second, you can drop the ball in the bunker where
the water is most shallow, but the ball will be hard
to play and you may still end up getting wet. The
last and best option is to drop the ball outside

» Bunker specialist
Bobby Jones, widely
considered to be one
of the best golfers in the
history of the game, was
a master of recovering
from awkward bunker
shots during his short
playing career in
the 1920s.

⏶ **Plugged ball** Taking a drop in a bunker invariably leads to this depressing conclusion, the ball semi-buried in its own pitch mark.

the bunker; however, by doing this you will incur a penalty stroke. In effect, you are having to treat your submerged ball as an unplayable lie (*see* p.176). This is perhaps the harshest rule in golf.

Two balls in the bunker

If two balls come to rest in the sand close to each other, it creates something of a dilemma. One ball is almost certainly going to interfere with the other, making it hard for the player whose turn it is to execute the shot. Not only that, but playing the shot may affect the lie of the golfer who has to play the other ball, which would be unfair.

Decide which of the two balls is most practical to play first. Mark the other with a tee peg and lift the ball out of the way. Once the first shot has been played, the original lie of the second ball should be restored. Rake the sand if the original lie was perfect. If the ball was plugged, then it must be plugged when you put it back in the sand.

Obstructions and impediments

Obstructions are no cause for concern; if a cigarette butt or candy wrapper lies next to your ball in the bunker, move it out of the way before playing. If the ball moves in the process, put it back on its original spot and continue as normal.

Another obstruction that often interferes with play in sand is the bunker rake. If your ball comes to rest up against the rake, you are entitled to relief. Before lifting and moving the rake out of the way, if there is a chance that the ball might move, mark the position of the ball with a tee peg in the sand. That way, you can avoid any doubt as to its exact location when replacing the ball (*see* p.169). Remember also that you may place the ball in the sand, recreating as accurately as possible the original lie. You are not required to drop it in this instance.

You are not allowed to move loose impediments such as leaves and twigs, even if they interfere with your stroke (*see* p.167). The only exceptions are stones. At most clubs, a local rule exists that allows you to move them from around your ball, in the interests of safety.

◀ **Swinging through the sand** When executed correctly, this recovery shot sends the ball up and over the front lip on a cushion of sand. According to the rules, though, your clubhead must not touch the sand at address or through your backswing.

Unplayable ball

When faced with an unplayable ball, the exact course of action is to some degree determined by a player's ability. In other words, it is up to the player to decide whether a ball is unplayable. What the beginner thinks is unplayable might not be for an accomplished golfer. Once the ball is declared unplayable, there are three options available and each incurs a one-stroke penalty.

⚠ **The ultimate unplayable lie?** These cacti bear the scars of many a wayward stroke. No chance of even retrieving a ball from here.

Drop the ball

The first option you have is to drop a ball within two club-lengths of the spot where the unplayable ball is lying. This is generally the preferred option, because it is the least severe penalty. First, determine where you intend to drop the ball. Mark with a tee peg the exact spot where the ball is lying, then, using your longest club (for maximum relief), measure two club-lengths toward the nearest point of relief—no closer to the hole—and mark that spot with a second tee peg.

You must then drop the ball within the margins of those two tee pegs. Assuming it strikes the ground within these two parameters, and then does not come to rest closer to the hole, the ball is deemed to be "in play" once more.

If the ball comes to rest more than two club-lengths from that spot, then you must re-drop. Unfortunately, if the ball rolls back into the very same unplayable lie, or indeed any other

⚠ **Aiming too high** When Nick Faldo's ball lodged up a tree at Pebble Beach during a US Open, he had to first positively identify it before attempting to shake it down.

unplayable lie, you do not get another chance to drop. This is why it pays to think carefully and consider your options before you drop the ball to prevent this from happening. If the ball is in the middle of thick gorse bushes, for instance, then not even two club-lengths will be enough to get you into a playable lie. You will then have to resort to one of the other two options.

The second option for the unplayable ball is to return to the spot where you played your last shot, and be penalized one stroke. This is called a stroke-and-distance penalty (see p.171). If you are going back to the tee you can make use of the entire teeing ground; you do not have to tee off again from precisely the same spot. Anywhere else on the course, though, and you have to use your memory. Be honest and drop the ball as near as possible to the spot where you think you struck the offending shot.

The final option is to walk back away from the green, keeping the point where the ball lies and the flag in a straight line, dropping your ball somewhere along an extension of that line. There is no limit to how far you are allowed to go back under this option, so always be on the lookout for the best possible lie as you walk back. It may well be worth going back an extra 20–30 yards (18–27m) if that means you can drop the ball on a closely mown area, instead of in deep rough

closer to the green. If you are in a bunker and exercising either the first or third option, the ball must be dropped in the bunker.

⏶ **Measuring two club-lengths** Use the longest club in the bag, the driver, when measuring two club-lengths for a penalty drop. This will ensure the best chance of dropping well clear of the hazard.

TAKING THE DROP

There are precise rules on how to drop a ball. It used to be that you would drop a ball over your shoulder, with your back to the target, but that was changed in the mid-1980s. Today, you must stand upright with your arm outstretched at shoulder height. Then let the ball fall out of your hand. You cannot spin the ball or throw it. Simply let gravity take its course.

The ball must strike the ground within the confines of the two tee pegs. Providing the ball then comes to rest within two club-lengths of the spot where it first hit the ground, no closer to the hole, the ball is then deemed to be in play.

The correct way to drop is shown here by French tour professional Thomas Levet. Hold your arm outstretched at shoulder height, and simply release the ball.

The putting green

The smooth, manicured surfaces of the putting green are not a safe haven from the complexities of golf's rule book. There is plenty of scope for penalty strokes for any golfer who steps out of line, inadvertently or otherwise. This can include repairing spike marks on your line of putt and accidentally nudging the ball.

» Attending the flag
You can ask another member of your group to attend the flag. He or she must pull it from the hole before the ball goes in, though, otherwise there is a two-stroke penalty.

Holding the flagstick

You can either have the flagstick out or, in the case of a long putt where you might not be able to see the hole, you can have it attended. This means someone stands by the flag, holding it, ready to take it out of the hole when your ball—hopefully—goes in. If you choose to have the flag out, make sure you place it well out of harm's way on the green. If your ball then strikes the flag, there is a two-stroke penalty in stroke play or loss of hole in match play. If you accidentally drop the flag and it hits your ball, moving it off its spot, you are penalized one stroke. If you choose to have the flag attended, it needs to be pulled out before the ball goes in the hole. If the ball strikes the flag, you incur a two-stroke penalty.

Addressing the putt

If the ball moves in the process of your taking up, or having completed, your address position, this can be a problem. This is where a split second can make all the difference. If the ball moves after you have properly addressed it (in other words, grounded the club behind the ball), then you are deemed under the rules to have been responsible

---

DOS AND DON'TS

Do
- Do place a tee marker or coin behind the ball before you move it to mark, lift, and clean it. Under no circumstances should you ever lift your ball on the green without first marking it.
- Do repair an old hole plug or pitch mark on the green. You are not allowed to repair pitch marks off the green, even on the apron where you might be choosing to putt.
- Do replace a damaged ball with another, as long as there is agreement from your fellow competitor or opponent.
- Do brush aside leaves, twigs, and loose sand using your hand or the putterhead.

Do not
- Do not repair a spike mark on the line of your putt, although there is nothing to stop you from tapping down spike marks once you and your group have holed out.
- Do not test the putting surface of the green by rolling a ball along it—for example, to assess the pace or the undulation.
- Do not play your ball while another ball is in motion.
- Do not cause damage to the green when putting down bags.
- Do not brush aside early morning dew or frost—these are not loose impediments.

for it moving. You incur a one-stroke penalty, plus you have to put the ball back on its original spot. If a ball moves before you have addressed it—for example, because of a sudden gust of wind—then you have to play it from wherever it comes to rest, even if it is not to your advantage. No penalty applies in this case.

It is frustrating when your ball looks as though it is about to go in, only to stop on the very edge of the hole. The rules are strict on this point. You are allowed as long as it takes you to get to the hole (but you must not take the long way around the green), and then a further ten seconds once you get to your ball. If the ball does not succumb to gravity in that time, tap it in and take another stroke in the process.

Casual water

The rules relating to casual water on the green are often misunderstood. Casual water is any temporary accumulation of water on the course not in a water hazard, such as puddles of rain on the surface. You are not allowed to brush aside casual water or mop it up from the line of play. If your ball is on the

« Rules breach
In October 2013 Simon Dyson was handed a two-month suspended ban after illegally tapping down a spike mark during a Tour event in China.

green and casual water interferes with the line of your ball to the hole, move the ball to an area of the green where the water ceases to become an obstruction. You cannot go closer to the hole. It is not permissible to brush aside early morning dew or frost. If you do, there is a two-stroke penalty. Many amateur golfers fall foul of this rule.

If there has been so much rain that the hole has actually filled up with water, the rules allow you to scoop some of it out, although in so doing you must avoid touching the actual line of your putt.

« Removing the flagstick from the hole It is advisable to leave the flagstick farther away from the hole than shown here when putting, because if the ball hits the flagstick, the golfer will incur a penalty.

Golf **Tournaments**

Tournaments have changed dramatically since the early days of golf. If the early pioneers could see the huge grandstands, hundreds of journalists and photographers from all around the world, and wall-to-wall television coverage, they would be stunned. This chapter details all the notable competitions open to both professionals and amateurs.

The Masters' Trophy

One of the more unusual among golf trophies, the prize for the Masters is a replica of the Augusta clubhouse.

The Masters

The US Masters marks the start of the golfing season. It is the first of four Major championships that the professionals play, and in many people's eyes is the ultimate golf tournament. Every April, amid the dogwoods and azaleas of Augusta National (*see* pp.222–3), Southern charm and beauty come face to face with the multi-million-dollar golf circuit. Invariably, what results is an unforgettable week.

Augusta National

It was Lionel Herbert, a US Tour player in the 1950s and 1960s, who said: "This is the only course I know where you choke when you come in the gate." Just walking up the drive, known as Magnolia Lane, to the clubhouse is enough to make the hairs on the back of your neck stand to attention. Augusta National is an extraordinarily beautiful and grand place, and the Masters Tournament is quite unlike any other tournament. Out of all the Major golfing tournaments, the Masters is unique because the competition takes place on the same course every year.

Course architect
The expatriate Scottish doctor Alister MacKenzie was the architect of Augusta National course, appointed in 1930 by the course founder Bobby Jones.

The Augusta National golf course is the Mecca of the golfing world, an ultra-exclusive course, which you are not allowed to play unless you do so in the Masters or as a member's guest. Ask anyone who has swung a club which course they would like to play for the rest of their lives and some will say St. Andrews, others Pine Valley, but most will plump for the immaculate fairways of Augusta.

US Masters' Program This cover of the 1933 US Masters' program, features Bobby Jones.

The first thing you notice about Augusta is the color. The previous owner, Louis Berckman, was an ardent horticulturist, which is borne out in the azaleas, and the magnolias, pines, and dogwoods, all of which provide an awe-inspiring backdrop.

The beginnings

After Bobby Jones retired in 1930, having won the Grand Slam—the four Open and Amateur championships held that year—he decided there was nothing more for him to achieve as a player, and he set his sights on creating his own tournament. It was to be for his golfing friends and acquaintances, by invitation only; however, he first needed a golf course. After a conversation with a friend, a New York banker named Clifford Roberts, an option was obtained on a fruit nursery at a price of $70,000.

Jones wanted it to be the "ideal golf club," full of members he thought of as the right type. He also wanted to build the ultimate golf course, and with this in mind, he invited Alister MacKenzie, an expatriate Scot, to work on the project. MacKenzie was a medical doctor, who had studied the art of camouflage while serving during the Boer War in South Africa; it was an art he frequently used during his design work. He had built Alwoodley and Moortown in England, and had received rave reviews for his work on Cypress Point in California.

Jones took a very hands-on approach to the design and spent a considerable time hitting balls and working out shot values and tee positions as the course was evolving. Small amounts of gold were found during the construction, but when it was finished, in December 1932, everyone who saw it agreed that it had been turned into a priceless piece of golfing real estate.

In March 1934, the First Annual Invitation Tournament was a fairly informal affair, and just 72 players teed up. It was Clifford Roberts' idea to call it the Masters, an idea that Bobby Jones initially thought showed a touch of arrogance, and did not like. By the end of the decade, however, Jones had relented, and in 1939 the title of the tournament was officially changed to the Masters.

Initially, Jones did not even want to play in the event, and preferred to be an official. However, the members of the club eventually persuaded him to tee up, which he did so more out of a sense of duty than with any intention of winning. In the 12 tournaments in which he took part, Jones never shot under 72, and his best position was a tie for 13th place. After Gene Sarazen's double eagle in 1935, the Masters took on immediate gravitas. It was as if the tournament, only in its second year, had already "arrived." Although it would take a couple more decades before it was thought of as a Major championship, it received huge interest every April and became an essential part of the golfing calendar.

Gene Sarazen Arguably the greatest of all US Masters' competitors, Gene Sarazen hit one of the most famous shots in golf, a double eagle, at the second event held at Augusta in 1935.

Spring colors at Augusta The US Masters is always played at Augusta National in April, when the hallmark plants and trees are at their most magnificent.

The course

Despite the prevailing peace and serenity of the atmosphere, nothing much stays still at Augusta, and the golf course is constantly changing and evolving. Every year alterations are made; a few mounds are put in here, a tee is shifted, or a green is resurfaced and reshaped. And, in typical Augusta fashion, when they want to put in a few trees (as they did recently on the right of the 15th fairway), they put them in full-grown, with no expense spared. For a place with such a "conservative" image, the one thing Augusta is never frightened of is change.

In the late 1940s, the 16th hole, for example, was completely restructured by the great designer Robert Trent Jones. Then, in 1980, all the greens went from having Bermuda grass on them to bentgrass, with the result that they became even quicker. And, more recently, the course has been lengthened by 300 yards (275m). But, despite all these changes, much of the philosophy behind Alister MacKenzie's original design still remains. The course has very wide fairways, very large greens, and very little rough—although there have been attempts to make the rough more severe since the late 1990s. As MacKenzie intended, it is the sort of course that is not too daunting for the club handicapper off the tee, but it can still be a severe test for the best professionals, especially around the greens, which are fast and have huge contours on them.

The course does not rely too much on its bunkering to protect it, although the bunkers are invariably big and deep. At the first tournament in 1934, there were only 22 bunkers; today, there are still only about 50. But, the fact that there is little rough means players with imagination invariably triumph. And, although the fairways are wide, you need to drive the ball in the right places in order to get the best line in to the flag on your approach. The two loops of nine were switched after the first tournament. So, in 1934, the hole at which Sarazen would make a double eagle a year later was in fact the 6th rather than the 15th. Today, it is the back nine, with water in play on the 11th, 12th, 13th, 15th, and 16th, that causes much of the excitement every April.

GREAT ROUNDS

Jack Nicklaus: Masters 1986

At the age of 46, Jack Nicklaus won his sixth Masters title, and his 18th Major with a final round 65. It will be remembered by everyone who saw it. After a slowish start, he birdied the 9th, 10th, and 11th, with putts of 10ft (3m), 20ft (6m), and 25ft (7.5m). A two-putt birdie at the 13th put him on the leaderboard, and then he eagled the 15th, put his tee shot to 3ft (1m) at the 16th for another birdie, and sank a slippery birdie putt on the 17th.

Jack Nicklaus, one of the greatest golfers ever, won the US Masters on an extraordinary six occasions.

⯅ **The reign of Spain** The Spaniard Seve Ballesteros lit up the world of golf in the early 1980s, winning the US Masters on two memorable occasions, in 1980 and 1983.

Controversy

Despite the fact that it does not court controversy, Augusta National has seen its fair share of it. Clifford Roberts, the first chairman, ruled the club with an iron fist. Although Roberts committed suicide by shooting himself in the head while at the club one evening in 1977, his autocratic nature lives on. Basically, players do what the members of the club want them to do, or they do not get invited the following year. This applies as much to television executives as it does to players or spectators. The rules are there to be obeyed and if, like the TV commentator Gary McCord, you describe the 17th green as being so fast it "must have bikini wax" on it, you will find yourself banned from the tournament. For many years, television commentators were not allowed to mention prize money or anything similarly vulgar.

The 1968 tournament ended in a tie between the Argentinian Roberto de Vicenzo and the American Bob Goalby, until it was discovered that de Vicenzo had signed for a 4 on the 17th when he had actually taken a 3. The rules of golf left no room for such a mistake, and Goalby won the championship. Because Georgia is in the deep South and for years no black player had ever played in the Masters (only since 1975, when

⟪ **The Par-3 Tournament** On the eve of every Masters, the competitors warm up with an event on the beautiful par-3 course. No one has ever won this and the main event.

Lee Elder was invited), civil rights campaigners have for a long time complained that the club pursued a racist policy. Black golfers were only allowed to become club members in 1990.

The championship

The Masters may be the youngest of the modern Majors, but there are a whole host of traditions that make it very different from every other tournament. For instance, you cannot just turn up to watch it; season tickets are passed on from generation to generation. And there are strict rules for spectators, who are not allowed to run on the premises. The Masters has a smaller, more select field than the other three Majors; and a handful of amateurs always get an invitation, in recognition of the founder of the tournament, Bobby Jones, who was an amateur. The winner gets a Green Jacket that is presented to him by the previous year's winner, and on the day before the tournament many of the competitors play in the Par-3 Tournament, on the stunningly beautiful par-3 course.

Only three men in the history of the event have won back-to-back victories at Augusta; Jack Nicklaus (1965 and 1966), Nick Faldo (1989 and

⚑ Handing on the Green Jacket The previous year's winner, Germany's Bernhard Langer, helps the 1994 winner, Spain's José Maria Olazabal, put on the time-honored Green Jacket.

1990), and Tiger Woods (2001 and 2002). Nicklaus won six Masters' titles in all, most memorably in 1986, when he was a relatively mature 46 years old. Seve Ballesteros' victory in 1980, at the age of 23, made him the youngest winner of a Green Jacket, until Tiger Woods came along in 1997. Playing in his first-ever Major as a professional, 21-year-old Woods beat almost every record in the book, shooting 18-under-par to win by 12 shots. Golf and the Masters would never be the same again.

The Masters' greatest shot

It was late afternoon in Georgia and there was a chill in the air. The final round of the 1935 US Masters was drawing to a close. Gene Sarazen, playing with Walter Hagen, was walking down the 15th fairway, when suddenly there was a huge roar up by the 18th green. Craig Wood had just made a birdie to finish at 6-under-par 282, and was being hailed as the victor.

Sarazen turned to his caddie, Stovepipe, and asked what he needed to win. "Four 3's, Mr. Gene," came the reply. When Sarazen arrived at his ball, the first thing he noticed was that the lie

⏩ Tiger Woods' historic win in 1997 The phenomenon that is Tiger Woods really exploded into life at Augusta in 1997, when the 21-year-old became the youngest player ever to win— by 12 shots.

was far from good. Stovepipe calculated that the 235-yard (215-m) distance would usually be a 3-wood, but he also knew that, out of this lie, his boss might not get the ball up high enough to clear the pond in front of the green. They agreed on the Turfrider 4-wood.

Sarazen ripped into the shot, a fierce low drive, and the ball never got more than about 10 yards (9m) above the ground. It landed on the front edge, bounced a couple of times, and made its inexorable way towards the flag. Sarazen ran forward to see how close it would get, and then the 23 people around the green let out a big cheer. The ball had disappeared into the hole. Sarazen made pars at the final two holes to equal Craig Wood's score of 6-under-par, and the next day he won the 36-hole playoff by five shots.

‹‹ **Phil Mickelson— winner in 2004** After years of near misses at the very pinnacle of the game, the US player Phil Mickelson finally won his first Major tournament at Augusta in 2004.

TOURNAMENT STATISTICS

The table below lists the winners of the US Masters for a ten-year period, from 2004 to 2013. The US Masters is unique in that the venue is the same every year—the Augusta National. The winning player's combined score is given in each case.

Year	Venue	Winner
2013	Augusta	**Adam Scott (Aus)** *With a total score of 279 over the four rounds.*
2012	Augusta	**Bubba Watson (US)** *With a total score of 278 over the four rounds.*
2011	Augusta	**Charl Schwartzel (SA)** *With a total score of 274 over the four rounds.*
2010	Augusta	**Phil Mickelson (US)** *With a total score of 272 over the four rounds.*
2009	Augusta	**Angel Cabrera (Arg)** *With a total score of 276 over the four rounds.*
2008	Augusta	**Trevor Immelman (SA)** *With a total score of 280 over the four rounds.*
2007	Augusta	**Zach Johnson (US)** *With a total score of 289 over the four rounds.*
2006	Augusta	**Phil Mickelson (US)** *With a total score of 281 over the four rounds.*
2005	Augusta	**Tiger Woods (US)** *With a total score of 276 over the four rounds.*
2004	Augusta	**Phil Mickelson (US)** *With a total score of 279 over the four rounds.*

Most wins: 6, Jack Nicklaus (US); 1963, 1965, 1966, 1972, 1975, 1986
Biggest Victory Margin: 12 strokes, Tiger Woods (US) 1997
Lowest Winning Aggregate: 270 (-18), Tiger Woods (US) 1997
Lowest Round 63 (-9), Nick Price (Zim) 1986 and Greg Norman (Aus) 1996
Youngest Winner: Tiger Woods (US), 21
Oldest Winner: Jack Nicklaus (US), 46

The Open

It is, quite simply, the oldest and most prestigious tournament in the game. Considered by many to be the ultimate Major championship, the Open is more "open" than the Masters (which has a restricted field), and the USPGA Championship (which has no amateurs in the field). It is also more cosmopolitan than the US Open, and the ultimate test for the game's leading players.

⏏ **The Claret Jug**
First awarded in 1873, the Claret Jug replaced the original Championship Belt, made from Moroccan leather.

Traditional golf

The Open Championship reflects the simplest and purest form of the game of golf, played as it always is on old, traditional British links courses. It is golf as it used to be played, golf without all the trimmings of so many other modern competitions. The courses are the most natural-looking you will find, blending as they do into the surrounding countryside. Whereas US Opens and other Majors tend to be held near large airports and metropolitan areas, the Open is held in little seaside villages, such as Sandwich or Gullane, Troon or Turnberry. Massive television compounds gather in places more used to selling beach balls.

Like the US Open, golfers need to qualify. Anyone with a handicap of scratch or better can enter. The Open is very different from every other week on the golfing calendar; there are no pristine fairways, no greens like billiard tables. Instead, wind, rain, sun, sleet, and hail will often go hand in hand with the tournament, along with quirky roly-poly courses and lots of ice cream.

Wind and the natural elements play a vital part in any Open. There is luck involved, and it can really matter which half of the draw you are in if there is a storm in the morning and the wind drops in the afternoon. And yet, despite all the injustices, most of the world's top players, including Tiger Woods, Ernie Els, and Phil Mickelson, go misty-eyed at the mention of links golf. It is a form of the game that enables them to use their imagination, and they love it.

The early years

The best golfer in the middle of the 19th century was without question the Scot Allan Robertson. He was the first man to break 80 at St. Andrews, and was the undisputed golfer of his age. When he died in 1859, there was no obvious successor.

Major J. O. Fairlie, who was a member at Prestwick, decided it would be a good idea to hold a tournament that would effectively decide who had taken over Robertson's mantle. The tournament was first held at Prestwick in 1860, and the Open was born.

The first few Opens were effectively held between Tom Morris and Willie Park, both of whom won the Open four times. When Morris won for the last time in 1867, he became (and still remains) the oldest winner at 46 years, 99 days. A year later, Morris' son, Young Tom, won his first title at the age of 17 years, 161 days; he is still the youngest-ever champion.

⏩ **Royal Troon**
The course at Troon in Scotland, which has hosted the Open seven times, is a quintessential links that offers the world's best golfers one of their toughest challenges.

Young Tom Morris was a prodigy. In 1868, he recorded the championship's first ever hole-in-one, and by 1870 he had won three times and retained the Moroccan belt that was the original prize for the winner.

Prestwick Golf Club, the Royal & Ancient, and the Honourable Company of Edinburgh Golfers decided to take turns holding the championship. They bought a silver claret jug for about $150, which is still played for today, and Young Tom's name was the first to be inscribed on it in 1872.

John Ball became the first English champion, when he won at Prestwick in 1890. He was also the first amateur to win. The only other amateurs to win the Open have been Harold Hilton (twice) and Bobby Jones (three times).

The Great Triumvirate

By the 1890s, prize money was increasing dramatically (to over $500), and the Open was doubled in length to 72 holes and played over two days. It was also taken to other courses.

❮❮ Bobby Jones
Widely regarded as the finest amateur golfer of all time, Bobby Jones was the Open champion in 1926, 1927, and 1930.

The two decades before World War I were dominated by three men who became known as the Great Triumvirate. Harry Vardon (a smooth-swinging player from the island of Jersey), James Braid (a modest man from Fife), and J. H. Taylor (a strong, stocky, bad-weather player from Devon) were all born within a year of each other. Between 1894 and the outbreak of World War I in 1914, they won an extraordinary 16 of the 21 Opens that were played.

James Braid won his first in 1901, and within ten years became the first man to win five. Harry Vardon still remains the only man to have clinched six Open championships. One exception to this domination occurred in 1907, when Frenchman Arnaud Massy became the first overseas player to have his name inscribed on the Claret Jug.

⌃ **Harry Vardon**
Part of the Great Triumvirate, Harry Vardon won the open six times between 1896 and 1914.

Prize money

The exponential rise in prize money at the Open is an indication of the huge growth in the sport that has taken place in recent years. Commercially, the

❮❮ **Australia's finest**
The most successful Australian player ever to compete in the Open, Peter Thomson won the event no fewer than five times, in 1954, 1955, 1956, 1958, and 1965.

Open is now big business, and you only have to take a look at the huge tented village at each tournament to see how many satellite industries depend on the championship.

At the first three Opens there was no prize money available, and when it was finally introduced in 1863, the winner, Willie Park, received about $40 and a gold medal. By 1920, the winner picked up roughly $300 in an overall purse of $900. The first winner to receive over a thousand pounds sterling (then about $3000) was the Australian, Peter Thomson, in 1955, when he won the second of his five Open titles. When Tom Watson won the first of his five titles, in 1975, he took home about $15,000. Compare that with the 2004 winner, US player Todd Hamilton, who collected a first prize of about $1.3 million.

Crossing the Atlantic

Between the two World Wars, the Claret Jug would find itself making an annual pilgrimage across the Atlantic to the US. Jock Hutchison (1921) became the first resident of the US to win the title, even though he was born in Scotland. The tweed jacket brigade at St. Andrews found it difficult to come to terms with the fact that US golfers were widely acknowledged to be the best in the world. Between 1921 and 1934, only one championship went to a home-grown player, Arthur Havers (1923).

US players Walter Hagen, Gene Sarazen, and Bobby Jones all crossed the Atlantic to dominate the Open during this period. Hagen first won in 1922, and again two years later, holing a 5-ft (1.5-m) putt to beat Ernie Whitcombe. Sarazen, like so many before and after him, took some time to appreciate the beauty of links golf. He eventually won the Open Championship at Prince's in 1932. Bobby Jones, the best amateur (some say, the best player) ever to play the game was also not taken with links golf immediately. He won the Open in 1926, 1927, and 1930, the year of his famous Grand Slam.

The postwar period

After World War II, South Africa's Bobby Locke won four titles, and Australian Peter Thomson won five; but the top US players stayed at home—put off by the travel, eccentric courses, odd food, and wild weather. All this changed when one of the world's best golfers, Arnold Palmer, decided to travel across the Atlantic for the centennial Open in 1960 at St. Andrews. He was virtually the only US player to enter, but he went on to win the tournament twice, in 1961 and 1962.

Palmer's fellow Americans gradually began to follow him over the Atlantic. The Open had been in danger of being discarded as a Major championship by the top players. Without the support and influence of Arnold Palmer, it certainly would not have enjoyed the status and prestige that it does today.

« Winning at the Open
A popular three-time winner, Seve Ballesteros was victorious in 1979, 1984, and 1988.

⌃ Sudden-death winner South African Ernie Els won the Open at Muirfield in 2002, beating three other players in a playoff.

The modern era

In 1970 at St. Andrews, US player Doug Sanders wrote himself into the record books when he missed a putt from under 3ft (1m) to win. He lost by a shot to Nicklaus in the playoff the next day. But Sanders was certainly not the only player to lose out on the Claret Jug. In 1972, the local favorite, Tony Jacklin, looked certain to win the title, until Lee Trevino chipped in twice down the final stretch. Jacklin was never the same player again after that match.

The greatest Open of the decade—some say it was the greatest Open ever—was the "Duel in the Sun" at Turnberry in 1977. The two leading players in the world, Jack Nicklaus and Tom Watson, went head-to-head for 36 holes, with Watson eventually winning by the narrowest of margins.

Watson reigned supreme in the early part of the 1980s, winning three times in four years (1980, 1982, and 1983). He would probably have won again at St. Andrews in 1984 if he had not found himself up against it on the Road Hole (the 17th) in the final round. Watson's demise, and a birdie by Spaniard Seve Ballesteros on the final hole, gave the latter his second of three Opens, and marked the end of the Watson era.

A year later, European golf received a further boost when Sandy Lyle became the first resident Scot to win the Open since James Braid in 1910. Two years later, in 1987, Englishman Nick Faldo won the first of his three Open titles. Faldo's determination at Muirfield will be remembered for his 18 relentless pars in the final round, which saw him finish a shot clear of US player Paul Azinger. In 1990 at St. Andrews, Faldo became only the second Englishman (behind J. H. Taylor) to win at the Home of Golf.

When the Open returned to St. Andrews five years later, it produced a memorable championship, with the unlikely figure of US player John Daly eventually lifting the Claret Jug. Needing a birdie 3 on the last hole to tie Daly's score, the Italian Costantino Rocca scuffed his second shot into the Valley of Sin. Then, just as everyone thought it was all over, he holed a huge long putt to take Daly into a playoff. Rocca banging his fists in disbelief on the hallowed turf is an image which will live on. Sadly for him, the four-hole playoff was an anticlimax, and he was easily beaten.

Since 2005 there have been back-to-back victories for both Tiger Woods and Padraig Harrington, and career-defining wins for Darren Clarke and Phil Mickelson. But the most

⌃ Tiger Woods at the Open One of the world's most celebrated golfers, Tiger Woods has had a somewhat checkered history at the Open. When he won in 2000, he broke the record for the lowest total in a Major, but the Open has also been the scene of his worst-ever round as a professional golfer.

memorable staging of the Open Championship in recent times was notable for the man who came second. In 2009, Tom Watson, last a winner in 1983, and now a few weeks short of his 60th birthday, rolled back the years to lead almost from start to finish. But needing a par on the 72nd hole to close out victory, his approach bounced through the green, and he went on to make bogey.

Stewart Cink beat the fans' favorite in the playoff but he will always be the forgotten champion due to Watson's heroics.

Missed opportunities
In one of the classic breakdowns in golfing history, Frenchman Jean Van de Velde played into a water hazard to ruin his chances of winning the 1999 Open.

TOURNAMENT STATISTICS

Golf's oldest and most prestigious championship has seen winners of many different nationalities in its long history. However, in the last ten years, only players from the US, UK (Northern Ireland), Ireland, and South Africa have triumphed, at a number of different courses.

Year	Venue	Winner
2013	Muirfield	**Phil Mickelson (US)** *With a total score of 281 over the four rounds.*
2012	Royal Lytham & St. Anne's	**Ernie Els (SA)** *With a total score of 273 over the four rounds.*
2011	Royal St. George's	**Darren Clarke (NI)** *With a total score of 275 over the four rounds.*
2010	St. Andrews	**Louis Oosthuizen (SA)** *With total score of 272 over the four rounds.*
2009	Turnberry	**Stewart Cink (US)** *With a total score of 278 over the four rounds.*
2008	Royal Birkdale	**Padraig Harrington (Ire)** *With a total score of 283 over the four rounds.*
2007	Carnoustie	**Padraig Harrington (Ire)** *With a total score of 277 over the four rounds.*
2006	Royal Liverpool	**Tiger Woods (US)** *With a total score of 270 over the four rounds.*
2005	St. Andrews	**Tiger Woods (US)** *With a total score of 274 over the four rounds.*
2004	Royal Troon	**Todd Hamilton (US)** *With a total score of 274 over the four rounds.*

Most wins: 6, Harry Vardon (GB); 1896, 1898, 1899, 1903, 1911, 1914
Biggest Victory Margin: 13 strokes, Tom Morris Sr. (GB) 1862
Lowest Winning Aggregate: 267, Greg Norman (Aus) 1993
Lowest Round: 63, achieved by a number of different players
Youngest Winner: Tom Morris Jr. (GB), 17
Oldest Winner: Tom Morris Sr. (GB), 46

The US Open

For US players, this is the ultimate Major championship. They grow up dreaming about a short putt to win their national title. For everyone else in the world, being called the US Open champion is one of the most important of accolades. Like the Open Championship in Britain, this is also one of the most open Opens.

⌃ **The US Open trophy**
The original cup was destroyed in a fire in 1946. Today, a copy is awarded to the winner.

The beginnings

In the 1890s, golf was still in its infancy in the US, and it was mostly played by the wealthy. The first golf club to be formed was the St. Andrews Golf Club in Yonkers, New York, in 1888. These were the days when rich Americans employed expatriate British golf professionals to design their courses and make their equipment. These pros were treated like servants by the employers, but there was also a certain amount of pride taken in the professionals' golfing prowess.

Inaugural year

The first official US Open took place at Newport Golf Club in Rhode Island in 1895 and was a bit of an afterthought to the Amateur Championship. It was played over 36 holes (four times around the nine-hole course) on October 4, with a field of 11—ten professionals and one amateur. The President of the United States Golf Association (USGA), which still runs the championship, paid the players' expenses, to ensure that the best players attended.

The early years of the championship were dominated by expatriates—players such as Fred Herd and Willie Smith, Willie Anderson, and Laurie Auchterlonie. Anderson was the best of the bunch, winning in 1901 and then consecutively from 1903 to 1905. Only three other men have won the US Open four times: Bobby Jones, in 1923, 1926, 1929, and 1930; Ben Hogan, in 1948, 1950, 1951, and 1953; and Jack Nicklaus, in 1962, 1967, 1972, and 1980. No player except Anderson ever achieved the distinction of winning three in a row. He would surely have added to his titles if he had not contracted arteriosclerosis and died at just 30 years old in 1910.

In its early years, the US Open could not match its older brother, the Open Championship, which had started in 1860 on the other side of the Atlantic. But, as the popularity of the game exploded in the US, its reputation grew. Both

Opens have had their ups and downs, and while the Open took 32 years to extend its championship to 72 holes, the US Open took only four.

Often, the best professionals would be playing exhibition matches all over the US in the summer, and would break off to play in the US Open, adding to the stature of the event. Harry Vardon, for instance, won the title in 1900 while on a tour of the US promoting Spalding's new Vardon Flyer golf ball. He shot rounds of 79, 78, 76, and 80 to win by two from J. H. Taylor, and the crowd sang "Auld Lang Syne" to him in the clubhouse.

When John J. McDermott won in 1911, it was a momentous breakthrough for US golf, because he became the first home-grown American to win

⌃ **Walter Hagen** Two-time winner of the US Open, the American Walter Hagen was a leading player for many years.

the title. And a year later, in 1912, he won a second time. The 16-year stranglehold by foreign-born professionals had finally been broken.

An open Open

The US Open and the Open are rightly widely regarded as the two most important Major championships in the world. Like the Open, one of the distinguishing features of the US Open is that it really is open to anyone who is good enough. The USGA, which runs the event, regularly receives over 6,000 applications to enter the tournament. Through a series of qualifying events, this is whittled down to a final field of 156. Although the eventual champion is likely to be a touring professional, the US Open Champion knows he has beaten everyone who thinks they can play the game, and not simply a select few who have been invited to take part.

In contrast to the Open Championship, which so far has been held at 14 different courses, the US Open has been held at nearly 50. It has been suggested that the USGA reduce the rota to just a handful of traditional courses, but with such a big country, they take the view that they need to spread the play around.

Walter Hagen once said: "Any player can win a US Open, but it takes a helluva player to win two." Hagen himself won two, in 1914 and 1919.

A surprising champion

When the unknown amateur, Francis Ouimet, beat arguably the two best players in the world, Harry Vardon and Ted Ray, in 1913, it was an upset of gigantic proportions and final proof that the balance of power was shifting from Britain to the US.

Francis Ouimet was a 20-year-old who lived across the road from the Country Club where the Open was held, and he used to caddie there. He had no plans to play in the Open, because he had just played in the Amateur (in which he was knocked out in the second round) and could not take any more time off from his job at the Wright and Ditson sporting goods store.

However, his manager eventually agreed to let him play. On the eve of the tournament, he went out to practice with a couple of friends and shot two 88s—not ideal preparation. Amazingly, his four rounds of the Championship proper added up to

304, the same score as Harry Vardon (who had won five Open Championships by this time), and Ted Ray (who had won one).

All week Ouimet had a 10-year-old named Eddie Lowery carrying his bag, but on the morning of the playoff, one of Ouimet's friends, Frank Hoyt, saw how the youngster was struggling and suggested it might be better if he carried the bag in the playoff.

"That's something you'll have to take up with Eddie," was Ouimet's reply. Hoyt tried a second time, and Ouimet was on the verge of giving in, when he looked at the 10-year-old and saw tears in his eyes. "Little Eddie Lowery will caddie for me in the playoff," said Ouimet. Ouimet shot 72 in the playoff, to Vardon's 77 and Ray's 78, though he was only one ahead of Vardon with two holes to play. It was a sensational victory. Suddenly golf, which had been described as "cow-pasture pool" in some quarters, caught the imagination of the US public. Ouimet's humble social status and modest manner made him a hero overnight, and hugely helped to broaden the appeal of the game.

⬢ **The unknown amateur** Previously unheard of, Francis Ouimet came from nowhere to win in 1913.

GREAT ROUNDS

Arnold Palmer: US Open, 1960
Seven shots behind the leader, US player Mike Souchak, with one round to play, Palmer came into the clubhouse for his lunch (they played 36 holes in one day). He asked a journalist, Dan Jenkins, what might happen if he drove the first green, made a birdie, and shot a 65 to finish on 280. "Doesn't 280 always win the Open?" he asked. "Only when Hogan shoots it," came the reply. Palmer did drive the 1st green, did make a birdie, and duly won the event.

Arnold Palmer worked out his tactics to win a famous victory in Colorado.

⌃ **Jack Nicklaus**
An exultant Jack
Nicklaus celebrating
a putt in 1980, when
he won in New Jersey.

The premier championship

By the 1920s, golf was much stronger in the
US than it was in Great Britain. It was the age of
Bobby Jones, Gene Sarazen, and Walter Hagen.
They helped make the US Open the premier
event in world golf.

The championship was becoming so popular
that tickets for spectators were sold for the first
time in 1922. And the USGA had to introduce
sectional qualifying as early as 1922, because
they were receiving so many entries.

In 1933, John Goodman became the fifth and
last amateur to win, following Ouimet in 1913,
Jerome D. Travers in 1915, Charles Evans Jr.
in 1916, and Bobby Jones. As well as winning
four titles, Jones lost four (two of the losses
coming in playoffs).

The list of winners of US Opens reads like a list
of the best players of every era; and yet one great
player never managed to lift the trophy. In the same
way that Arnold Palmer and Tom Watson could
never win the USPGA Championship, so fellow
US player Sam Snead could never win a US Open.

Course philosophy

Just as the Royal & Ancient like to prepare a "fast
and running links," so the USGA has very strict
guidelines on how they like to see a course set up
for a US Open. Invariably, US Open courses will have
narrow fairways—usually about 24 yards (22m)
wide—with long rough—"long enough to penalize
a player about half a shot"—either side. "A player
should be accurate as well as long," says the USGA.
"We penalize a player's inaccuracy."

Any inaccuracy is also penalized around the greens, where the rough is invariably very thick, lush, and long. And the greens are usually very firm and very fast. The USGA says it tries to set up a course that "ensures that a player is called upon to use all, or at least most, of his clubs during his round." They say they want a "stern but fair" test. But critics suggest that too often the USGA verge on being "stern" rather than "fair," and that it pays too much attention to "par," and getting hurt and insulted if the winner shoots a lot under par.

Highs and lows
After Arnold Palmer had made his extraordinary comeback victory in 1960 at Cherry Hills (when he came from seven shots off the lead to shoot a final round 65 to win by two from Jack Nicklaus), Briton

Tony Jacklin hit the headlines ten years later at Hazeltine. Jacklin won by seven shots on a course which had a plethora of blind shots and 13 doglegs. One journalist asked the US golfer Dave Hill what he thought the course needed and the reply from the dry Hill was: "Eighty acres of corn and a few cows." A year after his Open Championship victory, Jacklin became the first Briton to win the US Open since Ted Ray exactly 50 years before.

Twelve years later, in 1982 at Pebble Beach, Jack Nicklaus came within a whisker of winning his fifth US Open. Indeed, he would have if Tom Watson, playing a couple of groups behind him, had not played some extraordinary shots in his final round. Watson sank enormous putts on the 10th, 11th, and 14th holes and then rubbed salt in Nicklaus' wounds by chipping in, from thick rough, on the penultimate hole.

≪ Classic playoff in 1990 The Medinah Country Club at Medinah, Illinois, was the scene of a classic playoff in 1990, when Hale Irwin edged out the unlucky Mike Donald.

The playoff

The US Open is the only one of the four Majors to still persist with an 18-hole playoff. Their argument is that a Major championship is of such importance that it should not be decided by something as arbitrary as a sudden-death playoff, or even a three- and four-hole playoff.

The problem with the 18-hole playoff is that it inevitably turns out to be an anticlimax. The championship proper is scheduled to end on a Sunday night, and yet everyone has to return on Monday morning to perform the last rites. The crowd is inevitably hugely reduced, with the winner often being known well before the end. Contrast that with the instant excitement seen at the 2004 USPGA playoff, or the 1989 Open Championship playoff, and it is not difficult to see which the crowds prefer.

There have been 33 playoffs in US Open history, the most recent one in 2008, when Tiger Woods (71) beat fellow US player Rocco Mediate (71) at Torrey Pines. One of the closest playoffs took place in 1990 at Medinah, when after the 18 holes, US players Hale Irwin and Mike Donald were still level. Ultimately, the title was decided by sudden death, with Irwin sinking an 8-ft (2.5-m) putt for victory at the first extra hole.

Recent years

Although the US Open celebrated its centennial in 1995, the two suspensions (1917–18 and 1942–45) because of the two world wars unwittingly determined that the 100th US Open would also take place in the year 2000. The great links course at Pebble Beach in California hosted the historic occasion, and the championship that resulted was an epic.

Tiger Woods, who was enjoying an extraordinary run of form at the time, was unbelievably dominant. He seemed not to miss a putt from under 15ft (4.5m) all week. Woods conquered a course that looked nearly impossible to everyone else in the field. In the process, he broke just about every record in the book, eventually winning by an astonishing 15 shots, the largest victory ever in a Major (Old Tom Morris won the 1862 Open

▼ **American** Payne Stewart was lost to the world of golf in a plane crash in October 1999. He won the US Open on two occasions, in 1991 and 1999.

⌃ **Winning from the rough** South African Ernie Els has been one of the most consistently successful golfers in recent years. His victories in the US Open came in 1994 and 1997.

Championship by 12 shots). The previous largest margin of victory in a US Open was 11, when Willie Smith won in 1899. Another crushing victory was registered by Northern Ireland's Rory McIlroy at Congressional Club in 2011, the second consecutive victory for the nation, following Graeme McDowell's win at Pebble Beach in 2010. McIlroy won by eight shots from Australia's Jason Day. His performance, both physically and mentally, was all the more remarkable because it came only two months after the Irishman had blown a four-shot lead in the final round of the US Masters.

« South African victor
Retief Goosen won the US Open for the second time at Shinnecock Hills, New York, in 2004. His previous win was in 2001.

TOURNAMENT STATISTICS

Players from the US have dominated their own Open tournament for most of its existence, although several South African players have been notably successful in the event. The winners of the last ten years are listed below.

Year	Venue	Winner
2013	Merion	**Justin Rose (GB)** *With a total score of 281 over the four rounds.*
2012	Olympic Club	**Webb Simpson (US)** *With a total score of 281 over the four rounds.*
2011	Congressional	**Rory McIlroy (NI)** *With a total score of 268 over the four rounds.*
2010	Pebble Beach	**Graeme McDowell (NI)** *With a total score of 284 over the four rounds.*
2009	Bethpage State Park	**Lucas Glover (US)** *With a total score of 276 over the four rounds.*
2008	Torrey Pines	**Tiger Woods (US)** *With a total score of 283 over the four rounds.*
2007	Oakmont	**Angel Cabrera (Arg)** *With a total score of 285 over the four rounds.*
2006	Winged Foot	**Geoff Ogilvy (Aus)** *With a total score of 285 over the four rounds.*
2005	Pinehurst No. 2	**Michael Campbell (NZ)** *With a total score of 280 over the four rounds.*
2004	Shinnecock Hills	**Retief Goosen (SA)** *With a total score of 276 over the four rounds.*

Most wins: 4: Willie Anderson, Robert T. Jones, Ben Hogan, Jack Nicklaus
Biggest Victory Margin: 15 strokes, Tiger Woods (US) 2000
Lowest Winning Aggregate: 268, Rory McIlory (NI) 2011
Lowest Round: 63, achieved by a number of different players
Youngest Winner: John J. McDermott (US), 19
Oldest Winner: Hale Irwin (US), 45

The USPGA Championship

Held every August, the USPGA Championship is chronologically the fourth Major championship of the year. For many years it was also the fourth Major in terms of both status and prestige, but in recent times, it has enjoyed a significant revival.

⌃ **The Wanamaker Trophy** Awarded every August to the winner of the USPGA, the trophy is named after the founder of the tournament.

The beginnings

Rodman Wanamaker was the department store magnate whose idea it was to create the Professional Golfers Association of America. In January 1916, he invited 40 luminaries of the golf world, including Walter Hagen, to lunch at the Taplow Club in New York City. During this meeting it was decided to hold an annual tournament for professionals. Wanamaker was originally attracted by the merchandizing possibilities of such an organization as the PGA of America, but the primary aim of the group was to help the growth of the game and to look after the interests of the many golf professionals throughout the country.

It was Wanamaker's idea that the tournament would be a 36-hole elimination match play tournament, along the lines of the British News of the World Tournament. Both the Open and the US Open were 72-hole stroke play events, and he wanted his tournament to be a bit different.

Despite an illustrious history which dates back to 1916 (when an expatriate Cornishman, Jim Barnes, beat another expat, Jock Hutchison, by one hole in the final), the USPGA Championship has had a roller-coaster ride and its very existence has at times seemed doubtful. The advent of World War I meant that the second USPGA Championship did not take place until 1919, when it was again won by Jim Barnes.

The Wanamaker Trophy

By far the biggest trophy of the four Majors, the Wanamaker Trophy is 28in (70cm) high, 10½in (26cm) in diameter, 27in (68cm) from handle to handle, and 27lb (12kg) in weight. The great showman, Walter Hagen, had won the trophy in 1927, and when the time came to present it to the 1928 winner, Leo Diegel, officials discovered that it had vanished. Hagen was asked where it was, and he replied that it was lost. After being presented with it at Cedar Crest Country Club in Dallas, he had apparently entrusted it to a taxi driver, who was told to take it to his hotel room. For a couple of years, the winner of the PGA did not receive a trophy. Then, in 1930, workers discovered it by accident in a leather trunk in a warehouse belonging to the Walter Hagen Golf Company.

The early champions

The 1920s were dominated by Walter Hagen, who was also a founder of the PGA of America. He won the championship five times and, between 1924 and 1927, became the only man in the 20th century to win the same Major in four consecutive years.

» **Five-time winner** An indisputable star of early 20th-century golf, Walter Hagen won the USPGA five times in the 1920s.

During this winning streak, the "Haig" won 22 consecutive matches, before finally being beaten in the semifinals in 1928 by Leo Diegel. But even before all this, he had won the title in 1921, defeating fellow US player Jim Barnes. Hagen was also involved in one of the all-time great finals in 1923. That year, Hagen was two down with three holes to play, but still managed to take Gene Sarazen to extra holes.

Sarazen, too, dominated the USPGA Championship for many years, and his record is extraordinary because of its longevity. When he beat Emmet French in 1922, he was the youngest champion at the age of 20. He qualified for the match play version of the championship on 28 occasions, winning a total of 57 times in 82 matches. When the championship switched to stroke play in 1958, he played four times, before finally hanging up his spikes after an appearance in 1972, by which time he was 70 years old. In 1930,

Ben Hogan One of the great US golfers of the 1940s, Ben Hogan won the USPGA on two occasions.

Teeing off at the USPGA The USPGA is played at a different club every year, and all over the US. This is the beautiful setting of the Medinah Country Club in Illinois, which hosted the tournament in 1999, when it was won by Tiger Woods.

Sarazen lost a memorable final to Scottish golfer Tommy Armour, and three years later, in 1933, won the last of his three titles by beating Willie Goggin.

The year 1945 will always be remembered for Byron Nelson's extraordinary streak of 11 victories in a row. His victory over Sam Byrd in the PGA Championship that year was the 9th win in the run. Nelson also won the Championship in 1940, and to add to his two wins, he reached the final three times.

Great championships need great champions, and as well as these three, the celebrated Sam Snead won three titles and Ben Hogan won two.

Change of format

The PGA of America decided to change the format of their blue ribbon championship from match play to stroke play in 1958, although calls for a change had been requested in the early 1950s. Indeed, alarm bells started ringing for the PGA Championship when Ben Hogan (champion in 1946 and 1948), chose to play in the 1953 Open Championship at Carnoustie, rather than go to Baltimore to compete in the PGA Championship in Birmingham, Michigan. Both events were held in the same week so it was impossible to play in them both; yet the fact that Hogan chose to cross the Atlantic to Great Britain— and play in a different championship there—was seen as a huge rebuff to the PGA Championship.

As a result of a terrible car accident in February 1949, Hogan could not play the 36 holes a day required at the PGA Championship. Consequently, he had not entered the USPGA for the previous four years. But despite this, if Hogan, who was undoubtedly the best golfer in the world at the time, could not be bothered to turn up for it, the future of the PGA Championship was in question.

However, there was more to the change in format than this. One of the big problems with match play events is that they have a history of throwing up unpredictable winners. A quick look at the short history of the World Golf Championship (WGC) World

Match play event, which has already been won by such luminaries as Steve Stricker and Kevin Sutherland, shows that the best players do not always make it to a final.

Television was becoming increasingly important in the 1950s, and this was just one of many reasons why television producers disliked match play events. For good viewing figures, they want the world number one and two to meet in the final, but even if it is seeded carefully, this seldom happens. In the 1953 USPGA Championship, the relatively unknown Walter Burkemo met Felice Torza in the final, and this did not attract high viewing figures.

It is also impossible to predict where a match might finish in a match play championship. Often the television company would put a camera on the 18th green, and the match might end on the 15th. What was more, they had no idea how long a match would take and at what time it would finish, which invariably played havoc with television schedules.

As a consequence of all this, a change to stroke play was initiated in 1958. However, by changing the format, the USPGA Championship had lost the one element that helped distinguish it from the other Major championships.

Problematic tournament

There is very little difference between a USPGA Championship and a US Open. Both are 72-hole stroke play events, held every year in the US. Even the courses are set up the same, with narrow fairways, long rough, and fast greens.

Until the creation of the WGC World Match Play in the 1990s, there were many who argued that the USPGA Championship should schedule itself before the Masters, and revert to match play. By making these changes, it would have gained an identity and given itself a realistic chance of overtaking some of the other Majors in terms of stature. As it is, it will now always be the fourth Major, albeit of a very elite group.

⌃ **Lee Trevino**
The colorful Trevino dominated the USPGA during the 1970s.

Through what was a combination of bad luck and bad management, the PGA Championship had to put up with fierce criticism in the 1970s and 1980s. Mark Calcavecchia went on record as saying he would rather win the Western Open than the USPGA Championship. Sandy Lyle, when he was one of the best players in the world in the late 1980s, never used to turn up because he did not like the heat and the courses.

The 1987 USPGA Championship is widely thought of as the worst Major championship held in modern history. It took place at the PGA National, in Palm Beach Gardens, Florida, immediately next door to the PGA's headquarters. There was nothing wrong with this in principle, except that the course was in terrible shape. Add to that the fact that the weather was almost unbearable, with stifling humidity and temperatures soaring above 110°F (43°C), and there was a recipe for disaster.

Traditionally, there has always been a problem with the scheduling of the USPGA Championship. Although it has been held in August since 1972, historically it has been held at many different times of the year. Indeed, the only months in which the USPGA Championship has not been held in are January and March. In 1929, it was held in December, and as recently as 1971, it took place in February. Even the August date, which it has now

◄◄ Paul Azinger in 1993
The size of the enormous Wanamaker Trophy can be fully appreciated in this picture of Paul Azinger, who won the USPGA in 1993.

plumped for, is not ideal, because in August the Midwest tends to be very hot and humid, which is unpleasant for golfers and spectators alike.

Historically, the PGA have not only struggled with when to hold their tournament, but also where to hold it. Too often in the past, it has been held at an inappropriate course, either to promote some new facility, or for some other financial or political reason.

◄◄ Davis Love III in 1997
So often beaten at the last moment, Davis Love III won a famous victory in 1997 at Winged Foot in New York.

New life

Recently, the USPGA Championship has enjoyed a resurgence. Despite the fact that club professionals still play in the Championship, the number has fallen over the years and the field has been the strongest of all the Majors, attracting many of the top pros. What is more, the PGA seem no longer to be chasing the dollar. They appear to have realized that to capture people's imagination, old, traditional tournaments like their championship really should be played over old, traditional golf courses. In the 1990s the championship visited Inverness Country Club in Ohio (1993), Winged Foot in New York (1997), and Medinah Country Club in Illinois (1999).

Finally, either through luck or judgement, the list of winners since 1992—including Tiger Woods four times, Vijay Singh twice, Davis Love III, and Nick Price—has been very impressive. Tiger Woods' epic struggle against Sergio Garcia at Medinah in 1999 will live long in people's memories. It may have been the century's last Major, but it was also one of the very best ever played.

▲ **Unknown talent** Little-known Floridian Shaun Micheel surprised the golfing world by taking the prize at the 2003 USPGA at Oak Hill golf club in Rochester, New York.

The Daly factor

The 1991 USPGA Championship at Crooked Stick was one of the most extraordinary Major championships ever seen. It was a Cinderella story, right out of Hollywood, and served to put the championship, which was under fire at the time, right back in the spotlight.

Before his unbelievable victory, John Daly was unknown on the regular tour. He did not even warrant an invitation into the original field, but instead was the "ninth alternate." This meant that only if nine players pulled out of the tournament or did not show up would he be allowed onto the first tee.

By an extraordinary combination of circumstances, Daly made it into the championship, having to drive all night to make the start. From the outset, Daly drove the ball huge distances with his driver. While other players plotted their way round the Pete and Alice Dye design, Daly just "killed" the ball, driving over hazards and doglegs as if they never existed. And he hit it dead straight. Somehow the "Wild Thing"—as he is known—found fairways and greens, and then sank his fair share of putts.

Experts predicted that the pressure of the final round would find him out, but it did not seem to. He played so fast he never really gave himself time to think much about what was happening, and finally won by three shots.

GREAT ROUNDS

Sergio Garcia: USPGA 1999
During the 1999 USPGA Championship at Medinah, Spain's Sergio Garcia played what is widely regarded as one of the greatest shots ever seen. From behind a big tree he had to carry the ball 180 yards (165m) and put a huge left-to-right flight. With a 6-iron, and playing it with his eyes shut to avoid injury, he hit it absolutely perfectly up onto the green.

Sergio Garcia was not the victor at the USPGA in 1999—he was just beaten by Tiger Woods—but he played possibly the best-remembered shot of all time.

◄ **Vijay Singh in 2004**
The Fijian achieved the extraordinary feat of winning more than $10 million in 2004, including a victory at the USPGA.

TOURNAMENT STATISTICS

Although more club professionals compete in the USPGA than in any other Major tournament, few have ever won the competition. Instead, the event has been dominated by big names in recent years, with the occasional surprise result.

Year	Venue	Winner
2013	Oak Hill	**Jason Dufner (US)** *With a total score of 270 over the four rounds.*
2012	Kiawah Island	**Rory McIlroy (NI)** *With a total score of 275 over the four rounds.*
2011	Atlanta Athletic Club	**Keegan Bradley (US)** *With a total score of 272 over the four rounds.*
2010	Whistling Straits	**Martin Kaymer (Ger)** *With a total score of 277 over the four rounds.*
2009	Hazeltine	**YE Yang (Kor)** *With a total score of 280 over the four rounds.*
2008	Oakland Hills	**Padraig Harrington (Ire)** *With a total score of 277 over the four rounds.*
2007	Southern Hills	**Tiger Woods (US)** *With a total score of 272 over the four rounds.*
2006	Medinah	**Tiger Woods (US)** *With a total score of 270 over the four rounds.*
2005	Baltusrol	**Phil Mickelson (US)** *With a total score of 276 over the four rounds.*
2004	Whistling Straits	**Vijay Singh (Fiji)** *With a total score of 280 over the four rounds.*

Most wins: 5, Walter Hagen (US) and Jack Nicklaus (US)
Biggest Victory Margin: 8 strokes, Rory McIlroy (NI) 2012
Lowest Winning Aggregate: 265 (-15), David Toms (US) 2001
Lowest Round 63, achieved by a number of different players
Youngest Winner: Gene Sarazen (US), 20
Oldest Winner: Julius Boros (US), 48

The Ryder Cup

Ask any sports journalist to name the best sporting event they have ever been to, and a large proportion of them will say golf's Ryder Cup. It is the ultimate team event, three days of intense competition between the US and Europe, with (certainly in the recent past) hardly anything to separate the two teams.

The Ryder Cup Certainly the most famous team trophy in golf, if not in any sports, the Ryder Cup is unique.

Team challenge

The Ryder Cup is a three-day golf match that takes place every other year, and in which the best 12 professionals from the United States compete against the best 12 from Europe. What makes this event the most exciting and nail-biting sporting occasion on the golfing calendar is that the result is always impossible to predict. Indeed, the only predictable thing about the Ryder Cup is that in this modern era it is always extremely close; the last 11 Ryder Cups have been incredibly dramatic, with fantastic golf invariably providing thrilling entertainment for the huge crowds.

Money dictates so much of modern sports, but in the Ryder Cup players give of themselves for one week for free, with any revenue going toward a charity of their choice. There is something very refreshing about this—watching 24 millionaire superstars slugging it out toe-to-toe, for nothing more tangible than a small gold cup and a slice

of pride. Add to that the fact there is always a bit of "needle" between the two teams, and you have the perfect recipe for an unforgettable sporting event. The US players see themselves as superior golfers in terms of their records in Major championships and their positions in the World Rankings. The Europeans regard their US cousins as a touch arrogant and self-satisfied; great individual golfers, but not a "team" in the European sense. There is a definite edge and a fiery competitiveness, which seems to bring out the best in both teams.

Team spirit

In a magical way, the Ryder Cup is able to unlock normally very controlled and restrained sportsmen and suddenly make them all wear their hearts on their sleeves. Playing for a team, rather than for themselves, seems to bring out the emotion from even the most ice-cool of players. When

Sam Ryder The founder of the Cup, awarding the first-ever trophy.

All golf professionals spend 99 percent of their working lives playing as individuals, pursuing a very selfish dream. However, when they play in the Ryder Cup, they know that how they play will affect 12 other people (their 11 teammates and their captain). All Major championships have moments of great emotion, but they usually only happen down the final stretch, on the last couple of greens. In the Ryder Cup, such thrills and spills happen in every match, on every green, on all three days.

The early years

Samuel Ryder was an English businessman who had made a lot of money from selling packets of seeds. An unofficial match between Great Britain and Ireland (GB&I) and the US had taken place at Gleneagles in 1921, and when Ryder went to the second unofficial match at Wentworth in 1926, he was convinced this match should be repeated. Both the Gleneagles and Wentworth matches were won by the home side and, in the latter match, Ryder's personal golf coach, Abe Mitchell, was the star of the show. As a result, it is Mitchell's figure that appears on the small gold trophy, which Ryder had made for the match.

The first official encounter took place in 1927, in Massachusetts. It got off to a bad start for GB&I when Abe Mitchell fell ill with appendicitis, and could not make the trip over. Matters went from

⌂ **Spirit of the Ryder Cup** It is Abe Mitchell, not the founder Sam Ryder, whose image graces the Ryder Cup trophy. He was Sam Ryder's personal golfing coach.

David Duval arrived at the 1999 Ryder Cup, he had a reputation for being poker-faced and inscrutable behind his trademark sunglasses. And yet he reacted like a man possessed, dancing around the greens and punching the air with abandon.

« **Team United States in 1983** The Ryder Cup is famous for creating a powerful team spirit, bringing together golfers who spend the 51 other weeks of the year playing for themselves.

GREAT ROUNDS

Faldo and Woosnam: The Ryder Cup, 1989
In the 1989 tied match at the Belfry, the first fourballs match on Saturday afternoon was, according to those who witnessed it, the greatest match ever seen in a Ryder Cup. Nick Faldo and Ian Woosnam played extraordinary golf. They holed two chip shots and a bunker shot to be 9-under-par; and yet they still lost to Paul Azinger and Chip Beck.

bad to worse, and the final score was 9½–2½ to the US. This pattern was to be repeated for some time whenever the event was staged in the US; indeed, it was not until 1987 that the US players were finally beaten on their home soil.

In the second official match, revenge was wrought at Moortown, Leeds, with Henry Cotton winning the crucial point. In 1931, the heat in Ohio was too much for GB&I and an inevitable defeat ensued, but two years later, in 1933, at Southport & Ainsdale, there was one of the best finishes in the history of the event and the Cup was once more in the hands of GB&I. Two thumping US victories followed in 1935 and 1937, and in the immediate aftermath of World War II, the one-sided nature of the event was, if anything, even more pronounced. The balance of power in the golfing world had well and truly crossed the Atlantic.

The run of US victories continued. When they won at Ganton in 1949 it was their fourth consecutive victory, and at Pinehurst in 1951, the GB&I defeat was more emphatic. At Wentworth in 1953, it was even closer.

Finally, victory did arrive for GB&I at Lindrick in 1957; urged on by a massive Yorkshire crowd, the home side won by 7½–4½. Captaining GB&I, Welshman Dai Rees led from the front, winning his singles match. But such successes for GB&I were rare indeed. After 1957, the US team won nine of the next 10 matches, and the one they did not win was famously tied, in 1969, at Royal Birkdale.

By 1977, the event had become so one-sided that neither side was particularly enjoying the predictability of it all. Something had to be done if the match was not to die on its feet. After another big defeat for GB&I that year, Jack Nicklaus wrote to Lord Derby, President of the British PGA, suggesting that the GB&I team be expanded to include Europe. The European Tour had just been established and the young Spaniard Seve Ballesteros was just beginning to make waves, so such a move was only common sense.

The modern era

Although it took a couple of matches before the "European effect" was felt, the balance of power soon began to shift. This was for the better in terms of the matches as a whole. No longer did the US players have everything their own way, and new life was breathed into the event.

Much of the praise for this must go to Tony Jacklin, the European captain from 1983 to 1989. Jacklin insisted on doing the job his way, which meant having his players receive the best of everything. When they traveled to the US, they flew on the Concorde. Wherever

they were, they had the most comfortable clothes, the best food, and the best hotels. Suddenly, the Ryder Cup became a contest again, the most exciting week in the golfing calendar. In 1983 at PGA National in Florida, there was nothing between the two sides, and the match was eventually won when Lanny Wadkins of the US team played an extraordinary chip at the final hole, to halve his match with José Maria Canizares.

But, two years later, at the Belfry, the US team were finally beaten for the first time in 28 years, and comfortably, too—by 16½–11½ points. Two years after that, in 1987, there came ultimate proof, if it were needed, that parity had been restored, when the US lost for the first time ever on their home soil.

The Belfry in 1989 saw the second tied match in the history of the event. Christy O'Connor Jr., one of Tony Jacklin's "wild cards," played hero, and hit a 2-iron onto the final green to defeat Fred Couples.

Dave Stockton for the US and Bernard Gallacher for Europe were the captains for the infamous 1991 match at Kiawah Island, US, that was nicknamed "the War on the Shore" because of

Poor behavior
Probably the most controversial moment in the history of golf occurred at Brookline in 1999, when the US team and their partners invaded the 17th green at the finish.

» **Rocca and Torrance in 1995** Since the late 1980s the Europeans have enjoyed genuine parity with their US opponents. Here, Costantino Rocca and Sam Torrance celebrate in 1995.

Europe for the very first time. An inspirational Seve Ballesteros captained a European team to victory, again by a single point. Two years later, the US team won the Cup back in controversial fashion, again winning by the narrowest margin of a single point. The 2002 match, which was delayed by a year because of the atrocities in New York on September 11, 2001, saw the Europeans triumph again, this time under the leadership of Sam Torrance.

Ryder Cup controversy

The greatest team event in golf has seen more than its fair share of controversy over the years. In the 1947 match, the GB&I captain, Henry Cotton, created a storm when he accused the US team of having illegal grooves in their irons. After inspection, they were found to conform to all the rules, but two years later Ben Hogan, the US captain, reciprocated by accusing in turn two members of the GB&I side of having illegal clubs. This bickering went on for several matches afterward and set the tone for numerous subsequent incidents.

Seve Ballesteros was one of the all-time greats on the European side, but he did not always manage to stay clear of controversy. The 1989 match saw a well-publicized spat between the

the niggle that developed between the two teams. This bad-tempered affair was eventually won by the US team.

In 1993, Tom Watson, a favorite with British crowds, led a US team over to the Belfry again; and they successfully defended their title, once again defeating the luckless European captain, Bernard Gallacher. But the Scot, Gallacher, was to get his own back in 1995 at Oak Hill, in upstate New York, when his team won a very dramatic match by one point. In 1997, the match went to Continental

» **McGinley wins for Europe in 2002** Irishman Paul McGinley followed his winning putt in 2002 by diving into the lake beside the 18th green. On this occasion the Europeans beat the US by 15½–12½ points, at the Belfry course in Birmingham, England.

Spaniard and US player Paul Azinger. Two years later at Kiawah Island, Ballesteros accused Azinger and Beck of changing the compression of their ball between holes. The incident caused much ill will. "It was against the rules," said Azinger afterward, "but we weren't cheating. Seve is the king of gamesmanship."

Perhaps the most controversial moment in the history of the event took place in Brookline, US, in 1999. With the result delicately poised and with only a couple of matches still out on the course, José Maria Olazabal came to the penultimate green in his match with Justin Leonard all-square. The US player was first to putt, and when his 45-ft (14-m) effort fell into the hole, the watching US team rushed onto the green to congratulate him (*see* pp.208–09). What they had forgotten was that Olazabal still had a putt to make. Play was disrupted for several minutes as the green was cleared and eventually Olazabal missed his putt. Although in the end the Spaniard halved the match, it was a crucial moment in the US victory, and the European reaction to it was bitter and heated.

The excitement surrounding the Cup reached new heights in the 2012 match played at Medinah (*see* pp.228–9) when the European team, led by José Maria Olazabal and buoyed by memories of his compatriot, the late Ballesteros, came from a huge four points behind in the final day singles to steal victory. German Martin Kaymer coolly stroked home a six-foot putt to seal the crucial point. The "miracle at Medinah" was complete.

⌃ **Monty triumphs in 2004** Scotsman Colin Montgomerie savors the winning moment at Oakland Hills in September 2004.

TOURNAMENT STATISTICS

What was once a thoroughly one-sided event—with the US team winning easily in seemingly endless succession—has in recent years become a nail-biting roller coaster of an event with an unpredictable result. Today, the Europeans give as good as they get, both at home and away.

Year	Venue	Winner
2012	Medinah Country Club, Medinah, Illinois	*The European team won by a margin of 14½–13½ points.*
2010	Celtic Manor, Newport, Wales	*The European team won by a margin of 14½–13½ points.*
2008	Valhalla Golf Club, Louisville, Kentucky	*The United States team won by a margin of 16½–11½ points.*
2006	K Club, County Kildare, Ireland	*The European team won by a margin of 18½–9½ points.*
2004	Oakland Hills, Michigan	*The European team won by a margin of 18½–9½ points.*
2002	De Vere Belfry, Birmingham, England	*The European team won by a margin of 15½–12½ points.*
1999	Brookline, Boston	*The United States team won by a margin of 14½–13½ points.*
1997	Valderrama Sotogrande, Spain	*The European team won by a margin of 14½–13½ points.*
1995	Oak Hill, Rochester, NY	*The European team won by a margin of 14½–13½ points.*
1993	De Vere Belfry, Birmingham, England	*The United States team won by a margin of 15–13 points.*

Most wins: 25, US
Biggest Victory Margin by US: 15 points, Champions Golf Club, Houston, Texas, 1967
Biggest Victory Margin by GB&I or Europe: 9 points, Oakland Hills Country Club, Michigan, 2004 and K Club, Country Kildare, Ireland, 2006

Other tournaments

There is a golf tournament, professional or amateur, taking place somewhere in the world every second of every day. Although these may not be the Majors, there are many other championships, including the biggest event in women's golf, the Solheim Cup.

⟫ WGC World Matchplay, 2000
Darren Clarke, from Northern Ireland, beat Tiger Woods in the final of the WGC Accenture World Matchplay tournament at La Costa, San Diego, California, in 2000.

WGC Accenture World Match Play Championship

There are four WGC (World Golf Championship) events on the professional calendar; these are the four "Minors"—not as important as the four "Majors," but nevertheless more important than many other tournaments.

Ever since the USPGA Championship switched from stroke-play to match-play format in 1958, the dreary monotony of 72-hole stroke-play events on the professional circuits has been very much in evidence. In theory, match-play events are great, because they pitch player against player, and are full of excitement and thrills. In practice, they are not favored because they are unpredictable, and television (which runs professional sports) does not like them.

How refreshing it was, then, when in 1999 the first World Match Play Championship, in which the world's top 64 players compete in a knockout event, was held. The players are seeded, so that the number one player in the world plays the number 64, the number 2 plays the number 63, the number 3 plays the number 62, and so on.

In that first event, the old foibles of match-play tournaments emerged as little-known Jeff Maggert beat the equally little-known Andrew Magee. Their match went to the 38th hole, but few were interested in the result. However, since then the event has grown in stature, despite being held on the rather unspectacular resort course at La Costa, San Diego, California, for five of the first six years. Although there have been other journeymen winners after Maggert (Steve Stricker 2001, Kevin Sutherland 2002), there have also been some big-name victors. Tiger Woods has won the event three times (2003, 2004, and 2008), and reached the final in 2000, when he was beaten by Irishman Darren Clarke.

WGC–Bridgestone Invitational

Held every August, this tournament has taken place at Firestone Country Club in Akron, Ohio, for almost all the years it has been a WGC event. It made a single excursion to Sahalee, Washington, in 2002. It has a restricted field, and is open to the top 50 players in the world, as well as Ryder Cup and Presidents Cup players. And there is no cut, so everyone who plays gets a big, fat check. For the first three years, the tournament was dominated by Tiger Woods. In 1999, he shot a 10-under-par 270 to win by a stroke from Phil Mickelson. But it was a year later, in 2000 (the year he won three out of the four Majors), that he really took the event apart, shooting an amazing 21-under-par 259. Right from the start, Woods established his iron grip on the field, and if ever there was a case of there being two tournaments within a single tournament, this was it. There was the one Woods was playing in, and then there was the race for second place, which everyone else was playing for. Eventually, Justin Leonard and Phillip Price finished in a tie for second place, some 11 shots behind Woods. When Tiger won for the third successive year in 2001, it was in a dramatic playoff with Jim Furyk. To date, he has had two streaks of three consecutive wins, the second occurring 2005–07.

WGC–Cadillac Championship

This has a restricted field, and is open to the top 50 players in the world, as well as the top 30 players on the US Money List, and the top 20 on the European Tour Volvo Ranking. It usually takes place in September and was held at Valderrama Golf Club in southern Spain (scene of the 1997 Ryder Cup) for the first two years. In its inaugural year—1999—the one and only Tiger Woods beat the local favorite Miguel Angel Jimenez in a

playoff. And the following year, left-handed Canadian Mike Weir won by two shots over Lee Westwood.

In 2001, the tournament was canceled because of the atrocities in New York on September 11, but a year later, at Mount Juliet in Ireland (host club for the 2004 event as well), Tiger Woods won once again, by a shot from Retief Goosen. Tiger has gone on to dominate the tournament, triumphing eight times in total including at Doral, Florida, in 2013, 14 years after his first victory.

ISPS Handa World Cup

The Ryder Cup and Presidents Cup aside, there are precious few team competitions on the golfing calendar. The World Cup is an old tournament with a rich heritage, which was called the Canada Cup when it started in 1953. In 1967, it became the World Cup, and then in 2000 it was given World Golf Championship status.

⌃ **The popular champion** US player Stewart Cink won the WGC NEC (now the Bridgestone) Invitational at Akron, Ohio, in August 2004.

⌄ **Japanese victory** Japan's Shigeki Maruyama and Toshimitsu Izawa celebrate winning the EMC World Golf Championship (now the ISPS Handa World Cup) in 2002.

Karsten Solheim
Founder of the eponymous team cup, which is the best event in women's golf, Karsten Solheim is also the man behind the world-famous Ping brand.

The format has been tinkered with over the years, but today, two-man teams play fourballs on Thursday and Saturday, and then foursomes on Friday and Sunday.

In the first WGC World Cup, held in Buenos Aires, Argentina, Tiger Woods and David Duval underlined the US's reputation as the strongest golfing nation with a resounding victory. A year later in 2001, at the Taiheiyo Club in Gotemba City, Japan, the South African pairing of Ernie Els and Retief Goosen was victorious. Then, in 2002, the Japanese pair of Shigeki Maruyama and Toshi Izawa won in Puerto Vallarta, Mexico.

In 2003, the South Africans became the only team to win two WGC World Cups, at Kiawah Island, South Carolina (host to the infamous 1991 Ryder Cup). No single nation has won more than once in the years since, with Jason Day and Adam Scott adding Australia to the roster of winning countries at Royal Melbourne Golf Club in 2013.

Solheim Cup

This is the female version of the Ryder Cup, and was the brainchild of Karsten Solheim, the manufacturer of Ping clubs. Like the Ryder Cup, it is a biennial transatlantic team match-play competition, and is the biggest team event in women's golf. The first match took place in 1990 in

Florida, and although the US team won that match comfortably, the home team enjoyed a thrilling victory in the second match, much against the odds.

There have been some epic encounters between the US and European teams since, and in its short history the Solheim Cup has not been short of controversy. Dottie Pepper (née Mochrie) was the first US player to get under European skins. She is a feisty competitor who behaves aggressively on the golf course, yelling when her putts go in, and screaming with delight when her opponents miss. Before the 1992 match, US competitor Beth Daniel told a US magazine that she thought only two Europeans would be good enough to qualify automatically for the US team, a sentiment which the European team was understandably very angry about.

Then, at Loch Lomond in 2000, there was further serious controversy during the final fourball match. Sweden's Annika Sorenstam was playing with Scotland's Janice Moodie against US players Pat Hurst and Kelly Robbins, and the match reached its climax on Sunday morning, after heavy rain the previous evening. The US team were one-up on the 13th, when Sorenstam spectacularly chipped into the hole for a birdie. The momentum of the match seemed to have changed, except that the US team was in discussion about whether the

Europe wins Solheim Cup In a close-fought contest held in Sweden in September 2003, the European women's team triumphed over the US team after winning the singles matches.

⌃ **Dottie Pepper celebrating** The ebullient American player Dottie Pepper is renowned for her enthusiastic celebrations and loud outbursts.

Swede might have played out of turn. The US team captain, Pat Bradley, was brought in, and she told her players to insist that Sorenstam play her shot again. It was within the strict rules of the game for the US team to insist on this procedure, but probably against the spirit of the match. Sorenstam replayed the shot, with tears streaming down her cheeks, and the Europeans eventually lost the match.

"Match play is about great shotmaking and mental toughness," said Bradley afterward. "We have the greatest respect for the rules of the game, and we followed the rules." Sorenstam, understandably, saw the situation from a very different viewpoint. "I am disgusted," she said. "The more I think about it, the more mad I get. I like these two girls, but this will take me a long time to forget. We are all asking ourselves 'Is this how badly they want to win the Cup?'" Once again, the US team were accused of unsportsmanlike behavior and the sore festered for some time afterward. In 2011 and 2013, the European team won but the US still has eight wins to their five overall.

Walker Cup

Golf is predominantly an individual game, but just occasionally team events are held and are invariably a success. The Walker Cup is the amateur version of the Ryder Cup, with a few differences. Instead of two teams of 12 men, it

TOURNAMENT STATISTICS

The Solheim Cup is the women's equivalent of the Ryder Cup, a biennial match between Europe and the US. Now that most of Europe's best competitors play on the LPGA Tour in the US, the Solheim Cup is a very keenly contested, eagerly awaited event.

Year	Venue	Winner
2013	Colorado Golf Club, Colorado	**Europe** *The European team won by a margin of 18–10 points.*
2011	Killeen Castle, Ireland	**Europe** *The European team won by a margin of 15–13 points.*
2009	Rich Harvest Farms, Illinois	**US** *The United States team won by a margin of 16–12 points.*
2007	Halmstad GK, Sweden	**US** *The United States team won by a margin of 16–12 points.*
2005	Crooked Stick, Indiana	**US** *The United States team won by a margin of 15½–12½ points.*
2003	Barseback, Sweden	**Europe** *The European team won by a margin of 17–10 points.*
2002	Interlachen Country Club, Minnesota	**US** *The United States team won by a margin of 15½–12½ points.*
2000	Loch Lomond, Scotland	**Europe** *The European team won by a margin of 14½–11½ points.*

is played by two teams of 10. And, instead of the US against Europe, it is the US against Great Britain & Ireland (GB&I), just as the Ryder Cup used to be played.

Like the Ryder Cup, the Walker Cup is held biennially on alternate sides of the Atlantic. The most recent match took place in 2013 at the National Golf Links of America, with the US winning a decisive 17–9 victory. After three wins in a row for GB&I between 1999 and 2003, it has mainly been a strong tournament for the US.

In early 1921, George Herbert Walker, the president of the USGA, invited all golfing nations to compete for his trophy, but for a variety of reasons, none of them put a team together. An unofficial match was played in 1921, at Hoylake, between the amateurs from GB&I and the amateurs from the US. The US team was victorious, with a score of 9–3. It was largely due to the success of this inaugural competition that the Walker Cup came into being.

A year later, in 1922, the Royal & Ancient sent a GB&I team across to the US, to play the first official match. It took place at Walker's home club, the National Links on Long Island, New York. The British team did not take any reserve players with them, and when captain Robert Harris fell ill, his place was filled by Bernard Darwin, the golf correspondent of *The Times*, who had traveled out to the

US to cover the matches for his newspaper. Quite how some of today's golfing journalists would fare under such circumstances does not bear thinking about, but after losing his foursomes match, Darwin, incredibly, managed to beat the US captain.

The only tied match in this competition took place at Five Farms Golf Club, Maryland, in 1965, when Britain's greatest-ever amateur,

The US team triumphs in 1951
In 1951, the US team won the Walker Cup, when team captain Willie Turnesa received the trophy from H. F. Simpson, Captain of the Birkdale golf club.

TOURNAMENT STATISTICS

The US dominated the Walker Cup in the early years, but things have been much closer more recently. In the 45 matches, GB&I has only won eight times, including three in a row between 1999 and 2003.

Year	Venue	Winner
2013	**National Golf Links of America, New York**	**US** *The United States team won by a margin of 17–9 points.*
2011	**Royal Aberdeen, Scotland**	**GB&I** *The Great Britain & Ireland team won by a margin of 14–12 points.*
2009	**Merion, Ardmore, Pennsylvania**	**US** *The United States team won by a margin of 16½–9½ points.*
2007	**Royal County Down, Northern Ireland**	**US** *The United States team won by a margin of 12½–11½ points.*
2005	**Chicago Golf Club, Illinois**	**US** *The United States team won by a margin of 12½–11½ points.*

⌃ Michael Bonallack
Pictured in 1971 at the Walker Cup, this Englishman is known as "Britain's greatest-ever amateur," although he never quite attained the heights of his US equivalent, Bobby Jones.

« Walker Cup winning team The victorious GB&I Walker Cup team of 2003, poses on the steps of the clubhouse at Ganton golf club in Yorkshire, England, the scene of many famous golfing dramas over the decades.

Michael Bonallack, was the star of the GB&I team. It was not until 1989 that the US lost on home soil, in a dramatic match at Peachtree, Georgia, when the unheralded Scot Jim Milligan famously chipped in to turn the match to GB&I's advantage.

The Walker Cup is the premier amateur team event—certainly in terms of its long and distinguished history—and it is only fitting that the greatest-ever amateur golfer, US player Bobby Jones, played a significant part in the history of the event. He played for the US team in four matches between 1924 and 1930 and had an outstanding record. He lost only one foursomes match (his first), and at singles he was unbeatable.

In those days, matches were played over 36 holes, and in 1926 he thrashed Tolley. Two years later, in Chicago, similar treatment was handed out to Perkins, who lost to Jones by an even worse score.

« Gary Wolstenholme
This evergreen British player was an important part of the team that won the Walker Cup at Ganton in 2003.

⌃ Teenage sensation
US prodigy Michelle
Wie reacts to a putt
on the 17th green during
the first morning at
foursomes at the 2004
Curtis Cup held at
Formby golf club
in England.

The Curtis Cup

This is the women's version of the Walker Cup,
which has effectively been played in one form or
another for many decades. Women amateurs
from the US and Great Britain were playing
unofficial matches against each other as far back
as the beginning of the 20th century. The first
one in the record books seems to have taken
place on the eve of the British Women's Amateur
Championship at Cromer, Norfolk, in 1905. Two
sisters, Harriot and Margaret Curtis, played in
the US team on that occasion, and they were
subsequently instrumental in arranging several
other matches on both sides of the Atlantic,
which took place in the period up to 1930.
Eventually, the Curtis sisters put up for a
trophy, and the first official match (6-a-side)
took place at Wentworth, Surrey, in 1932. The
US team won by 5½–3½ points.

Rather like the early years of the Ryder Cup
and the Walker Cup, the history of the Curtis
Cup has been dominated by the US. Of the 37
matches played, GB&I has only won seven of
them, while three others were tied. A 16-year
run of dominant form by the US was ended in
2012 by a 10½–9½ result for GB&I. That year,
European teams held the Curtis, Solheim, Ryder,
and Walker Cups simultaneously.

The GB&I team had to wait until the 1952
match at Muirfield, Scotland, before they
recorded their first victory, by the slender margin
of 5–4, although they had tied a memorable
match at Gleneagles in 1936. Four years after the
famous Muirfield victory, there was another win
for the home team at Prince's golf course in Kent,
England, again by the narrowest of margins.
Two years later, at Brae Burn, in Massachusetts,
the British team really should have won again,

but eventually finished in a tied match of 4½
points each. These have only been little British
splashes in a sea of US victories.

However, in 1986, at Prairie Dunes, Kansas, the
British made history by becoming the first team
ever, male or female, to win on US soil. This set
the tone for dramatic victories by the European
Ryder Cup team (1987), and the British Walker

**» US team wins
Curtis Cup** The US
team eventually won
a close-fought series of
matches 10–8 in the 2004
Curtis Cup in Formby,
Lancashire, England,
in June of that year.

TOURNAMENT STATISTICS

The Curtis Cup, which was first held in 1932
at Wentworth, is a biennial match between
the amateurs of GB&I and the
amateurs of the US. Of
the 37 matches, only seven
have been won by the British
and Irish side, with another two
matches being tied.

Year	Venue	Winner
2012	**Nairn Golf Club, Nairn, Scotland**	**GB&I** *The Great Britain & Ireland team won by a margin of 10½–9½ points.*
2010	**Essex Country Club, Manchester, Massachusetts**	**US** *The United States team won by a margin of 12½–7½ points.*
2008	**St. Andrews, Fife, Scotland**	**US** *The United States team won by a margin of 13–7 points.*
2006	**Bandon Dunes Golf Resort, Oregon**	**US** *The United States team won by a margin of 11½– 6½ points.*
2004	**Formby, Lancashire, England**	**US** *The United States team won by a margin of 10–8 points.*

Teeing off at Wentworth Spaniard Seve Ballesteros teeing off during the Toyota World Matchplay tournament at Wentworth, England, in October 1994.

Cup team (1989) on foreign shores. Belle Robertson, aged 50, was the oldest ever player to take part in the Curtis Cup, and she won both the matches she played in the 1986 match. Since this heady week, the GB&I team has tasted success four times on home soil, in 1988 at Royal St. George's, in 1992 at Hoylake, in 1996 at Killarney, and in 2012 at Nairn.

Volvo World Match Play Championship

Held in the fall at Wentworth, Surrey, this tournament is another with a rich heritage. It dates back to 1964, when Arnold Palmer won it. In fact, the list of winners is really a list of golf greats from the latter half of the 20th century. Vijay Singh, who has won once, Arnold Palmer and Nick Faldo (twice), Greg Norman and Ian Woosnam (three times), Gary Player and Seve Ballesteros (five times), and Ernie Els (seven times) have all tasted success in the World Match Play.

The tournament was the brainchild of Mark McCormack, the founder of the International Management Group, and he envisaged getting the best golfers in the world to compete head-to-head.

In the 1960s and 1970s, the world's top players did all congregate at Wentworth. With the increasingly crowded golfing calendar, it has been difficult to get the best 12 golfers in the world to appear. After being held twice in Malaga, Spain, in 2013 the tournament moved to Bulgaria, and will henceforth be held in different European countries.

First world match play Arnold Palmer of the US beat Gary Player of South Africa in the final of the Piccadilly World Matchplay at Wentworth in 1964.

Golf Courses **of the World**

The "royal and ancient" game of golf can truly be described as a global activity—it is played on every continent and in almost every climate. This chapter covers championship courses, many of which are famous from television coverage, but also include many lesser-known, yet strikingly scenic layouts.

Augusta

AUGUSTA, GEORGIA

This private club is the home of the Masters Tournament, one of the most important events on the golfing calendar. To play here is an ambition of every golfer. Augusta is known for its colorful foliage, and hole names such as Carolina Cherry, and Azalea, reflect this.

A relatively modest start

Soon after capturing his historic Grand Slam in 1930, Bobby Jones set about creating his dream course. He longed for a private club where he and his friends could play away from the public gaze, and he also wanted to host an event for some of the game's top players. A former nursery in Augusta, called Fruitlands, was the ideal site. Jones teamed up with Scottish course designer Alister MacKenzie (*see* p.227) to fulfill his dream, and the rest is history. Fruitlands became Augusta, and, when every great golfer wanted to play in Jones's event, the tournament was named "the Masters" (*see* pp.182–7). This event has been staged at Augusta each year since 1934 (except 1943–5); the winner is presented with the famous Green Jacket.

Capacity to dazzle

The factors that make Augusta so challenging are the speed and contouring of the putting surfaces. Otherwise, Augusta is in many ways a straightforward golf course. Its fairways are wide, there are relatively few bunkers (none particularly deep), and the greens are large. Moreover, for 51 weeks of the year, neither Rae's Creek nor Amen Corner are so treacherous and intimidating as when a coveted Green Jacket is at stake—and when the whole world is watching.

Flowering fruit trees and shrubs

Clubhouse

COURSE CARD					
Hole	Yards	Par	Hole	Yards	Par
1	445	4	10	495	4
2	575	5	11	505	4
3	350	4	12	155	3
4	240	3	13	510	5
5	455	4	14	440	4
6	180	3	15	430	5
7	450	4	16	170	3
8	570	5	17	440	4
9	460	4	18	465	4
Out	3,725	36	In	3,710	36
Total 7,435 yards, par 72					

⌂ **The clubhouse** At the end of Magnolia Drive lies Augusta's clubhouse. It is a modestly scaled building, in keeping with the club's small and private membership.

Ben Hogan Bridge

⌃ **The par-3 12th** Rae's Creek is spanned by the Ben Hogan Bridge at the 12th hole. The bridge is named after the four-time US Open champion, who won the Masters in 1951 and 1953. Hogan (along with Sam Snead) dominated golf in the decade after World War II.

⌃ **Amen corner** The 11th, 12th, and 13th holes—known as Amen Corner—feature hazardous bunkering and Rae's Creek. Many Masters' titles are decided at the 13th.

» **The par-5 15th** Named Firethorn after the orange pyracantha planted nearby, the par-5 15th also has a water hazard.

The Country Club

BROOKLINE, BOSTON

Located in the leafy Boston suburb of Brookline, the Country Club—a founding member of the US Golf Association (USGA)—has been the scene of historic clashes. On three occasions here, US golfers have achieved major victories over their European counterparts.

Place in history

Golf came to Brookline in 1892, and 21 years later the club staged its first US Open. The outcome of that event is regarded as a seminal moment in US golf history. Francis Ouimet, a 20-year-old local amateur, defeated British legends Harry Vardon and Ted Ray in an 18-hole playoff. In 1988, there was another epic battle, when Curtis Strange of the US outlasted the Briton Nick Faldo. European golfers also lost the 1999 Ryder Cup here, when Ben Crenshaw's US side staged a remarkable, final-day comeback.

Old-style course

The Country Club is old by New World standards. It is small in scale, featuring tiny greens and narrow, tumbling fairways. Nine holes were added in 1927 (making 27 in total), and changes were made before the 1988 US Open; however, Brookline still retains a 19th-century flavor.

» **Classic golf** One of the oldest golfing venues in the US, the Country Club is eminently capable of testing the world's best. When the rough is grown, and the width of the fairways is reduced, Brookline becomes a classic course for the US Open.

⌃ **The par-4 9th** One of the finest holes at Brookline, the 9th may look relatively flat from a distance, but its roller-coasting terrain is referred to by players as "the Himalayas."

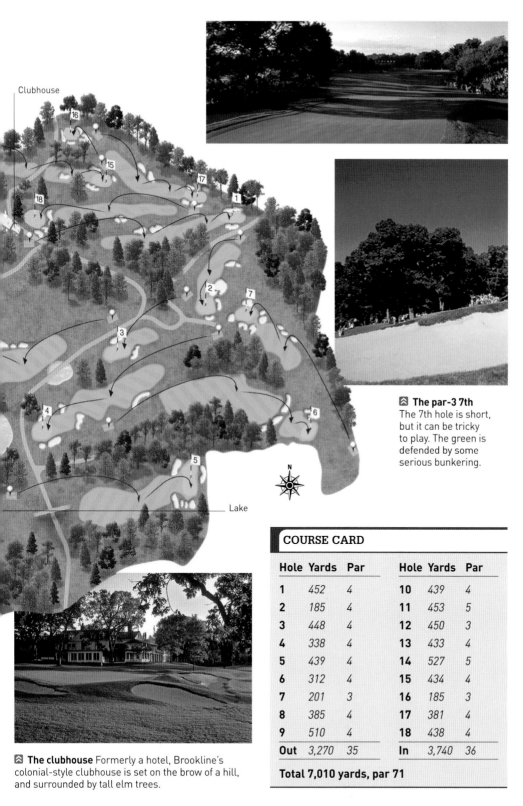

Clubhouse

N

Lake

◁ The par-4 17th
Golfing history has been made at the 17th: a birdie by Francis Ouimet, effectively won him the 1913 US Open, and, 86 years later, Justin Leonard's 45ft (14m) putt won the Ryder Cup for the US.

⌃ The par-3 7th
The 7th hole is short, but it can be tricky to play. The green is defended by some serious bunkering.

⌃ The clubhouse Formerly a hotel, Brookline's colonial-style clubhouse is set on the brow of a hill, and surrounded by tall elm trees.

Hole	Yards	Par	Hole	Yards	Par
COURSE CARD					
1	452	4	10	439	4
2	185	4	11	453	5
3	448	4	12	450	3
4	338	4	13	433	4
5	439	4	14	527	5
6	312	4	15	434	4
7	201	3	16	185	3
8	385	4	17	381	4
9	510	4	18	438	4
Out	*3,270*	*35*	**In**	*3,740*	*36*

Total 7,010 yards, par 71

Cypress Point

SEVENTEEN MILE DRIVE, PEBBLE BEACH, CALIFORNIA

Anyone who has traveled along California's Seventeen Mile Drive will understand why the 19th-century novelist Robert Louis Stevenson ranked the Monterey Peninsula "the finest meeting of land and sea in the world." Such is the setting of Cypress Point Golf Club.

MacKenzie's masterpiece

The beautiful course at Cypress Point was designed in the late 1920s by the famous golf course architect Alister MacKenzie, who had just returned from planning the much-heralded course at Royal Melbourne in Australia (see pp.342–3). MacKenzie once said of his California creation: "I do not expect anyone will ever have the opportunity of constructing another course like Cypress Point, as I do not suppose anywhere is there such a glorious combination of rocky coast, sand dunes, pine woods, and cypress trees."

>> **The par-3 15th**
The first of storied back-to-back par 3s, the 15th clings to the coast and provides a stunning, yet gentle, foretaste of things to come.

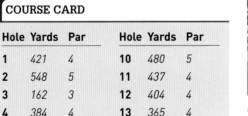

COURSE CARD					
Hole	Yards	Par	Hole	Yards	Par
1	421	4	10	480	5
2	548	5	11	437	4
3	162	3	12	404	4
4	384	4	13	365	4
5	493	5	14	388	4
6	518	5	15	143	3
7	168	3	16	219	3
8	363	4	17	393	4
9	292	4	18	346	4
Out	3,349	37	In	3,175	35
Total 6,524 yards, par 72					

<< **The par-4 17th** The dog-legged 17th is played from the tip of Cypress Point to a green that nestles on a precipice above the Pacific Ocean.

Tantalizing layout

Cypress Point could not be regarded as a long golf course—especially by modern championship standards—but MacKenzie's use of the rich variety of terrain both teases and tantalizes the player. The most memorable holes are the incredible oceanside sequence from the 15th to the 17th. The centerpiece of this, the 16th, is possibly North America's toughest par 3 and also its most photographed golf hole.

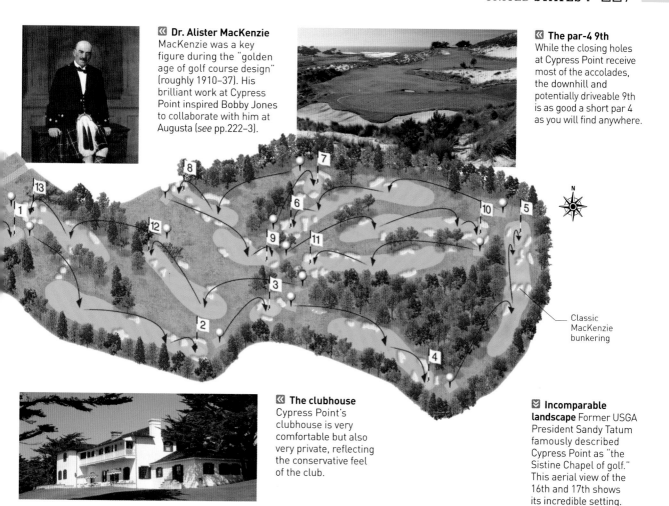

« Dr. Alister MacKenzie
MacKenzie was a key figure during the "golden age of golf course design" (roughly 1910–37). His brilliant work at Cypress Point inspired Bobby Jones to collaborate with him at Augusta (*see* pp.222–3).

« The par-4 9th
While the closing holes at Cypress Point receive most of the accolades, the downhill and potentially driveable 9th is as good a short par 4 as you will find anywhere.

Classic MacKenzie bunkering

« The clubhouse
Cypress Point's clubhouse is very comfortable but also very private, reflecting the conservative feel of the club.

☑ Incomparable landscape Former USGA President Sandy Tatum famously described Cypress Point as "the Sistine Chapel of golf." This aerial view of the 16th and 17th shows its incredible setting.

Medinah

NO. 3 COURSE, MEDINAH, CHICAGO, ILLINOIS

In the late 1920s, an extraordinary group of individuals, known as the Shriners, created a monument to the game of golf in the suburbs of Chicago. The exclusive Medinah Country Club has three courses, of which No. 3, designed by Tom Bendelow, is the most magnificent.

A golfing shrine

Medinah was founded by the Shriners—a philanthropic, fraternal organization more properly known as the Ancient Arabic Order of Nobles of the Mystic Shrine of North America. Shriners take their golf seriously, as shown by the vast scale of Medinah's clubhouse. The group built 54 holes of golf here, including the outstanding No. 3 Course, which has hosted three US Open championships. Hale Irwin won Medinah's most recent Open in 1990, and in 1999 Tiger Woods captured his first PGA Championship at this prestigious course.

Challenging parkland golf

Set in a beautiful, mature landscape studded with elegant elms and spreading oaks, Medinah's No. 3 Course is revered as one of America's toughest parkland challenges. The layout is heavily bunkered and brutally long from the back tees. At a number of places—most dramatically at the signature par-3 holes—the player must also engage in a watery duel with Lake Kadijah. More golfers lose than win this contest.

Lake Kadijah

Clubhouse

18

The par-4 18th The tree-lined finishing hole curves gracefully from right to left, with its championship tee protruding back into Lake Kadijah.

COURSE CARD

Hole	Yards	Par	Hole	Yards	Par
1	433	4	10	578	5
2	192	3	11	440	4
3	412	4	12	476	4
4	463	4	13	245	3
5	536	5	14	609	5
6	509	4	15	390	4
7	617	5	16	482	4
8	201	3	17	193	3
9	432	4	18	449	4
Out	3,795	36	In	3,862	36

Total 7,657 yards, par 72

⌃ **The clubhouse** Medinah's extraordinary Byzantine-style clubhouse was designed by Richard Schmidt, the architect of several Shriner buildings.

⌃ **The miracle at Medinah** The 2012 European Ryder Cup team celebrates an unlikely victory snatched at the last moment and known as "the miracle at Medinah."

⌄ **Water at the par-3 17th** Created just before the 1990 US Open, Medinah's 17th hole is similar to the 13th—but its watery defenses are even more intimidating.

《 **The par-3 13th** Negotiating the 13th is like trying to find a way through to a besieged fortress. The green is almost totally encircled with sand, and the tee shot has to be fired over a long, thin section of Lake Kadijah.

Merion

EAST COURSE, ARDMORE, PENNSYLVANIA

No golf course in the US has a more celebrated history than the East Course at Merion. Built in 1912 on a compact site, this course is where Bobby Jones completed his Grand Slam in 1930 and where, 20 years later, Ben Hogan achieved his most impressive victory.

Compact course

Merion was designed by Hugh Wilson (1879–1925), an expatriate Scot who turned novice architect for the sake of his home club. At 125 acres (50ha), the East Course is short in comparison with modern courses, most of which occupy about 200 acres (80ha). But what it lacks in length, the course makes up for in other ways. It is a sublime shot-maker's golf course—one that rewards precision, imagination, and intelligent play in equal doses.

Making history

The 1st hole at Merion is a cleverly conceived short par 4. Also memorable is the 11th, where, in 1930, Bobby Jones won the final of the US Amateur and secured his historic Grand Slam (winning the US Open, British Open, and both Amateurs in one year). The 16th, called the Quarry Hole, is a formidable par 4. The final hole was immortalized by Ben Hogan in 1950—just 12 months after surviving a near-fatal car crash, Hogan made a superb shot onto the 18th green as a prelude to winning the US Open.

◄ **Wicker baskets** Merion uses wicker baskets instead of traditional flagsticks. Because of this, the golfer has few clues as to the direction and strength of the wind.

Hole	Yards	Par	Hole	Yards	Par
1	350	4	10	303	4
2	556	5	11	367	4
3	256	3	12	403	4
4	628	5	13	115	3
5	504	4	14	464	4
6	487	4	15	411	4
7	360	4	16	430	4
8	359	4	17	246	3
9	236	3	18	521	4
Out	3,736	36	In	3,260	34

COURSE CARD

Total 6,996 yards, par 70

⌃ **The par-4 7th** The 7th is a relatively short par 4 and its fairway curves gracefully from right to left. It is sited at the farthest point from the clubhouse on Merion's compact layout.

GREAT ROUNDS

Bobby Jones: 1930 US Amateur

The game's greatest amateur player is indelibly linked with Merion. This course was where, in 1916, Jones competed in his first US Amateur, aged just 14; where in 1924 he won his first US Amateur; and where he again won in 1930 to complete the final leg of his incredible Grand Slam.

The par-4 16th With its all-or-nothing second shot across an old overgrown quarry, the 16th, or Quarry Hole, is very intimidating.

The par-4 18th The finishing hole is played over the crown of a hill to a green set between bunkers. This is where Hogan clinched the 1950 US Open.

Clubhouse

Justin Rose Justin Rose lifts the US Open trophy after becoming the first Englishman to win it for 43 years in 2013.

Green at the par-3 9th The 9th is a good example of the brilliant bunkering and elegant green settings that define Merion. The tee shot needs to be hit over water at this hole.

Muirfield Village

DUBLIN, COLUMBUS, OHIO

Inspired by the course at Augusta, Jack Nicklaus first conceived the idea for Muirfield Village in 1966, naming his course in Ohio after the famous Scottish links on which he had just won the Open. A decade later, the world's top golfers were playing on his masterly layout.

Striking similarities

Of all the celebrated courses that he has designed around the world, none means as much to Jack Nicklaus as Muirfield Village, which lies close to his hometown of Columbus, Ohio. It is often said that imitation is the greatest form of flattery, and in many respects Muirfield Village is a northern version of Augusta (*see* pp.222–3). Maintained in the same pristine condition, it too hosts an important, invitation-only event. The Memorial Tournament is traditionally held in late spring or early summer, and is now regarded as the biggest event on the golfing calendar to fall between the Masters and the US Open. However, Muirfield Village has little in common with the Scottish Muirfield (*see* pp.280–1).

Stream

The fabulous 14th

There are several echoes of Augusta in the course design. For instance, the spectacular par-3 12th hole is very similar to Augusta's fabled 16th. However, the best hole of all at Muirfield Village is a true original. Fashioned by a wandering creek, the 14th is a short par 4, where the approach shot rarely requires much more than a 9-iron or wedge, but precision is everything.

☑ **The par-4 14th** Water and sand combine to defend the cleverly angled 14th green. Rated one of the finest short par 4s in golf, it is a hole that yields comparatively few birdies due to its intimidating nature. Most golfers play very defensively and rarely attack the pin.

☑ **The par-3 12th** Stand on the tee at the par-3 12th and you could imagine yourself playing in the Masters. Like Augusta's 16th, the hole calls for a do-or-die shot across water to a severely sloping green.

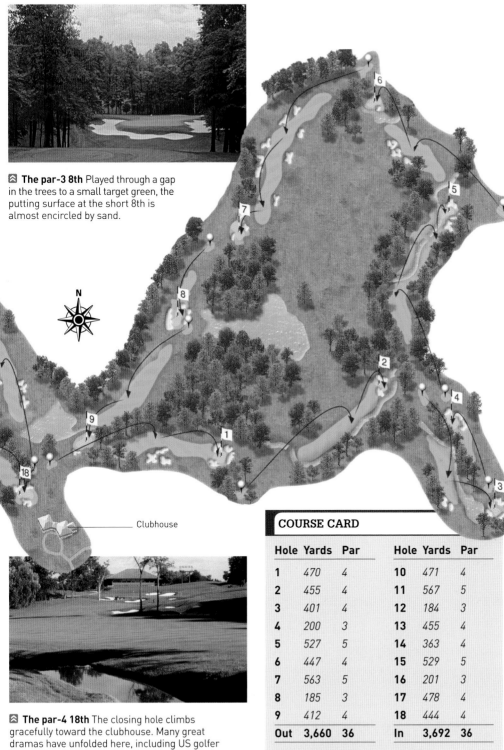

The par-3 8th Played through a gap in the trees to a small target green, the putting surface at the short 8th is almost encircled by sand.

Jack Nicklaus Not only has Nicklaus had the most successful playing record in the history of golf, but he has also carved out an exceptional career as a course architect.

N

Clubhouse

The par-4 18th The closing hole climbs gracefully toward the clubhouse. Many great dramas have unfolded here, including US golfer Paul Azinger's famous holed bunker shot to win the 1990 Memorial.

COURSE CARD					
Hole	Yards	Par	Hole	Yards	Par
1	470	4	10	471	4
2	455	4	11	567	5
3	401	4	12	184	3
4	200	3	13	455	4
5	527	5	14	363	4
6	447	4	15	529	5
7	563	5	16	201	3
8	185	3	17	478	4
9	412	4	18	444	4
Out	3,660	36	In	3,692	36
Total 7,352 yards, par 72					

Oakmont

OAKMONT, NEAR PITTSBURGH, PENNSYLVANIA

Built in 1903–04, Oakmont has always reveled in its reputation as the most difficult golf course in the US. The severity of the course is such that golfers need to be masochistic to enjoy playing here. It is one of the country's finest and most historic championship venues.

Punishing design

The only golf venture of industrialist Henry Fownes is a legacy of the "penal school" of course design, which was fashionable in the early 1900s. Everything is difficult. The Church Pews are notorious bunkers, and nowhere else has faster greens. Lew Worsham, the club's former professional, once said: "This is a course where good golfers worry about their second putt before they hit their first one."

◁ The par-4 1st It has been said that Oakmont starts tough and gets tougher. The opening hole is a long but downhill par 4.

A major venue

Oakmont is a historic venue. Bobby Jones, Ben Hogan, and Jack Nicklaus won national titles here, while Gene Sarazen and Sam Snead won USPGA Championships. Johnny Miller scored an amazing 63 to steal the 1973 US Open, and the popular South African Ernie Els achieved his first Major success after a playoff with Loren Roberts and Colin Montgomerie at the 1994 US Open.

▽ Church Pews Arguably the most notorious bunker complex in golf, the Church Pews lurks between the 3rd and 4th fairways.

Church Pews

COURSE CARD

Hole	Yards	Par		Hole	Yards	Par
1	482	4		10	435	4
2	341	4		11	379	4
3	428	4		12	667	5
4	609	5		13	183	3
5	382	4		14	358	4
6	194	3		15	500	4
7	479	4		16	231	3
8	288	3		17	313	4
9	477	5		18	484	4
Out	3,680	36		In	3,550	35

Total 7,230 yards, par 71

The clubhouse
Oakmont's clubhouse has hosted the winning celebrations of eight US Opens and three USPGA Championships.

Clubhouse

Typically fearsome fairway bunkering

Big Mouth bunker

The par-4 18th Oakmont's excellent last hole features a vast, intricately contoured, superslick green. This marks the tricky finish to an exceptionally difficult course.

GREAT ROUNDS

**Ernie Els:
1994 US Open**
In the 1994 US Open at Oakmont, Els began his third round by scoring birdie-birdie-par-eagle-birdie. An eventual 66 gave him his first Major victory, after defeating Loren Roberts and Colin Montgomerie in a 20-hole playoff.

Pebble Beach

PEBBLE BEACH, CALIFORNIA

It has been said that the finest courses often produce the best championships and reveal the greatest champions. Certainly, the story of Pebble Beach suggests as much. Gloriously sited on the Monterey Peninsula, it has been hosting Major tournaments since the 1970s.

Vintage US Opens

Created in the early 1920s, during what is often described as the Golden Age of golf course architecture, Pebble Beach finally hosted the US Open 50 years later. Jack Nicklaus, the supreme golfer of the day, triumphed in the club's first Open in 1972. The championship returned to Pebble Beach 10 years later, and on this occasion Nicklaus was eclipsed by his great rival and heir apparent, Tom Watson. Tom Kite captured the stormy 1992 Open, and, in June 2000, Tiger Woods emphatically underlined his world's number one status when he won by an astonishing 15-stroke margin. Nicklaus, Watson, Kite, and Woods: they are the "awesome foursome" of Pebble Beach.

Stunning holes

The holes that define Pebble Beach are the glorious oceanside sequence from the 4th to the 10th, and the closing holes. Most dramatic of all are the short, scary 7th—its

tiny green so exposed to the elements—and the par-4 8th; its approach was hailed by Jack Nicklaus as the most spectacular second shot in all of golf.

Steep hill (blind shot)

COURSE CARD

Hole	Yards	Par	Hole	Yards	Par
1	380	4	10	495	4
2	502	4	11	390	4
3	404	4	12	202	3
4	331	4	13	445	4
5	195	3	14	580	5
6	523	5	15	397	4
7	109	3	16	403	4
8	428	4	17	208	3
9	505	4	18	543	5
Out	3,377	35	In	3,663	36

Total 7,040 yards, par 71

The par-3 17th Although Jack Nicklaus effectively lost the 1982 US Open here, the 17th was kind to him in the final round of the 1972 US Open. Nicklaus' 1-iron tee shot struck the pin and stopped on the edge of the hole.

The par-5 18th The 18th is a heroic par 5; it can be reached in two shots, but only if a bold drive across the edge of the Pacific Ocean has been played by a skillful golfer.

GREAT ROUNDS

Tom Watson: 1982 US Open
Major championship golf in the late 1970s and early 1980s featured a number of titanic confrontations between Jack Nicklaus and Tom Watson. On one memorable occasion in the 1982 US Open at Pebble Beach, Nicklaus appeared set to win a record fifth title until Watson chipped in for an unlikely two at the penultimate hole.

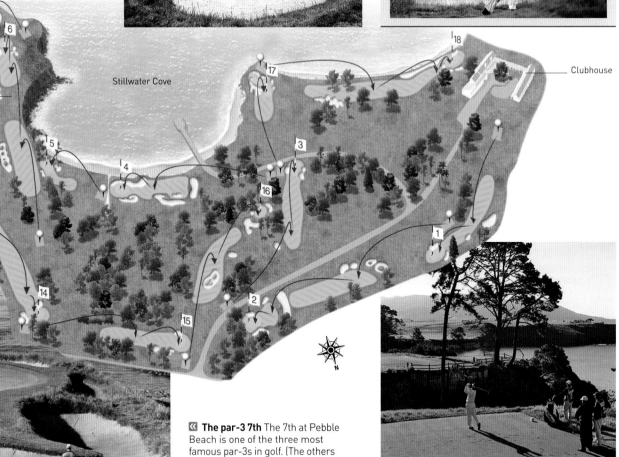

Stillwater Cove

Clubhouse

N

The par-3 7th The 7th at Pebble Beach is one of the three most famous par-3s in golf. (The others are the Postage Stamp 8th at Troon and the 12th at Augusta.) It is downhill and very short, but the green is set above steep slopes.

The par-3 5th The short 5th is a relatively new hole. It was designed by Jack Nicklaus and unveiled in 1998.

Pinehurst

NO. 2 COURSE, PINEHURST, NORTH CAROLINA

Widely regarded as the ultimate US golfing resort, Pinehurst was the idea of New Englander James Tufts. It became famous in the early 1900s through the influence of Scottish golf course designer Donald Ross. The jewel in Pinehurst's crown is the fabled No. 2 Course.

The ultimate golf resort

Visitors to Pinehurst have no fewer than eight golf courses from which to choose. Everyone wants to play No. 2—"the fairest test of championship golf I have ever designed," according to Donald Ross, who was the most prolific golf architect in the US. Ross was originally from Dornoch in Scotland, and there are many similarities between Pinehurst No. 2 and Royal Dornoch (see pp.282–3). Both are ranked among the top dozen courses in the world. Despite this, Pinehurst was long regarded as too remote for an Open Championship. It was finally awarded the US Open in 1999.

Crowning glory

Pinehurst is known for its crowned putting surfaces. These are often slightly above the level of the fairway, with the green surrounds mown tightly. Strategic play is rewarded, which is why Pinehurst No. 2 has a reputation as the "thinking-person's course."

COURSE CARD

Hole	Yards	Par	Hole	Yards	Par
1	406	4	10	619	5
2	503	4	11	486	4
3	389	4	12	451	4
4	569	5	13	385	4
5	476	4	14	479	4
6	223	3	15	205	3
7	429	4	16	534	5
8	490	5	17	208	3
9	190	3	18	453	4
Out	3,675	36	In	3,820	36

Total 7,495 yards, par 72

⌃ **The par-4 3rd** The course has little rough, but the sandhills of North Carolina offer up a range of natural hazards.

The par-4 14th It has been said that you need a driver and a cannon to reach the green in two at the 14th hole on Pinehurst No. 2.

The par-3 9th Some classic bunkering designed by Donald Ross defends the green at the 9th. This may be the shortest hole on Pinehurst No. 2, but it is not the easiest.

Raised greens

Clubhouse

Donald Ross (1872–1948) Born in the far north of Scotland, Ross journeyed to the US in 1899 and went on to become the country's foremost golf course architect. From Seminole in Florida to Oakland Hills in Michigan, he designed courses in almost every state—413 in all. Pinehurst No. 2 is his most celebrated creation.

Raised green at the par-4 18th Most of the putting surfaces on the No. 2 Course are crowned. An errant approach shot at the finishing hole will invariably be deflected off the green.

Pine Valley

CLEMENTON, NEW JERSEY

Built in 1912–18 by the hotelier George Crump, Pine Valley is voted by many experts as the best course in the world. The severity of its terrain is legendary. The club hosted the Walker Cup in 1936 and 1985, but space constraints make it unsuitable for most championships.

Secret domain

George Crump's creation, located deep in a secluded wood on the fringes of Philadelphia, has been described as a vast, 184-acre (74-ha) bunker. The fairways and greens appear as islands; all else is sand, scrub, and pine forest. The club is private, so few golfers get the chance to play on this magnificent course. Moreover, there is little room for crowds on the course, so Pine Valley has never hosted a US Open or USPGA Championship.

Incomparable holes

It is difficult to single out individual golf holes at Pine Valley because each one is memorable. The course has the world's finest collection of par 3s, and the two par 5s are both extraordinary. As for the two-shot holes, there is great variety, ranging from the

short and arrow-straight, but formidable 2nd, to the long and spectacularly curving 13th. Finally, the par-4 18th is one of the best holes at Pine Valley and one of the greatest finishing holes of all time.

☑ **The par-3 14th** The one hole where water is more of a hazard than sand is the dramatic, downhill 14th. As with many holes at Pine Valley, the only place of relative safety is the green.

Typically severe terrain—a punishing mixture of sand and scrub

N

Railroad track

≪ Sand at the par-5 7th
A massive expanse of sand ensures that no golfer is likely to reach the green in two shots at the 7th, which is called Hell's Half-Acre.

COURSE CARD

Hole	Yards	Par	Hole	Yards	Par
1	427	4	10	146	3
2	367	4	11	392	4
3	181	3	12	344	4
4	444	4	13	448	4
5	232	3	14	184	3
6	388	4	15	591	5
7	567	5	16	433	4
8	319	4	17	338	4
9	427	4	18	428	4
Out	3,352	35	In	3,304	35

Total 6,656 yards, par 70

Clubhouse

⌃ The challenging par-3 5th It takes a very talented golfer to make a three at the 5th. This is a long, uphill par 3, that crosses a stream to reach a putting surface defended by sand and scrub.

⌃ Bunker at the par-3 10th The green at the 10th is home to one of the deepest and most awkwardly shaped bunkers in golf. The nickname for this hazard is the Devil's Ass-hole.

≪ The par-4 18th The 18th at Pine Valley is a spectacular par 4 played from an elevated tee. After a drive across a sandy waste, the approach is played over a creek (and yet more sand) to a raised green.

Shinnecock Hills

SOUTHAMPTON, LONG ISLAND, NEW YORK

One of the five founding members of the USGA and host to the second US Open in 1896, Shinnecock has aged gracefully and today ranks alongside Pine Valley, Augusta, and Pebble Beach as one of the four greatest courses in North America.

A US links

Although often described as a New York course, Shinnecock is farther from the Big Apple than, for example, Royal St. George's (see pp.262–3) is from London. Indeed, Shinnecock resembles that famous English links course more than it does a classic New York layout. It occupies a sandy, windswept site near Peconic Bay on Long Island, and looks similar to Muirfield (see pp.280–1)— another great British links—with its greeny-brown fairways framed by gold-tinted native roughs.

Championship quality

Shinnecock has been a truly great course since the late 1920s, when the original layout was revised by William Flynn. The works were completed in the 1930s by Dick Wilson. In 1977, the course gained acclaim when it staged the Walker Cup. Since then, three US Opens have been held here: in 1986, 1995, and 2004, when the South African Retief Goosen overcame trying conditions to win his second Open title in four years.

《 Water at the 6th A large pond to the right of the 6th fairway is the only water hazard at Shinnecock.

》 The par-3 17th A diagonal line of bunkers bar entry to the green at the 17th. Greg Norman (1995) and Phil Mickelson (2004) dropped shots here in their final rounds, losing them the chance of winning their first US Opens.

⌃ **Fast greens** Shinnecock invariably plays firm and fast-running. The greens are prepared to be especially quick during a Major championship.

COURSE CARD

Hole	Yards	Par	Hole	Yards	Par
1	391	4	10	412	4
2	221	3	11	158	3
3	456	4	12	469	4
4	409	4	13	372	4
5	529	5	14	447	4
6	456	4	15	408	4
7	184	3	16	542	5
8	361	4	17	169	3
9	411	4	18	426	4
Out	3,418	35	In	3,403	35

Total 6,821 yards, par 70

⌃ **The par-5 16th** Big hitters may regard the three-shot 16th as a potential birdie opportunity, but the putting surface is significantly contoured and fiercely defended by bunkers.

Clubhouse

⌃ **The par-4 9th and clubhouse** The 9th is one of Shinnecock's finest. A dramatic uphill approach is played to a stagelike green in front of the wonderfully appointed clubhouse.

⌃ **The 2004 US Open** In a summer when three of golf's four Grand Slam events were staged on links-style courses, Shinnecock hosted its fourth US Open.

TPC at Sawgrass

STADIUM COURSE, PONTE VEDRA, FLORIDA

In 1978, the members of the PGA Tour decided to build a course at Sawgrass specifically to stage the Players Championship. Pete and Alice Dye, the leading US golf architects of the day, designed an extraordinary golf course here.

Dream course

The TPC (Tournament Players Club) at Sawgrass has spawned a number of imitations, but the course remains a true original. It is the ultimate stadium course. Island greens, such as the par-3 17th, are an emblematic feature of this type of course. Target golf reigns supreme—a drive at the 18th has to flirt with water bordering the entire left side of the fairway. The Dyes have produced a spectacular golf course that encourages and rewards attacking play.

Players' favorite

No tournament attracts a stronger field than the Players Championship, and it has become one of the most eagerly awaited events on the golfing calendar. In recent years, Tiger Woods, Davis Love, Fred Couples, Sergio Garcia, and Greg Norman have all won at Sawgrass. Norman set a record score of 264 (24 under par) in 1994.

⌃ Tropical scenery
The palm trees at Sawgrass are typical of northern Florida. However, before the Dyes created the course, parts of the land were underwater.

Clubhouse

≫ The par-4 4th
Though it is probably best known for its dramatic finishing holes, Sawgrass also offers a rich variety of more subtle holes, including the excellent drive-and-pitch, short par-4 4th.

⏫ **Island green at the par-3 17th** One of the best-known and most feared short holes in the world, the 17th demands an ultraprecise shot to an island green.

COURSE CARD

Hole	Yards	Par		Hole	Yards	Par
1	423	4		10	424	4
2	532	5		11	558	5
3	177	3		12	358	4
4	384	4		13	181	3
5	471	4		14	481	4
6	393	4		15	449	4
7	442	4		16	523	5
8	237	3		17	137	3
9	583	5		18	462	4
Out	3,642	36		In	3,573	36

Total 7,215 yards, par 72

Reclaimed swampland

◀ **The par-4 18th** Any golfer seeking to win the highly prestigious Players Championship has to successfully negotiate the water at Sawgrass's tough finishing hole.

◀ **Course architect** Many experts regard Sawgrass as Pete Dye's best course. His other layouts include Kiawah Island in South Carolina, Casa de Campo in the Dominican Republic, and Whistling Straits in Wisconsin.

◀ **Swampland** Some of the holes lie on reclaimed swampland and are comprised more of water than fairway.

Winged Foot

WEST COURSE, MAMARONECK, NEW YORK

The New York Athletic Club's brief to golf architect A. W. Tillinghast was succinct: "Build us a man-sized golf course." In fact, Tillinghast delivered two such courses at Winged Foot, one of which—the West Course—is today regarded by many as the ultimate US Open venue.

Tillinghast's epic test

Built in 1923, Winged Foot may not have the dramatic beauty of a Pebble Beach (see pp.236–7) or the elegance of a Pinehurst (see pp.238–9), but as a relentless test in precision, this course has no peers. It is the archetype of championship parkland golf. A.W. Tillinghast once said, "a controlled shot to a closely guarded green is the surest test of any man's golf." And sure enough, all but one of the greens on his West Course are defended by large bunkers on both flanks. Moreover, the putting surfaces on the course are ultrafast and severely contoured.

⤊ **The par-4 18th**
One of championship golf's most celebrated finishing holes, the 18th on the West Course sports a wickedly contoured green.

Venue for US Opens

Five US Opens have been held at Winged Foot. In 1929, Bobby Jones holed a difficult 12-ft (4-m) putt on the final green to tie the winning score, then promptly won the 36-hole playoff by 23 strokes. Billy Casper (1959), Hale Irwin (1974), and Fuzzy Zoeller (1984), all of the US, also triumphed here. The US Open returns to Winged Foot in 2020.

Clubhouse

⟫ **The clubhouse**
Winged Foot's magnificent clubhouse has the appearance of an elegant English country house. Built in stone, it is one of the most admired golf clubhouses in the US.

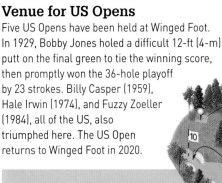

GREAT ROUNDS

Davis Love: 1997 USPGA Championship

Conditions were ideal for low scoring, but no one could foresee that Davis Love from North Carolina would shoot an 11 under par total at Winged Foot to win his first Major. Scoring 66-71-66-66, Love won by five shots and holed a 16-ft (5-m) birdie putt on the final green.

« Amazing architect
Born in Philadelphia, A. W. Tillinghast (1874–1942) was one of the greatest US architects of his time. Widely known as "Tillie," he designed the Winged Foot courses and such acclaimed layouts as Baltusrol, San Francisco, and Quaker Ridge.

⌃ The par-4 2nd
The West Course begins with two fairly testing par 4s. The 1st doglegs mildly to the left; the 2nd (above) turns slightly to the right.

⌃ The par-5 9th The 9th provides a strong conclusion to the front nine. It guides the golfer back to the clubhouse prior to starting the even more challenging back nine.

COURSE CARD

Hole	Yards	Par	Hole	Yards	Par
1	446	4	10	190	3
2	411	4	11	386	4
3	216	3	12	535	5
4	453	4	13	212	3
5	515	5	14	418	4
6	324	4	15	417	4
7	166	3	16	457	5
8	442	4	17	449	4
9	471	5	18	448	4
Out	3,444	36	In	3,512	36
Total 6,956 yards, par 72					

Tryall

HANOVER, MONTEGO BAY, JAMAICA

In the early 1990s, Scottish whisky producer Johnnie Walker decided to stage its World Championship event at the Tryall Club near Montego Bay. The tournament put Tryall and Jamaica on the world golfing map.

Sugar plantation

Located on the northwestern coast of Jamaica, overlooking Sandy Bay, Tryall's fairly hilly terrain was part of an 18th-century sugar plantation. US architect Ralph Plummer designed Tryall on this challenging site in 1957. Despite the abundant lush native vegetation, the course is exposed to the elements. It is said that when local surfers start gathering, the golfers know they are in for a testing, windswept round. Lengthened and in parts remodeled for the Johnnie Walker event, Tryall makes the most of the dramatic terrain. The back nine, in particular, includes several memorable holes.

Jamaica in December

Beginning in 1991 and always held in mid-December, five successive Johnnie Walker World Championships were played at Tryall. The US golfer Fred Couples won the inaugural event and he also triumphed in 1995. In between his successes, Nick Faldo of the UK, Larry Mize of the USA, and Ernie Els of South Africa claimed the coveted trophy. The tournament was not contested after 1995, but by then Tryall— and Jamaican golf generally—was world-famous.

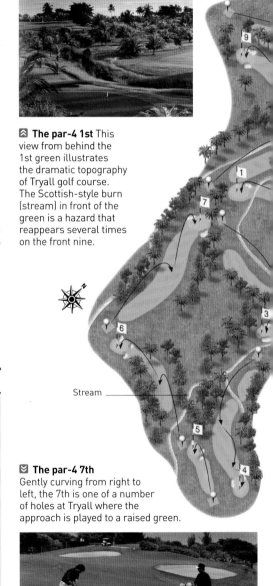

⌃ **The par-4 1st** This view from behind the 1st green illustrates the dramatic topography of Tryall golf course. The Scottish-style burn (stream) in front of the green is a hazard that reappears several times on the front nine.

Stream

⌄ **The par-4 7th** Gently curving from right to left, the 7th is one of a number of holes at Tryall where the approach is played to a raised green.

Hole	Yards	Par	Hole	Yards	Par
1	373	4	10	170	3
2	193	3	11	500	5
3	521	5	12	213	3
4	175	3	13	373	4
5	367	4	14	450	4
6	510	4	15	445	4
7	434	4	16	429	4
8	482	4	17	391	4
9	404	4	18	342	4
Out	3,459	35	**In**	3,313	35

COURSE CARD

Total 6,772 yards, par 70

The par-4 8th
At the exhilarating 8th hole, the drive is from an elevated tee directly toward the ocean.

Clubhouse

The par-4 14th The back nine steps up a gear at the par-4 14th, as the course turns spectacularly toward the ocean. This hole and the par-4 15th are two of Tryall's finest.

Fairway at the par-3 2nd
The fairways are generally wide at Tryall, and staying on them is strongly recommended. The bunkering is not overly penal, but playing out of the rough can be a struggle for golfers.

Banff Springs

STANLEY THOMPSON 18, BANFF, ALBERTA, CANADA

In the heart of the spectacular Canadian Rockies, Banff Springs has one of the finest and most famous golf courses in Canada. There are 27 holes in all, the most celebrated of which are the 18 designed by Stanley Thompson, Canada's greatest golf course architect.

Pioneering development

Today, the Canadian Rockies may seem an obvious location for a world-class resort. Back in the 1880s, however, the Canadian Pacific Railway Company had to take a calculated risk when it created the extravagant Banff Springs Hotel in this scenic but little-known region. The gamble paid off, and the pioneering hotel and its golf course are still central to the ever-expanding Fairmont Banff Springs Resort.

Thompson's layout

Nine holes were built at Banff Springs in 1911, and another nine were added a few years later. At that stage it was little more than a typical hotel golf course—fun to play, but not especially challenging or sophisticated. The layout that is familiar today did not really take shape until 1927, when the course was substantially redesigned by Stanley Thompson. In recent times, a further nine holes have been built, together with a stylish new clubhouse. The additional holes have affected Thompson's layout only in terms of configuration: it remains a masterpiece, with its 4th hole (formerly the 8th) one of the most admired and photographed par 3s in the world of golf.

☆ "The castle in the Rockies" Built in the style of a vast Scottish baronial castle, the Banff Springs Hotel is situated in the heart of the Canadian Rockies, 5,000ft (1,500m) above sea level.

COURSE CARD

Hole	Yards	Par	Hole	Yards	Par
1	414	4	10	218	3
2	171	3	11	417	4
3	528	5	12	442	4
4	192	3	13	225	3
5	424	4	14	440	4
6	373	4	15	475	4
7	602	5	16	414	4
8	150	3	17	374	4
9	501	5	18	578	5
Out	*3,355*	36	**In**	*3,583*	35

Total 6,938 yards, par 71

» The clubhouse
The stylish clubhouse at Banff Springs is relatively new. Completed in 1989, it commands fine views of the course.

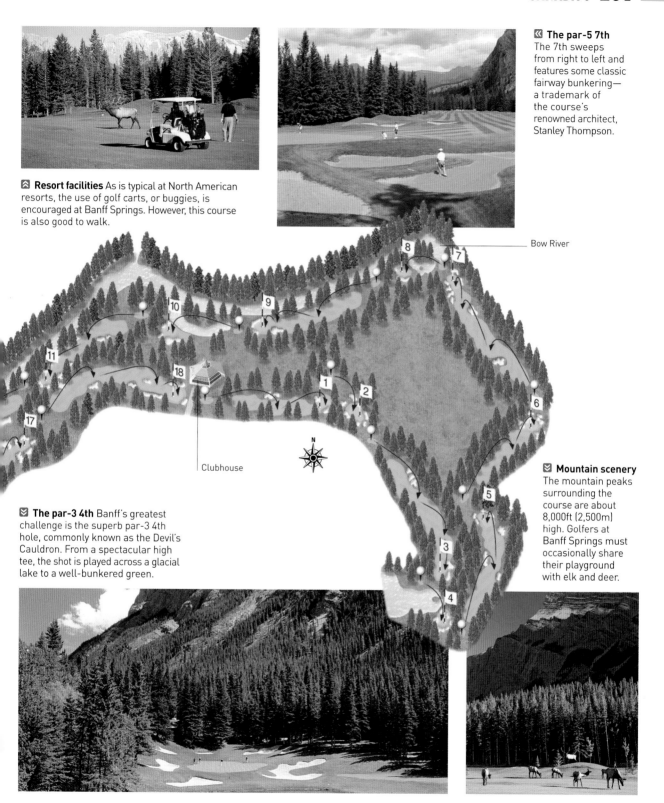

The par-5 7th The 7th sweeps from right to left and features some classic fairway bunkering—a trademark of the course's renowned architect, Stanley Thompson.

Resort facilities As is typical at North American resorts, the use of golf carts, or buggies, is encouraged at Banff Springs. However, this course is also good to walk.

Bow River

Clubhouse

The par-3 4th Banff's greatest challenge is the superb par-3 4th hole, commonly known as the Devil's Cauldron. From a spectacular high tee, the shot is played across a glacial lake to a well-bunkered green.

Mountain scenery The mountain peaks surrounding the course are about 8,000ft (2,500m) high. Golfers at Banff Springs must occasionally share their playground with elk and deer.

Glen Abbey

OAKVILLE, ONTARIO, CANADA

Designed by Jack Nicklaus in the mid-1970s, when he was at the peak of his career, Glen Abbey was one of the first public courses in the world to be created specifically for the purpose of staging a major professional tournament.

⌃ **Calm before the storm** Glen Abbey is a serene spot, but the course is anything but the proverbial "walk in the park."

Pioneering course

Located on the leafy fringes of Oakville, Ontario, Glen Abbey occupies mature grounds that were once home to an order of Jesuit priests (hence the club's distinctive "swinging monk" logo). In many ways, Glen Abbey pioneered what is now called the "stadium course," with its viewing mounds and amphitheater-like greens. The Canadian Open was first held here in 1977, and Glen Abbey is still the regular home of the tournament. The caliber of players who have won here, including Lee Trevino, Greg Norman, Nick Price, Tiger Woods, and Vijay Singh, bears testimony to the quality of the course.

Sixteen Mile Creek

The most admired stretch of holes is the sequence running from the 11th to the 15th, in which the course plunges into a valley and crisscrosses a stream known as Sixteen Mile Creek. The 18th provides a suitably strong finish and has witnessed a lot of drama, including a thrilling shot from a fairway bunker by Tiger Woods that clinched him the 2000 Canadian Open.

⌃ **The par-4 17th** A long par 4, the 17th is one of the most difficult holes at Glen Abbey. Bunkers threaten both sides of the fairway and protrude into the putting surface. This makes the green a relatively narrow target.

Sixteen
Mile Creek

The par-4 11th It has been said that golfers journey into another world when they head off down the 11th at Glen Abbey. "The Valley" holes are said to be the hardest stretch on the PGA tour.

The Canadian Open Crowds flock to Glen Abbey each year to watch Canada's premier golf event. Although many of the world's greatest players have won here, including Tiger Woods, who captured the 2000 championship in stunning fashion, Jack Nicklaus surprisingly never triumphed on the course he created at Glen Abbey.

COURSE CARD

Hole	Yards	Par	Hole	Yards	Par
1	502	5	10	443	4
2	414	4	11	452	4
3	156	3	12	205	3
4	417	4	13	558	5
5	527	5	14	457	4
6	437	4	15	141	3
7	197	3	16	516	5
8	433	4	17	436	4
9	458	4	18	524	5
Out	3,541	36	In	3,732	37

Total 7,273 yards, par 73

The par-3 3rd The short 3rd features an exciting shot across water and sand. Many golfers fail to live up to the challenge—it is said that the pond swallows up 15,000 golf balls each year.

The clubhouse Glen Abbey has a distinctive clubhouse that occupies a prime position overlooking the spectacular par-5 18th.

Ganton

GANTON, SCARBOROUGH, NORTH YORKSHIRE, ENGLAND

One of the greatest courses in the British Isles, Ganton is a golfing curiosity. Although situated 10 miles (16km) inland, its layout has many of the characteristics of a seaside links course. The course occupies open heathland and lies on a substratum of rich sand.

Gorse country

Ganton enjoys a wonderfully tranquil and picturesque setting, nestling in a quiet valley on the edge of the Vale of Pickering. Although surrounded by trees, the course itself is relatively clear, aside from the gorse, which has been allowed to run rampant. This "yellow peril" is a major feature of Ganton, but the bunkering is a much more significant hazard. There are more than 100 traps at Ganton, most of which are deep—some cavernous—and nearly all of them are strategically positioned.

Fabulous par 4s

If Ganton's layout has a weakness, it is that there are only two par 3s on the card. However, the two-shot holes more than compensate, and provide enormous variety. For example, there are two outstanding par 4s on the front nine, namely the 4th, with its superb plateau green, and the swinging, doglegged 7th. On the back nine is a spectacular run-in, beginning with the teasingly short, dramatically bunkered 14th.

⏫ **The par-4 17th** Ganton's penultimate challenge is a very short, yet fiercely defended par 4. It is a great match-play hole.

Clubhouse

⏬ **The par-5 6th** The heavily bunkered, right-to-left curving 6th hole is a good example of Ganton's strategic qualities.

COURSE CARD					
Hole	Yards	Par	Hole	Yards	Par
1	369	4	10	168	3
2	445	4	11	424	4
3	349	4	12	399	4
4	407	4	13	563	5
5	158	3	14	280	4
6	467	5	15	493	4
7	432	4	16	446	4
8	411	4	17	251	4
9	501	5	18	435	4
Out	3,539	37	**In**	3,459	36
Total 6,998 yards, par 73					

Gorse at the par-3 10th Just as Sunningdale (*see* pp.264–5) is famed for its mass of purple heather, so Ganton is renowned for its yellow-flowering gorse bushes.

The par-4 7th A dangerous nest of bunkers lurks just beyond the fairway of the 7th hole, at the corner of the dogleg.

The par-4 14th The 14th is a classic risk-reward hole. If you can negotiate the gargantuan bunker with a tee shot, you then have a straightforward approach to the green. Threes and fives are more common than fours.

Royal Birkdale

SOUTHPORT, LANCASHIRE, ENGLAND

Royal Birkdale vies with Royal St. George's (*see* pp.262–3) for the unofficial title of the best links course in England. Almost every fairway and green is framed by enormous sandhills—golfers playing here can easily imagine that they are performing in an amphitheater.

Fairest of links

As befits a regular venue for the Open, the Royal Birkdale course has a reputation for toughness, but is also praised for its fairness. Awkward bounces and uneven stances are almost unheard of, and there are no blind shots. The bunkers are deep, the rough is difficult, and the wind whistles down the dune-lined fairways. The reputation for fairness explains why professional golfers like Royal Birkdale, and why the Open Championship has been held here eight times since World War II.

Halcyon days

Founded in 1889, Royal Birkdale has had two particularly significant periods in its long history. The current championship links was shaped by renowned English architect Fred Hawtree in 1932. It was also around then that the wonderful Art Deco clubhouse was unveiled. Three decades later—from 1961 to 1971—Royal Birkdale hosted three Open Championships and two Ryder Cups, including a historic tie between the teams in 1969.

⏶ **The par-3 12th** Royal Birkdale's fine collection of par 3s includes the superb 12th. This hole is a favorite of Tom Watson, who won his fifth Open Championship at the course in 1983.

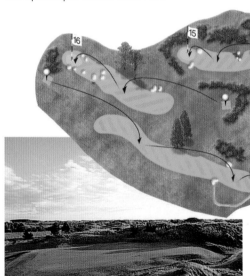

⏶ **Emerald fairways surrounded by dunes** Royal Birkdale's gently undulating fairways are beautifully maintained, in stark contrast to the surrounding dunes and rough, which are left wild.

COURSE CARD

Hole	Yards	Par	Hole	Yards	Par
1	450	4	10	408	4
2	421	4	11	436	4
3	451	4	12	184	3
4	201	3	13	499	4
5	346	4	14	201	3
6	499	4	15	544	5
7	178	3	16	439	4
8	457	4	17	572	5
9	414	4	18	473	4
Out	3,417	34	In	3,756	36

Total 7,173 yards, par 70

Strategically placed
fairway bunker

Clubhouse

☑ **Bunkers at the par-4 5th** The 5th hole is defended by a semicircle of bunkers. Many of Royal Birkdale's bunkers are deep and strategically positioned—golfers must carefully plot their way around this course.

◁◁ **The clubhouse** Royal Birkdale's Art Deco clubhouse was built in 1931. The building's striking, white façade—characterized by sweeping, clean lines, and huge, curvilinear windows—is a superb example of the architecture of that era.

Royal Liverpool

HOYLAKE, THE WIRRAL, MERSEYSIDE, ENGLAND

Hoylake—as the links at the Royal Liverpool Golf Club is known—dates from 1869, and is a venue steeped in history and tradition. The Open Championship staged here in July 2006 was the club's 11th such competition, after a gap of almost four decades.

In good company

The 10 Open Championships held at Hoylake between 1897 and 1967 produced 10 different victors. Among them are some of the greatest names in golfing history: Harold Hilton, John H. Taylor, Walter Hagen, and Bobby Jones. Jones's victory in 1930 came in the second leg of his historic Grand Slam. The popular Argentinian Roberto de Vicenzo won the 1967 Open.

Strategic course

Royal Liverpool's impressive clubhouse overlooks a course that, at first glance, seems unimpressive. But Hoylake merits closer inspection. The terrain may be generally quite flat (except at the far end of the links), but the layout is brimming with subtlety and strategy. The principal hazards are the ever-present wind, the superbly positioned bunkers, and an out of bounds area unusually sited inside the course, right next to the opening hole. Like Carnoustie (see pp.276–7) and Royal Lytham (see pp.260–1), Hoylake is renowned for its exacting closing stretch, which has two par 5s and three par 4s, any of which is capable of wrecking a good score.

⌃ **The par-5 8th** Royal Liverpool is not the most spectacular of courses, but the terrain becomes more turbulent at the far end of the links. The 8th is often played into a fierce headwind.

COURSE CARD					
Hole	Yards	Par	Hole	Yards	Par
1	429	4	10	448	4
2	372	4	11	198	3
3	535	5	12	456	4
4	202	3	13	161	3
5	483	4	14	576	5
6	433	4	15	459	4
7	198	3	16	560	5
8	534	5	17	457	4
9	393	4	18	456	4
Out	3,579	36	In	3,771	36
Total 7,350 yards, par 72					

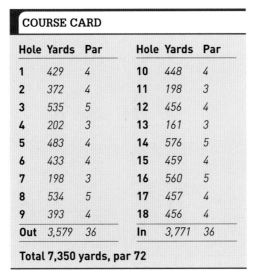

The par-3 11th
Angled in four different directions, Hoylake's four par-3 holes are excellent. The 11th is the star of the collection and the one played closest to the shore.

Bobby Jones
Jones won the Open Championship at Royal Liverpool in 1930. He also captured the US Open and the British and US Amateurs that year—an amazing feat.

Dee Estuary

Road

The par-5 3rd The 3rd has an impressive fairway bunker typical of Royal Liverpool—a course where hazards are very awkward. Of all the other great British links courses, only Muirfield has bunkers that are as elegantly sculpted.

Internal out of bounds area

The clubhouse
One of the oldest golf clubs in England, Royal Liverpool doubled as a horse-racing track in the 19th century. Memorabilia in the clubhouse includes a saddling bell.

Royal Lytham

LYTHAM ST. ANNES, LANCASHIRE, ENGLAND

Red-brick suburbia near Blackpool Tower is the unusual setting for a championship golf club steeped in history. In terms of character and challenge, the course at Royal Lytham is one of the world's finest.

Hallowed turf

To play golf at Royal Lytham is to tread on sacred ground. This is the links immortalized by Bobby Jones and twice conquered by Seve Ballesteros. It is where Gary Player putted left-handed from up against the clubhouse wall, and where Tony Jacklin rifled an arrow-straight drive down the 18th fairway en route to becoming the first "British" Open champion in 18 years.

Bobby Jones plaque at the 17th

Magical moment

Royal Lytham is somewhat nonconformist in beginning with a par 3 and including back-to-back par 5s on the front nine. The layout is also slightly lopsided, because the back nine invariably plays much longer and tougher than the outward half. But the closing sequence is marvelous, and the 17th hole is especially one to savor. It was here in the 1926 Open (and a plaque marks the precise spot) that Bobby Jones hit one of the most sensational shots in golfing history—a stroke that ultimately won him the title and caused his playing partner Al Watrous to declare: "There goes a hundred thousand bucks!"

⟪ The par-3 1st A grandstand view of the 1st hole: Royal Lytham Golf Club is the only Open Championship venue in the British Isles that begins with a par 3.

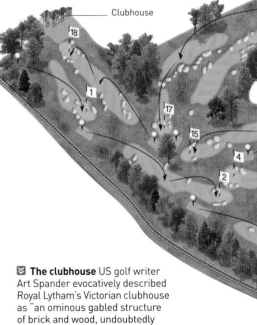

Clubhouse

⬇ The clubhouse US golf writer Art Spander evocatively described Royal Lytham's Victorian clubhouse as "an ominous gabled structure of brick and wood, undoubtedly the home of Count Dracula."

GREAT ROUNDS

Seve Ballesteros: 1988 Open Championship
The great Spanish golfer always had a special affection for Royal Lytham. It was here that he won his first Open in 1979, and where he achieved a hat trick of victories in 1998. The last of these triumphs came courtesy of a final round 65 that let him overtake his playing partner, Nick Price.

⌃ **The par-3 12th** The final par-3 at Royal Lytham is not long, but it can be the hardest on the course. A slippery green is angled away from the player and guarded by deep bunkers.

COURSE CARD

Hole	Yards	Par	Hole	Yards	Par
1	205	3	10	387	4
2	481	4	11	598	5
3	478	4	12	198	3
4	392	4	13	355	4
5	219	3	14	444	4
6	492	4	15	462	4
7	592	5	16	336	4
8	416	4	17	453	4
9	165	3	18	413	4
Out	**3,440**	**34**	**In**	**3,646**	**36**

Total 7,086 yards, par 70

Railroad track

≪ **The par-4 10th** The back nine starts with a short par 4 at the 10th, followed by a fairly benign par 5. But from then on there is no letup.

⌃ **Deep pot bunkers at the par-4 8th** Some of the bunkers at Royal Lytham are prodigiously deep. This one at the 8th punishes poor approaches to the green. Altogether, there are more than 100 bunkers on the championship course.

Royal St. George's

SANDWICH, KENT, ENGLAND

Royal St. George's is affectionately called "the patron saint" of English golf. No fewer than 12 British Amateur Championships and 13 Open Championships (including the first ever on English soil) have been contested over the links at Sandwich.

Traditional values

Depending on how you like your golf, Royal St. George's is either a classic links course or a quaint reminder of how golf used to be. The fairways are not laid out beside the sandhills. Instead, they clamber in among them, and sometimes charge over the top of them. Awkward stances, uneven lies, impossibly deep pot bunkers, and the occasional blind or semiblind shot are all typical features here. In style and spirit, Royal St. George's is as far removed from the world of big-headed drivers and broom-handled putters as you are likely to find.

Norman conquest

For a golf course condemned as "unfair" and "outmoded" by its critics, Royal St. George's has enjoyed a remarkably successful and eventful modern history. It has staged four Opens since the early 1980s. In 1993, it played host to one of the finest Major championships in living memory, when Greg Norman edged out Nick Faldo and Bernhard Langer courtesy of a brilliant final-day 64.

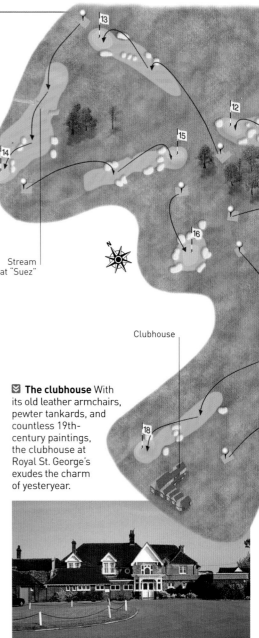

Stream at "Suez"

Clubhouse

⊻ **The clubhouse** With its old leather armchairs, pewter tankards, and countless 19th-century paintings, the clubhouse at Royal St. George's exudes the charm of yesteryear.

» **The par-5 14th** Known as Suez, the 14th has shipwrecked many promising rounds. A mischievous stream crosses the fairway, and the green is perilously close to an out of bounds fence.

The par-4 10th Like every other hole at Royal St. George's, the 10th has the flag of St. George on its pin. The red cross on a white background is the club's emblem.

The par-3 6th The most famous short hole at Royal St. George's is the 6th, otherwise known as the Maiden. The green here is almost totally encircled by deep pot bunkers.

Blind green at the 5th

The fairway bunker at the par-4 4th There are few more intimidating hazards in golf than the bunker to the right of the 4th fairway at Royal St. George's. It is the tallest and deepest bunker in the UK. This trap must be driven over from the back tees.

COURSE CARD

Hole	Yards	Par	Hole	Yards	Par
1	442	4	10	412	4
2	426	4	11	242	3
3	239	3	12	379	4
4	496	4	13	457	4
5	416	4	14	545	5
6	176	3	15	493	4
7	573	5	16	161	3
8	457	4	17	424	4
9	410	4	18	456	4
Out	**3,635**	**35**	**In**	**3,569**	**35**

Total 7,204 yards, par 70

Sunningdale

OLD COURSE, SUNNINGDALE, ASCOT, BERKSHIRE, ENGLAND

The most quintessentially English golf club of all, Sunningdale has hosted many important tournaments, including, in recent times, the Walker Cup and the European Open. The Old Course is the stage for these events and consequently is better known than the New Course.

Old and new

Sunningdale's Old Course dates from 1901, and its New Course dates from 1922. In terms of overall quality, most commentators agree that there is little to choose between the two courses. Both exemplify all that is good about English heathland golf. With fairways bordered by dense purple heather and framed by avenues of pine, oak, and silver birch trees, Sunningdale is characterized by a shock of color at every turn.

Unbelievable golf

Many great rounds of golf have been played on the Old Course, but two eclipse all the others. In 1926, the legendary American amateur Bobby Jones achieved a 66—an exceptional score at that time—and played a standard of golf described by *The Times* newspaper as "incredible and indecent." Almost 80 years later, England's Karen Stupples achieved a 64 on the way to winning the 2004 Women's British Open. Remarkably, she was five under par after the first two holes.

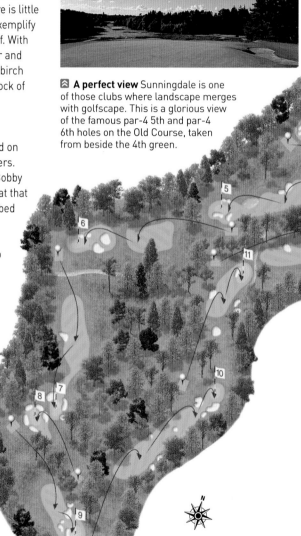

⏶ **A perfect view** Sunningdale is one of those clubs where landscape merges with golfscape. This is a glorious view of the famous par-4 5th and par-4 6th holes on the Old Course, taken from beside the 4th green.

⏵ **Harry Colt** The architect of many of England's finest heathland courses, Harry Colt revised the Old Course and laid out the New Course at Sunningdale.

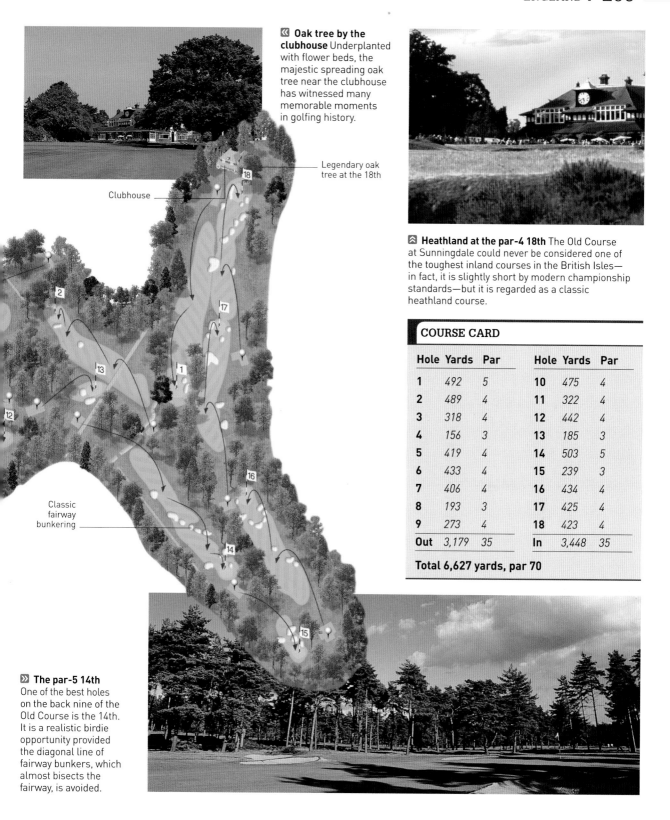

Oak tree by the clubhouse Underplanted with flower beds, the majestic spreading oak tree near the clubhouse has witnessed many memorable moments in golfing history.

Legendary oak tree at the 18th

Clubhouse

Heathland at the par-4 18th The Old Course at Sunningdale could never be considered one of the toughest inland courses in the British Isles—in fact, it is slightly short by modern championship standards—but it is regarded as a classic heathland course.

Classic fairway bunkering

COURSE CARD

Hole	Yards	Par	Hole	Yards	Par
1	492	5	10	475	4
2	489	4	11	322	4
3	318	4	12	442	4
4	156	3	13	185	3
5	419	4	14	503	5
6	433	4	15	239	3
7	406	4	16	434	4
8	193	3	17	425	4
9	273	4	18	423	4
Out	3,179	35	In	3,448	35

Total 6,627 yards, par 70

The par-5 14th One of the best holes on the back nine of the Old Course is the 14th. It is a realistic birdie opportunity provided the diagonal line of fairway bunkers, which almost bisects the fairway, is avoided.

Wentworth

WEST COURSE, VIRGINIA WATER, SURREY, ENGLAND

Located in the heart of leafy "stockbroker-belt" country, yet less than 30 miles (45km) from central London, the West Course at Wentworth is England's preeminent golfing venue. Its celebrity status comes from television coverage and the exploits of the world's finest golfers.

Classic Colt

The West Course—the best of three excellent courses at Wentworth—was designed by master-architect Harry Colt in the mid-1920s. It is normally referred to as a heathland layout, but parts of the course have a woodland and parkland feel. There is a wealth of classic golf holes, and the course is always well tended.

Annual rites

The golfing public sees Wentworth in all its glory twice a year. As spring turns to summer and the rhododendrons are in full bloom, the West Course hosts the PGA Championship—Europe's most important event after the Open. Then, as summer turns to fall, and the mists roll in, the same layout hosts the storied World Match Play Championship. Inaugurated in 1964, this event has a roll of honor that reads like a Who's Who of post-1960s golf history: Arnold Palmer, Jack Nicklaus, Gary Player, Greg Norman, Nick Faldo, Seve Ballesteros, and Ernie Els have each won this tournament at least twice.

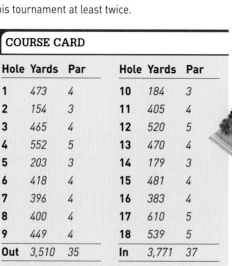

« **Master of Wentworth** Nick Faldo, who once lived on the Wentworth Estate, has won both the PGA Championship and the World Match Play tournament here.

Railroad track

COURSE CARD

Hole	Yards	Par	Hole	Yards	Par
1	473	4	10	184	3
2	154	3	11	405	4
3	465	4	12	520	5
4	552	5	13	470	4
5	203	3	14	179	3
6	418	4	15	481	4
7	396	4	16	383	4
8	400	4	17	610	5
9	449	4	18	539	5
Out	3,510	35	In	3,771	37

Total 7,281 yards, par 72

The long par-4 15th Formerly a short par 5, the left-to-right doglegging 15th demands a precise tee shot down the left side of the fairway. The approach to this mischievous hole is then played to a green that tilts from right to left.

The clubhouse A rhododendron-lined drive leads to Wentworth's castellated clubhouse, which is often described as "one of the most beautiful in England."

The par-4 3rd The West Course opens with three testing holes, the most difficult being the long, uphill 3rd. The green is severely contoured, and putting can be a lottery.

Clubhouse

The par-5 18th The 18th green becomes a vibrant and dramatic stage whenever tournaments are held on the West Course.

The par-4 8th Perhaps not one of the most difficult but certainly one of the prettiest holes at Wentworth is the 8th, where the second shot is played across an attractive pond.

Ballybunion

OLD COURSE, BALLYBUNION, COUNTY KERRY, EIRE

Ireland's largest and most impressive range of sandhills is to be found in a remote and beautiful corner of County Kerry. Located deep in these dunes—and occasionally bursting out along the Atlantic coast—is the magical Old Course at Ballybunion.

Fantasy golf

There are 36 holes at Ballybunion, but it is the Old Course that everyone wants to play. And little wonder, given that five-time Open champion Tom Watson described it as the finest seaside course he had ever seen. The Ballybunion coast has a wild beauty, and the Old Course could not be set closer to the ocean—some fairways run right alongside the cliffs. A game here always feels like a heroic battle with the elements. When the wind lashes in from the Atlantic, it is not a place for the faint of heart.

⊼ **The par-4 17th** One of the most exhilarating holes at Ballybunion is the short 17th, which is played from an elevated position down to a green that nestles beside the ocean.

Ballybunion's glorious 11th

The 11th is the most celebrated hole on the very memorable back nine of Ballybunion's Old Course. The sight from the tee at the 11th can be intimidating, however. Bordered by huge dunes to the left and the Atlantic Ocean to the right, the fairway drops in terracelike fashion until finally culminating on a windswept plateau green overlooking the sea. It is unquestionably one of the greatest two-shot holes in the world. The 2nd, 7th, and 8th on Ballybunion's Old Course are equally challenging.

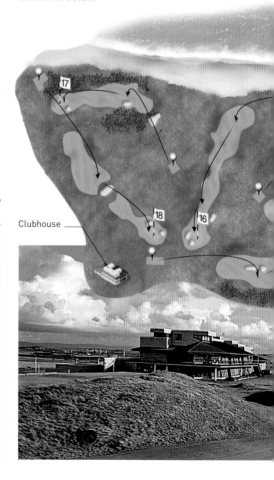

Clubhouse

COURSE CARD

Hole	Yards	Par	Hole	Yards	Par
1	408	4	10	364	4
2	445	4	11	473	4
3	224	3	12	214	3
4	533	5	13	488	5
5	560	5	14	133	3
6	396	4	15	216	3
7	434	4	16	509	5
8	163	3	17	398	4
9	462	4	18	382	4
Out	3,625	36	In	3,177	35

Total 6,802 yards, par 71

⌃ **The par-4 11th** The sheer drama of Ballybunion's windswept 11th has inspired many golf writers to include it in their choice of the world's greatest 18 holes.

⌃ **The par-4 7th** Shown here during the Irish Open, the 7th runs parallel with the shore and is one of the most exciting holes on the front nine.

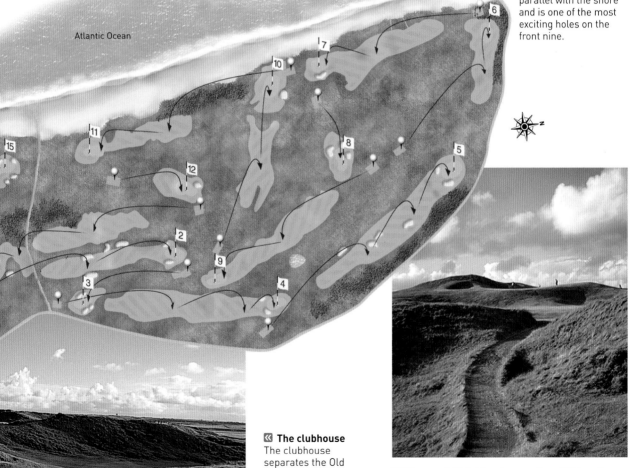

Atlantic Ocean

⌄ **The clubhouse** The clubhouse separates the Old Course from the newer Cashen Course, which was designed by Robert Trent Jones in 1980.

⌃ **The par-3 12th** After the amazing, cliff-hugging 11th hole comes a demanding, uphill par 3, which sends players clambering back into the dunes for the 12th green.

Portmarnock

PORTMARNOCK, COUNTY DUBLIN, EIRE

The spiritual home of Irish golf, Portmarnock is the country's premier championship venue, having hosted numerous Irish Opens as well as the World Cup and the Walker Cup. In the opinion of many, Portmarnock's staging of the Ryder Cup is long overdue.

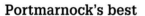

Serious challenge

Portmarnock is magnificent and formidable. Located on a peninsula to the north of Dublin, the links is surrounded by water on three sides, so the player is often at the mercy of the elements. To add to this, the course is very long and expertly bunkered.

Portmarnock's best

Portmarnock is often compared with Muirfield (*see* pp.280–1) because it is laid out in two loops of nine. Perhaps the most memorable sequence of holes on the first nine occurs between the 4th and the 8th. On the second nine, the toughest test is invariably the long, par-4 17th, but the finest hole on the course is generally thought to be the par-3 15th. It is played parallel to the shore, and if the wind is whipping in off the Irish Sea, you have to direct your tee shot out over the beach—a "white-knuckle" shot if ever there was one.

⟨⟨ The par-3 15th One of golf's most celebrated and intimidating short holes, the 15th at Portmarnock runs parallel to the Irish Sea.

⌃ Putting surfaces The subtly contoured putting surfaces at Portmarnock have a reputation for being quick and very true.

⟩⟩ The par-4 18th The final challenge at Portmarnock is to shoot onto a green that appears like an elevated stage. This is a fitting conclusion to a memorable round.

Clubhouse

The par-5 6th A small pond lurks to the left of the fairway at the long 6th, a danger to wayward second shots. Most golfers are relieved to achieve a regulation par 5 at this hole.

The par-3 7th Most links courses are exposed to the elements, with little in the way of tree cover, and they can seem like desolate, lonely places. Portmarnock is no exception—this view is from behind the green at the 7th.

The clubhouse Occupying a peninsula, Portmarnock has an islandlike setting. To reach the clubhouse, golfers at one time used to travel by boat; today there is access by road.

COURSE CARD

Hole	Yards	Par	Hole	Yards	Par
1	417	4	10	370	4
2	411	4	11	428	4
3	398	4	12	177	3
4	474	4	13	565	5
5	442	4	14	411	4
6	603	5	15	204	3
7	184	3	16	577	5
8	427	4	17	472	4
9	454	4	18	452	4
Out	3,810	36	In	3,656	36

Total 7,466 yards, par 72

Royal County Down

NEWCASTLE, COUNTY DOWN, NORTHERN IRELAND

Two esteemed English golf writers have encapsulated the appeal of Royal County Down. For Peter Dobereiner, the links is "exhilarating, even without a club in your hand." To Bernard Darwin, it offers "the kind of golf that people play in their most ecstatic dreams."

Extraordinary links

The famous links at Newcastle has often been declared more spectacular than Ballybunion (*see* pp.268–9); more natural and charming than Royal Dornoch (*see* pp.282–3); and more punishing than Carnoustie (*see* pp.276–7). Most golfers will be enthralled by such comparisons, and may well quake at the prospect of the last.

Spectacular scenery

Newcastle's setting is every bit as sensational as the golf. The links is fringed by the impressive sweep of Dundrum Bay and sprinkled with purple-flowering heather and gold-turning gorse. You can hear the crashing of waves as you set off to play the opening holes, and the imperious Mountains of Mourne provide a backdrop to much of the course. Laid out in two loops of nine, Royal County Down has at least seven truly great holes, namely the 3rd, 4th, 5th, 8th, 9th, 13th, and 15th.

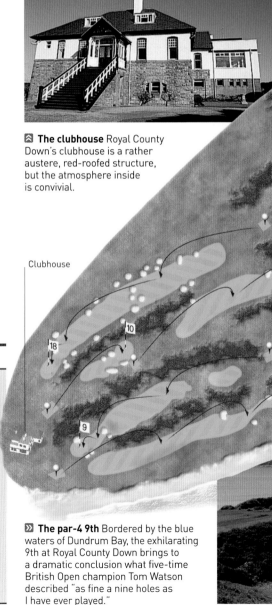

Clubhouse

⌃ **The clubhouse** Royal County Down's clubhouse is a rather austere, red-roofed structure, but the atmosphere inside is convivial.

⌃ **Extraordinary bunkers** Typically overgrown with marram grass and distinctly disheveled in appearance, Royal County Down's 130 bunkers display unique character.

⌃ **Gorse on the links** Thick gorse frames many of the fairways at Royal County Down. It looks attractive, but swallows up many balls.

⌗ **The par-4 9th** Bordered by the blue waters of Dundrum Bay, the exhilarating 9th at Royal County Down brings to a dramatic conclusion what five-time British Open champion Tom Watson described "as fine a nine holes as I have ever played."

COURSE CARD					
Hole	Yards	Par	Hole	Yards	Par
1	539	5	10	196	3
2	444	4	11	442	4
3	475	4	12	525	5
4	229	3	13	446	4
5	440	4	14	212	3
6	396	4	15	468	4
7	144	3	16	337	4
8	429	4	17	433	4
9	483	4	18	548	5
Out	**3,579**	**35**	**In**	**3,607**	**36**

Total 7,186 yards, par 71

The par-4 5th
One of the finest holes at Newcastle is the left-to-right curving 5th, beyond which the Mountains of Mourne provide a truly splendid backdrop.

The par-4 3rd Royal County Down has many formidable two-shot holes, but none is more challenging than the 3rd, which runs parallel to the shore. It features an unusual split-level fairway.

Royal Portrush

DUNLUCE COURSE, PORTRUSH, CO. ANTRIM, NORTHERN IRELAND

Situated on the scenic Antrim Coast—close to the ruins of Dunluce Castle and the geological oddity of the Giant's Causeway—is the magnificent links of Royal Portrush Golf Club. It was here, on the Dunluce Course in 1951, that Ireland's only British Open was staged.

Beauty and brains

If the Open Championship ever returns to Ireland, the Ailsa Course at Turnberry in Scotland (see pp.288–9) will have a serious rival in the beauty stakes. As with the famous Scottish links, there are two 18-hole courses at Portrush, the Dunluce links being the Ailsa's counterpart. Many critics believe that in terms of its architecture, the Dunluce links, fashioned by Harry Colt in 1933, is superior to the Ailsa. It is also said to be Colt's finest work.

Sensational golf

The front nine at Portrush is outstanding. The 4th hole is a strong par 4, and the famous 5th charges downhill from a spectacular tee to a green perched on the edge of the links, overlooking the sea. The 14th, "Calamity," provides the defining moment of the back nine and is a real "death or glory" hole. It is extremely long, and the direct line to the flag is across a vast ravine. Mis-hitting the shot can mean a penalty of playing the next stroke from 50ft (15m) below the hole.

⌃ **The valley course** Royal Portrush's second 18-hole links, the Valley Course, is visible beyond the 6th green on the Dunluce links. It is not as challenging as the Dunluce, but is a fine course nonetheless.

⟫ **Bunker at the par-5 17th** In a manner reminiscent of the famous 4th at Royal St. George's (see pp.262–3), this formidable bunker threatens the drive on the 17th. It guards the right edge of the fairway and should be given as wide a berth as possible.

Clubhouse

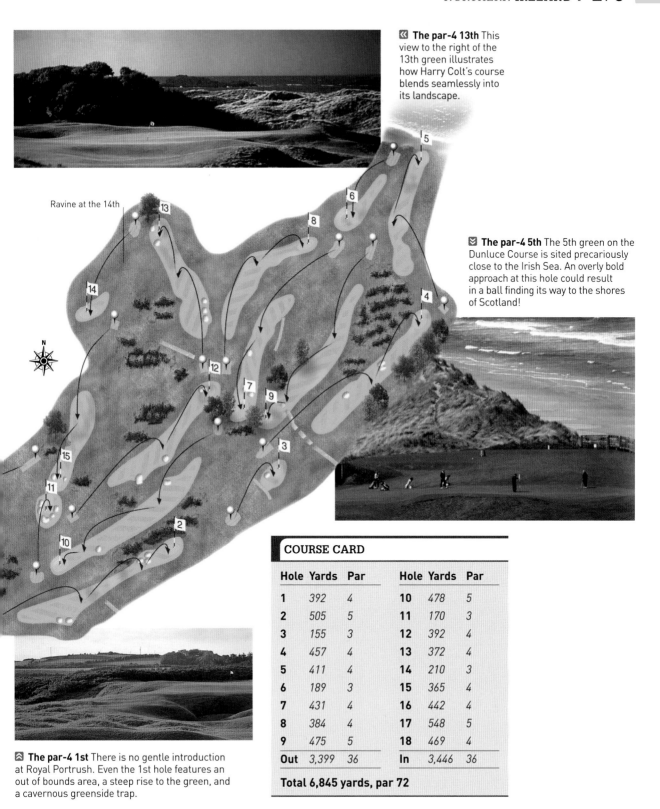

The par-4 13th This view to the right of the 13th green illustrates how Harry Colt's course blends seamlessly into its landscape.

Ravine at the 14th

The par-4 5th The 5th green on the Dunluce Course is sited precariously close to the Irish Sea. An overly bold approach at this hole could result in a ball finding its way to the shores of Scotland!

The par-4 1st There is no gentle introduction at Royal Portrush. Even the 1st hole features an out of bounds area, a steep rise to the green, and a cavernous greenside trap.

COURSE CARD

Hole	Yards	Par	Hole	Yards	Par
1	392	4	10	478	5
2	505	5	11	170	3
3	155	3	12	392	4
4	457	4	13	372	4
5	411	4	14	210	3
6	189	3	15	365	4
7	431	4	16	442	4
8	384	4	17	548	5
9	475	5	18	469	4
Out	3,399	36	In	3,446	36
Total 6,845 yards, par 72					

Carnoustie

CHAMPIONSHIP COURSE, CARNOUSTIE, TAYSIDE, SCOTLAND

There are difficult golf courses, there are very difficult golf courses, and then there is the Championship Course at Carnoustie. Described by one journalist as "a great big shaggy monster," this links is widely acknowledged as the most demanding course in Britain.

The ultimate test

As commentator Henry Longhurst was fond of saying, "golf takes us to such beautiful places," but no one ever visited Carnoustie to admire the scenery. Golfers want to play this links course for much the same reasons that runners enter a marathon or climbers seek to scale the heights of Mount Everest—Carnoustie represents a tremendous challenge.

Formidable hazards

There are several factors that add up to make Carnoustie tough. For one thing, every aspect of the links is on a grand scale. Many of the holes are exceedingly long, the greens are typically vast, and the rough is usually grown tall. Then there is the bunkering: Carnoustie is famed for its deep, steep-faced pot bunkers—even a skillful golfer might imagine that he is plotting his way through a minefield. And finally, there is the water: several other Scottish links courses feature a meandering burn (stream), but Carnoustie has two of them—Barry Burn and

Jockie's Burn. As many great golfers can attest, Carnoustie's burns make a habit of traversing the fairways in the most unfriendly of places.

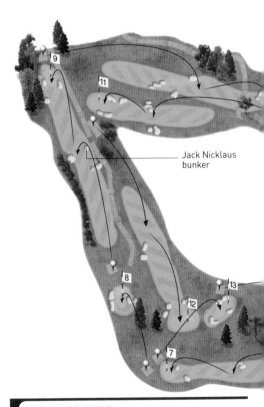

Jack Nicklaus bunker

The course

Carnoustie was judged as the greatest course in the British Isles by the legendary 1920s US golfer Walter Hagen.

COURSE CARD					
Hole	Yards	Par	Hole	Yards	Par
1	406	4	10	466	4
2	463	4	11	383	4
3	358	4	12	499	4
4	412	4	13	176	3
5	415	4	14	514	5
6	578	5	15	472	4
7	410	4	16	248	3
8	183	3	17	461	4
9	478	4	18	499	4
Out	3,703	36	In	3,718	35

Total 7,421 yards, par 71

GREAT ROUNDS

Ben Hogan: 1953 Open
Victorious in both the Masters and US Open, Ben Hogan traveled to Carnoustie in 1953, attempting to win golf's Triple Crown. Hogan had never experienced links conditions before, but he won with decreasing rounds of 73-71-70-68.

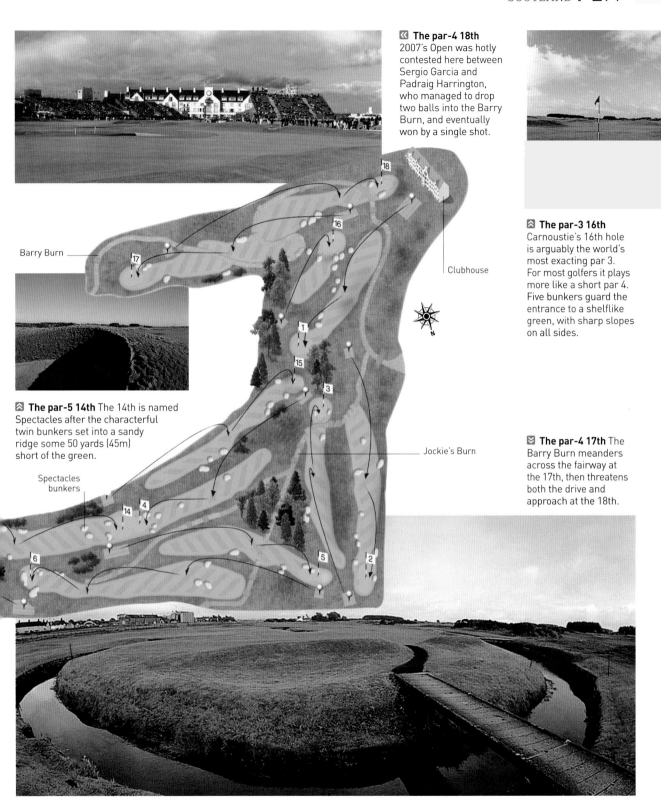

The par-4 18th 2007's Open was hotly contested here between Sergio Garcia and Padraig Harrington, who managed to drop two balls into the Barry Burn, and eventually won by a single shot.

The par-3 16th Carnoustie's 16th hole is arguably the world's most exacting par 3. For most golfers it plays more like a short par 4. Five bunkers guard the entrance to a shelflike green, with sharp slopes on all sides.

Barry Burn

Clubhouse

The par-5 14th The 14th is named Spectacles after the characterful twin bunkers set into a sandy ridge some 50 yards (45m) short of the green.

Spectacles bunkers

Jockie's Burn

The par-4 17th The Barry Burn meanders across the fairway at the 17th, then threatens both the drive and approach at the 18th.

Loch Lomond

LUSS BY ALEXANDRIA, DUNBARTONSHIRE, SCOTLAND

Scotland is famous for its beautiful blue lochs. To the Scottish themselves, there is no more exquisite place on Earth than Loch Lomond. In 1996, a new golf course built on the west bank of the loch became the talk of the world's golfing media.

High praise

Loch Lomond lies within the Trossachs National Park, about 25 miles (40km) northwest of Glasgow. Laid out within the ancestral homelands of the Clan Colquhoun, the new golf course was unveiled in 1996 and instantly showered with accolades. The owners arranged an inaugural tournament, inviting many of the world's top players, which certainly helped to focus media attention. However, once Nick Faldo and Colin Montgomerie respectively had described the course as "absolutely fabulous" and "faultless," it was clear that much of the hype was genuine. A decade on, Loch Lomond is still the most talked about "new" golf course in the British Isles.

Influence from the US

The course was designed by the acclaimed US architects Tom Weiskopf and Jay Morrish. Indeed, there is a strong US influence at Loch Lomond: the club operates along the lines of an exclusive US country club, and in style is more akin to Augusta (see pp.222–3) than clubs elsewhere in the Scottish Highlands. The ambience is wonderful. You could golf your way around each of the five continents and never find a more spectacular finish than the 17th and 18th at Loch Lomond.

⌃ **Eagle's-eye view of the course** The club's chairman, US entrepreneur Lyle Anderson, is reputed to have fallen in love with Loch Lomond at first sight.

Clubhouse

☑ **The 17th green** There can be few more idyllic spots in golf than the green at Loch Lomond's par-3 17th hole.

	COURSE CARD					
Hole	**Yards**	**Par**		**Hole**	**Yards**	**Par**
1	425	4		10	455	4
2	455	4		11	235	3
3	510	5		12	415	4
4	390	4		13	560	5
5	190	3		14	345	4
6	625	5		15	415	4
7	440	4		16	495	4
8	160	3		17	205	3
9	345	4		18	435	4
Out	**3,540**	**36**		**In**	**3,560**	**35**
Total 7,100 yards, par 71						

The par-5 6th Impressive trees line (and define) the route at the enormous 6th. At 625 yards, this is the longest hole in Scottish golf. The green at the hole is elevated and fairly close to the edge of the loch.

The par-3 5th Nick Faldo is seen here striking an explosive shot from sand at the 5th during the inaugural Loch Lomond World Invitational Tournament in 1996. The event was won by Thomas Björn of Denmark.

Course designer Together with his former partner Jay Morrish, Tom Weiskopf designed Loch Lomond in the early 1990s. Although he has won the Open and a US Senior Open, Weiskopf regards this course as his greatest contribution to the game.

The clubhouse The golf course occupies part of an ancient Scottish estate. A 500-year-old ruined castle stands beside the 18th green, and 19th-century Rossdhu House serves as Loch Lomond's palatial clubhouse.

Muirfield

MUIRFIELD, GULLANE, EAST LOTHIAN, SCOTLAND

Muirfield is the third home of the world's oldest private golf club. The Honourable Company of Edinburgh Golfers was founded in 1744; it moved to Muirfield in 1891 after previous bases at Leith and Musselburgh became overcrowded.

Ingenious layout

Modern Muirfield took shape in the 1920s, under British course designer Harry Colt (see p.264). A masterpiece in terms of golf architecture, it is usually rated among the top three British courses. The course is configured in two loops, with the front nine holes heading clockwise on the outer loop; the inner loop (the back nine) runs counterclockwise. This layout means the golfer confronts the prevailing wind from every direction. Muirfield's bunkering is also superb, and the course is always kept in an immaculate condition.

⏏ **Hazards** Muirfield has traditional British links-style hazards. There are no hidden traps or water features, but the bunkers are deep.

A champion's course

Of all the Open venues, Muirfield has consistently produced the finest championships and the greatest champions. Its postwar honor roll speaks volumes: Henry Cotton (1948), Gary Player (1959), Jack Nicklaus (1966), Lee Trevino (1972), Tom Watson (1980), Nick Faldo (1987 and 1992), and Ernie Els (2002). Clearly, Muirfield brings out the very best in the best.

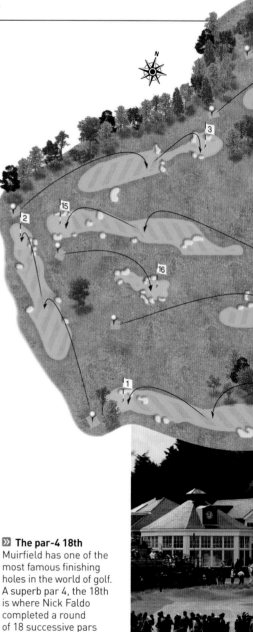

▷ **The par-4 18th** Muirfield has one of the most famous finishing holes in the world of golf. A superb par 4, the 18th is where Nick Faldo completed a round of 18 successive pars to win his first Open Championship in 1987.

COURSE CARD

Hole	Yards	Par	Hole	Yards	Par
1	450	4	10	472	4
2	367	4	11	389	4
3	379	4	12	382	4
4	229	3	13	193	3
5	561	5	14	478	4
6	469	4	15	447	4
7	187	3	16	188	3
8	445	4	17	578	5
9	558	5	18	473	4
Out	3,645	36	**In**	3,600	35

Total 7,245 yards, par 71

The par-3 13th The best of the short holes at Muirfield is generally considered to be the slightly uphill 13th. The green here is narrow and neatly wedged between two tall dunes.

Pot bunkers at the par-3 7th Elegantly sculpted pot bunkers are the trademark of Muirfield. Jack Nicklaus once described them as the most fastidiously built bunkers he had ever seen.

Wall at the par-5 9th An ancient stone wall runs along the left edge of the 9th fairway. It conspires with several cunningly placed bunkers to make the 9th a very strategic golf hole.

Clubhouse

5
11
13
12
7
6
10
17
8
18
9

Royal Dornoch

DORNOCH, SUTHERLAND, SCOTLAND

Two words are normally associated with Royal Dornoch: one is "great" and the other is "remote." Situated 50 miles (80km) north of Inverness, Dornoch enjoys a splendid isolation. It is a course that many golfers would like to play, but very few actually do.

A remote and natural course

Royal Dornoch may be geographically challenging, but this merely adds to its mystique. It has an almost theatrical setting, bordered by the Dornoch Firth and a glorious stretch of sand, with distant hills filling the horizon. Much of the links is blanketed in gorse—a glorious sight when it flowers in early summer. Another aspect that intrigues people is Dornoch's remarkable history: golf has been played in the area since at least the early 1600s. Most fascinating of all is the quality and character of the golf links itself, which is widely regarded as the most natural golf course in the world. The holes blend perfectly into their landscape: every bump, hollow, plateau, and other feature is either natural or appears to be so.

Seamless layout

Royal Dornoch is famous for its magnificent, contoured greens. The course flows wonderfully from tee to green. The 4th, 5th, and 6th holes are widely celebrated. And, once you have turned for home, the 10th, 14th, and 17th are also superb. But then it could be said that every hole at Royal Dornoch is a seaside classic.

⌃ **The par-4 18th** The 18th green is one of the largest on Royal Dornoch's golf course, overlooked by the clubhouse.

Clubhouse

⌄ **The par-4 16th** The approach to the 16th is sharply uphill, but the view from the green is well worth the climb.

The par-4 5th
This aerial view shows the 5th green at the center of the layout, and some of the early holes on the back nine, which run right alongside the Dornoch Firth.

The par-3 6th
Golden gorse frames the links—and sometimes encroaches on it—from late spring onward.

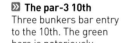

Gorse

Embo Bay

The par-3 10th
Three bunkers bar entry to the 10th. The green here is notoriously slippery and prone to shrugging a golf ball off down the slopes. Golfers hope that the wind is not at their back when they play this short hole.

The par-4 17th Few greens in the world of golf are as elegantly sited as the 17th at Royal Dornoch. The penultimate hole is also one of the finest on the course. It features a downhill, semi-blind drive, and an uphill approach that involves tackling two large bunkers mischievously placed in front of the green.

COURSE CARD

Hole	Yards	Par	Hole	Yards	Par
1	331	4	10	174	3
2	184	3	11	449	4
3	413	4	12	523	5
4	422	4	13	180	3
5	353	4	14	445	4
6	161	3	15	358	4
7	479	4	16	401	4
8	434	4	17	405	4
9	529	5	18	456	4
Out	3,306	35	In	3,391	35

Total 6,697 yards, par 70

Royal Troon

TROON, AYRSHIRE, SCOTLAND

Once overshadowed by neighboring Prestwick, Royal Troon is now a firm fixture on the Open Championship rota. It is a venue seemingly favored by golfers from the US, who have triumphed the last six times that the Open has been contested over the rugged Ayrshire links.

A classic challenge

Royal Troon dates from the 1870s and is a very traditional golf club. Its championship layout follows the classic Scottish links formula of nine holes out, starting hard by the coast, and nine holes back, returning inland. The return is invariably into the wind. A glance at the scorecard reveals that the first four holes are relatively benign. Indeed, they can have the effect of lulling the golfer into a false sense of security. Yet a good score really needs to be fashioned over these early holes, because Royal Troon has a formidable, "take no prisoners" type of finish.

Memorable golf

Royal Troon has a rich history. It was the scene of Tom Weiskopf's only Major victory (1973), Tom Watson's fourth Open success (1982), and, most recently, the 2004 championship, which featured a terrific final-day tussle between Ernie Els, Phil Mickelson and, the eventual winner, Todd Hamilton. Perhaps the most memorable moment of all occurred in the 1973 Open, when 71-year-old Gene Sarazen achieved a hole-in-one at Royal Troon's fabled "Postage Stamp" 8th hole.

⏫ **The par-5 16th** For most golfers, the 16th hole presents the last realistic birdie opportunity. After this come the extremely long par-3 17th and the demanding two-shot 18th.

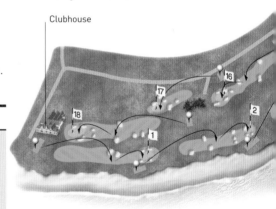

Clubhouse

COURSE CARD

Hole	Yards	Par	Hole	Yards	Par
1	370	4	10	438	4
2	391	4	11	490	5
3	379	4	12	431	4
4	560	5	13	472	4
5	210	3	14	178	3
6	601	5	15	483	4
7	405	4	16	542	5
8	123	3	17	222	3
9	423	4	18	457	4
Out	3,462	36	In	3,713	36

Total 7,175 yards, par 72

➡️ **Strong finish at the par-4 18th** The 18th green is protected by five deep bunkers, and the fairway bunkering is also menacing. The Australian Greg Norman found this out to his cost at the conclusion of the 1989 Open, when he lost to Mark Calcavecchia of the US.

Rugged country
Royal Troon is one of golf's great battle grounds. When the wind blows—as it invariably does on the Ayrshire coast—every hole becomes a serious test.

Railroad track

Firth of Clyde

GREAT ROUNDS

Todd Hamilton: 2004 Open Championship
Either Ernie Els or Phil Mickelson was expected to win the 2004 Open at Royal Troon, but Todd Hamilton pulled off a shock victory by scoring 71-67-67-69, before defeating Els in a playoff.

The par-3 8th: "Postage Stamp" Golfers miss the tiny green at the 8th at their peril. Gene Sarazen may have holed-in-one here, but most players are delighted to walk off the green with a par 3.

The par-4 2nd
Royal Troon's opening sequence comprises three short par 4s followed by a par 5. The golfer who struggles over these holes is in for a torrid round.

St. Andrews

OLD COURSE, ST. ANDREWS, FIFE, SCOTLAND

St. Andrews is acknowledged as the home of golf (*see* p.8). There is documentary proof that local folk were teeing up here in the 15th century, making the Old Course the oldest links course in the world.

**St. Andrews' crest
with crossed clubs**

Historic links

It is often said that a good test of a course's quality is the extent to which, after the first time of playing, you can remember each hole. This is not easy at St. Andrews, where the sense of history is distracting. However, the vast double greens, rippling fairways, and myriad pot bunkers are unforgettable.

Strategy reigns

The Old Course challenges every aspect of your game. On any course you hope to strike the ball well, but at St. Andrews it is also essential that you hit into the right places—and invariably these are not the obvious ones. You have to think your way around the golf course and, to score well, you must play imaginatively as well as skillfully.

A stroke played wisely one day is not necessarily such a clever shot the following day. Conditions are ever-changing, and with each change there is a new strategy to consider. In fact, you could play St. Andrews every day for a month and see 30 different courses.

Cockle bunkers

Coffin bunkers

COURSE CARD

Hole	Yards	Par	Hole	Yards	Par
1	376	4	10	386	4
2	453	4	11	174	3
3	397	4	12	348	4
4	480	4	13	465	4
5	568	5	14	618	5
6	412	4	15	455	4
7	371	4	16	423	4
8	175	3	17	495	4
9	352	4	18	357	4
Out	3,584	36	In	3,721	36

Total 7,305 yards, par 72

⌃ **An ancient links** Golf was being played at St. Andrews in 1400, which was long before Columbus sailed to America and two centuries before Shakespeare wrote *Macbeth*.

⏏ **The terrain** From a distance, the Old Course looks fairly flat. In reality, however, its fairways resemble crumpled blankets, and most of its greens are heavily contoured.

⏏ **The clubhouse** The most famous building in golf overlooks the opening drive on the Old Course, and looms up in front of the approach to the final green.

Hell bunkers

The Principal's Nose bunker system

The Valley of Sin

⏏ **Hell bunker on the par-5 14th** In many respects St. Andrews is a golfing obstacle course. You must plot your way around many hazards. A wide berth should be given to "Hell" on the 14th, the largest bunker on the Old Course.

⏎ **The par-4 17th** No championship at St. Andrews is won until the 17th—the Road Hole—has been successfully negotiated. It features a nerve-wracking drive beside the Old Course Hotel, then a long shot to a fiercely defended plateau green. The road that gives the hole its name runs behind the green.

Turnberry

AILSA COURSE, TURNBERRY, AYRSHIRE, SCOTLAND

Dating from the early 1900s, Turnberry's Ailsa Course is the better known of the club's two championship courses. Beautifully situated, with the Isle of Arran and the granite dome of Ailsa Craig filling the horizon, it boasts a litany of dazzling, world-famous holes.

Scotland's Pebble Beach

Many Scots say that Turnberry's Ailsa Course is without comparison because of its setting and the dramatic golf on offer. But there is one great course that is similar: California's Pebble Beach (*see* pp.236–7). Both courses made their Major debuts in the 1970s, and both feature a stunning sequence of oceanside holes. The two most celebrated holes on the Ailsa Course are the 9th, which lies next to a lighthouse, and the curving 10th.

Duel in the sun

Turnberry's 1977 Open debut proved to be a classic. Two of the finest golfers of the day, Jack Nicklaus and Tom Watson, pulled out in front and turned the final 36 holes into a marvelous head-to-head confrontation. Despite being two behind with six to play, Watson triumphed when he birdied the penultimate hole and then struck his approach to within 2ft (60cm) of the flag at the last. Turnberry's two subsequent Opens were won by Greg Norman in 1986 and Nick Price in 1994.

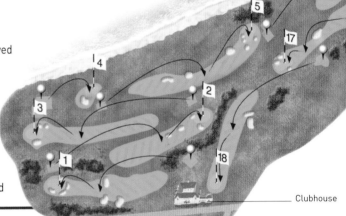

Clubhouse

COURSE CARD

Hole	Yards	Par	Hole	Yards	Par
1	354	4	10	456	4
2	428	4	11	175	3
3	489	4	12	451	4
4	166	3	13	410	4
5	474	4	14	448	4
6	231	3	15	206	3
7	538	5	16	455	4
8	454	4	17	559	5
9	449	4	18	461	4
Out	3,583	35	In	3,621	35
Total 7,204 yards, par 70					

⏏ **Turnberry Hotel** Turnberry is a luxury golfing resort. An opulent hotel perches on a hill behind the clubhouse, overlooking the links.

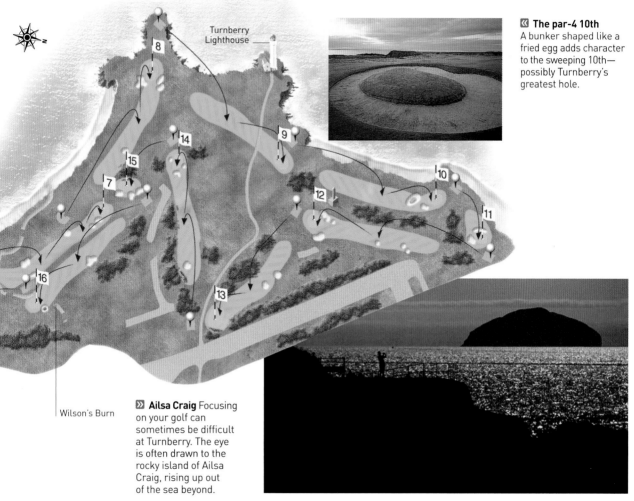

8

Turnberry
Lighthouse

14

15

7

9

12

10

11

16

13

Wilson's Burn

« The par-4 10th
A bunker shaped like a
fried egg adds character
to the sweeping 10th—
possibly Turnberry's
greatest hole.

» Ailsa Craig Focusing
on your golf can
sometimes be difficult
at Turnberry. The eye
is often drawn to the
rocky island of Ailsa
Craig, rising up out
of the sea beyond.

**« Turnberry
Lighthouse** A jewel
on the west coast of
Scotland, the Ailsa
Course has a unique,
rugged beauty. Its most
striking feature is an
old lighthouse, sited on
the headland between
Turnberry Bay and the
Firth of Clyde, just
beyond the 9th hole.

Chantilly

LE VINEUIL COURSE, CHANTILLY, FRANCE

Located about 25 miles (40km) north of Paris in a historic region famous for horse racing, the Vineuil Course at Chantilly, founded in 1888, is widely acknowledged to be the finest course in France. English architect Tom Simpson is chiefly responsible for its fame.

Simpson's commission

In the mid-1920s, Chantilly's owners engaged Tom Simpson to design another 18 holes to complement the club's established Vineuil Course. Simpson did produce an additional layout, but most of his energies became focused on what he envisioned to be the full potential of Le Vineuil. His redesign of the course was a masterpiece.

Strong and strategic

Le Vineuil is a difficult course, featuring deep bunkers and with thick woodland bordering many of its fairways. Among the best holes are a trio on the front nine, from the 6th to 8th, and a similar sequence on the back nine, from the 13th to 15th. The French Open has been played here several times. Winners include Britons Henry Cotton (1946) and Nick Faldo (1988 and 1989), and the Argentinian Roberto de Vicenzo (1964).

>> **Green at the par-4 13th** One of Chantilly's most challenging shots is the second shot at the 13th on the Vineuil Course. The approach to the green must be played over a grassy chasm.

>> **The par-4 2nd** After a stout opening hole, the Vineuil's 2nd is a much more gentle affair with a graceful right-to-left curve and an attractive approach to a slightly raised green.

Clubhouse

△ **The par-4 15th and clubhouse** The Vineuil Course has an unusual layout, which approaches the clubhouse at the 15th. It then makes a final loop of three holes and returns to the clubhouse. Five bunkers defend the 15th.

The par-4 7th The 7th is a fine par 4. Severe bunkering in front of and to the right side of the green is the key feature.

COURSE CARD

Hole	Meters	Par	Hole	Meters	Par
1	407	4	10	422	4
2	339	4	11	451	3
3	158	3	12	196	5
4	338	4	13	568	4
5	389	4	14	194	4
6	186	3	15	391	4
7	396	4	16	447	4
8	561	5	17	530	3
9	476	5	18	406	4
Out	3,250	36	In	3,605	35

Total 6,855m, par 71

The par-4 14th Le Vineuil's mighty six-hole finishing stretch begins with the very exacting 13th. The long, downhill 14th is followed by two strong par 4s, a formidable par 3, and the gigantic par-4 18th.

The par-4 15th The terrain is very dramatic at the 14th and 15th holes of the Vineuil Course. This view down a valley is taken from the elevated tee at the 15th hole.

Saint Nom-la-Bretèche

COMPOSITE COURSE, SAINT NOM-LA-BRETÈCHE, FRANCE

To the west of Paris, laid out in gently rolling grounds that once belonged to the Château of Versailles, Saint Nom-la-Bretèche is one of the finest golf facilities in Europe. Holes from two courses are used for the championship Composite Course.

⌃ **Well-defended greens** Some of the putting surfaces—such as the 5th, 7th, and 11th on the Composite Course—are cleverly guarded by sand, encroaching trees, and water.

First-rate layouts

Saint Nom-La-Bretèche Golf Club opened in 1959 with two excellent 18-hole courses—the Red and the Blue. Both layouts were designed by British architect Fred Hawtree. When the Trophée Lancôme is played here, 11 holes from the Red and 7 from the Blue are amalgamated to form a par-71 championship course.

Celebrity status

The club's first big event was the Canada Cup in 1963, which was won by the US team of Arnold Palmer and Jack Nicklaus. The French Open was played here in 1965 and 1969. However, it has been the Trophée Lancôme—an invitational tournament played here since 1970—that has put the club on the golfing world map. Attracting high-caliber fields, the event has been won by such legends as Tony Jacklin, Gary Player, and Seve Ballesteros.

⊳⊳ **The par-4 5th** The 5th fairway of the Composite Course, like many others at Saint Nom-la-Bretèche, is lined with mature trees.

⊲⊲ **The par-3 7th** The short 7th is a very enticing but potentially perilous hole. A water hazard guards the left side of the green and swallows many wayward shots.

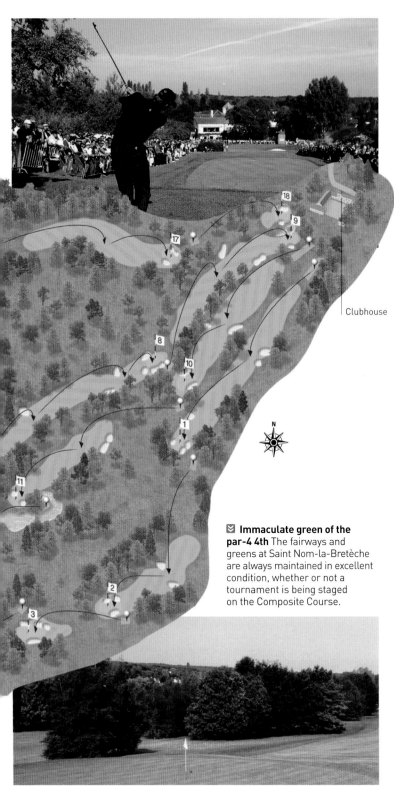

The par-3 18th A strong par 3 provides a dramatic conclusion to a round on the Composite Course. The outcome of the prestigious Trophée Lancôme has often been determined here.

Clubhouse

The clubhouse An attractive practice putting green lies right in front of the renovated 17th-century clubhouse.

Immaculate green of the par-4 4th The fairways and greens at Saint Nom-la-Bretèche are always maintained in excellent condition, whether or not a tournament is being staged on the Composite Course.

COURSE CARD

Hole	Meters	Par	Hole	Meters	Par
1	456	4	10	364	4
2	399	4	11	417	4
3	207	3	12	189	3
4	459	4	13	408	4
5	369	4	14	467	4
6	522	5	15	438	4
7	153	3	16	541	5
8	509	5	17	422	4
9	374	4	18	209	3
Out	3,448	36	In	3,455	35

Total 6,903m, par 71

FRANCE

Although the French golf club was founded in the mid-19th century, and some of the best courses in Europe were built in and around Paris in the 1920s and 1930s, it is only in the last 20 years that golf has become widely popular. The number of French courses has tripled and there are currently almost 500 of them—a similar number to Scotland.

Seignosse

The Aquitaine region is celebrated for the quality of its golf courses. Approximately a 45-minute drive north of Biarritz—an extremely stylish town that just happens to be twinned with Augusta in the US—is Seignosse, one of the finest layouts in Europe. The course has an enviable setting, located deep in a mature pine forest, yet also close to the sea. Sandy underfoot and undulating, the terrain is ideal for golf. Fairways weave their way in and out of the forest, culminating on greens that are typically fast and contoured. Among the best holes at Seignosse are the varied collection of par threes and the exhilarating par-3 18th hole with its tee sited fully 55 yards (50m) above the level of the fairway.

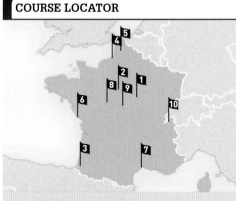

COURSE LOCATOR

1. **Chantilly**, Chantilly
2. **Saint Nom-La-Bretèche**, Versailles
3. **Seignosse**, Seignosse
4. **Le Touquet**, Le Touquet
5. **Hardelot**, Neufchatel-Hardelot
6. **Paris International**, Baillet en France
7. **Grande Motte**, Montpellier
8. **Golf National**, Guyancourt
9. **Les Bordes**, St. Laurent-Nouan
10. **Evian**, Evian-les-Bains

» **Thomas Levet** One of France's leading players, Levet was runner-up to Ernie Els in the 2002 British Open, and played in the 2004 Ryder Cup.

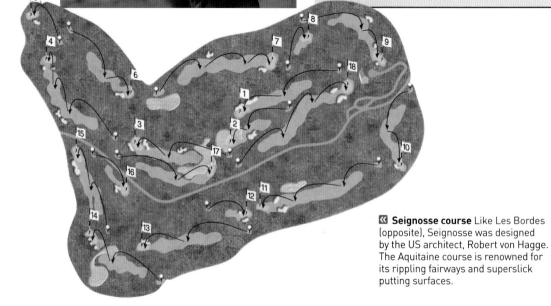

« **Seignosse course** Like Les Bordes (opposite), Seignosse was designed by the US architect, Robert von Hagge. The Aquitaine course is renowned for its rippling fairways and superslick putting surfaces.

Les Bordes

Enjoying a quiet, almost hidden location on the edge of the Loire Valley, Les Bordes is approximately 19 miles (30km) southwest of Orleans. The sense of isolation begins the instant you enter the grounds—the entrance passes through the ancient hunting ground of a medieval forest. Aside from golfers, the area's only residents are deer, wild boar, and an array of birdlife. Les Bordes was created by the visionary businessman and landowner Baron von Bic—the inventor of Bic pens—and the US architect Robert von Hagge, who designed the course. Always pristinely maintained, water is the dominant feature of the layout. The site has very few major changes in elevation, so the course twists and turns rather than tumbles, as it flows gracefully from tee to green to tee.

The par-4 1st at Les Bordes There is no gentle breaking in at Les Bordes—the degree of challenge is apparent from the outset with the 1st green almost encircled by a sea of sand.

Premier course Les Bordes is rated the number one golf course in France by the authoritative *Peugeot Golf Guide*.

Water hazards Built in a marshy environment and featuring water hazards on no fewer than 12 of the 18 holes, Les Bordes has been described as a "floating golf course."

Le Golf National

The Albatros Course at Le Golf National near Paris is the regular home of the French Open and is unquestionably one of the country's strongest course layouts. Its successful creation also represents a remarkable feat of engineering. Prior to its transformation during the late 1980s, the site was a vast, flat, featureless industrial wasteland. It is now far from flat and anything but dull. Roller-coasting, treeless, and exposed to the wind, British links-style golf meets US stadium golf head on. The Albatros Course is an extraordinary

cross between the Old Course at St. Andrews (*see* pp.296–7) and the TPC at Sawgrass (*see* pp.244–5). Le Golf National staged its first French Open in 1991; the tournament was won by Argentine Eduardo Romero, and he has been followed by an array of international champions.

French players

While France lacks a modern champion, recent years have seen French golfers—led by Thomas Levet, Jean Van de Velde, Marie Laure de Lorenzi, and Patricia Lebouc—become increasingly

The Albatros course
This aerial view of the spectacular Albatros Course was taken during a recent French Open championship that was held there.

successful. The most famous French golfer is probably Catherine Lacoste, the first amateur to win the Women's US Open in 1967.

Evian

Occasionally, a golf course is set in such beautiful surroundings that the degree of golfing challenge becomes almost irrelevant: the unique spa resort of the Royal Club Evian is a prime example. Situated close to Mont Blanc on the French shores of Lake Geneva, Evian has an understated elegance and an almost fairy-tale ambience. The century-old course was redesigned by Cabell Robinson in 1990. It has hosted the prestigious Evian Masters Tournament—a Major event on the Women's European Tour—since 1994.

» **Jean Van de Velde** In September 1999, Jean Van de Velde became the first Frenchman to play in the Ryder Cup when he qualified for the European team. Two months prior to this, Van de Velde had unfortunately squandered a two-shot lead at the final hole of the British Open at Carnoustie, losing the resulting playoff to Scotsman Paul Lawrie.

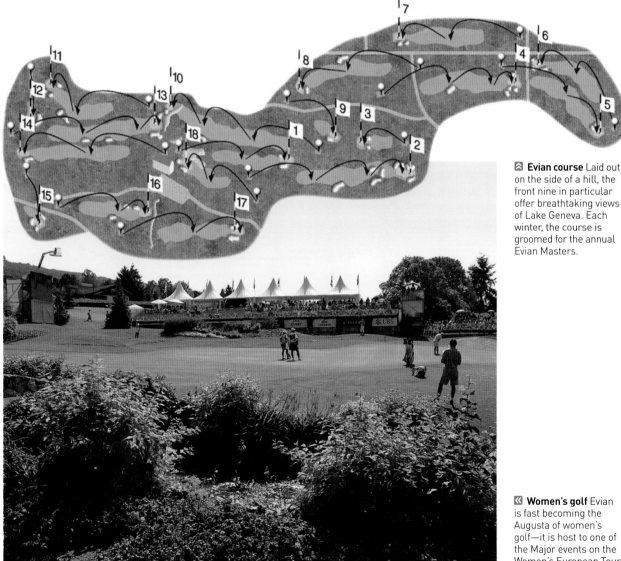

⌂ **Evian course** Laid out on the side of a hill, the front nine in particular offer breathtaking views of Lake Geneva. Each winter, the course is groomed for the annual Evian Masters.

« **Women's golf** Evian is fast becoming the Augusta of women's golf—it is host to one of the Major events on the Women's European Tour.

Club Zur Vahr

GARLSTEDT, BREMEN, GERMANY

Hewn from a dense pine forest near Bremen in the 1960s by leading German architect Dr Bernhard von Limburger, Club Zur Vahr's course at Garlstedt has staged three German Opens and is regularly rated among the country's top five courses.

A mighty challenge

Bernhard von Limburger—one of Europe's most celebrated golf course designers—was given an instruction by Club Zur Vahr to create a genuine championship test. The club owners wanted even the very finest players in Europe to find their course long and difficult. The site selected was well suited to such a task. Much of the countryside at Garlstedt comprises rolling woodland, and von Limburger essentially carved out the course from the forest. Most of the fairways on his layout are narrow, and several are shaped as doglegs. There are not many bunkers, but the penalty for inaccuracy is severe, because the forest sucks up stray golf balls. With many of the holes also being long—there are six par 5s—Club Zur Vahr rewards golfers who can hit the ball straight and far.

German Opens

Club Zur Vahr was selected to host its first German Open in 1971. The event attracted competitors from more than 20 countries and was won by the UK's Neil Coles. The tournament returned in 1975, this time the title going to Coles's Ryder Cup team-mate Maurice Bembridge. Club Zur Vahr hosted the German Open for a third time in 1985, when Bernhard Langer battled some horrendous weather to gain a popular home victory.

 The clubhouse
Situated immediately behind the 18th green and framed by attractive tall pine trees, Club Zur Vahr's clubhouse is renowned for its facilities and welcoming atmosphere.

Clubhouse

GREAT ROUNDS

Bernhard Langer: 1985 German Open
In the 1980s, Langer won four German Opens, including the 1985 championship at Club Zur Vahr. Torrential rain reduced the event to three rounds, but the German spectators had to cheer when their golfing hero lifted the coveted trophy.

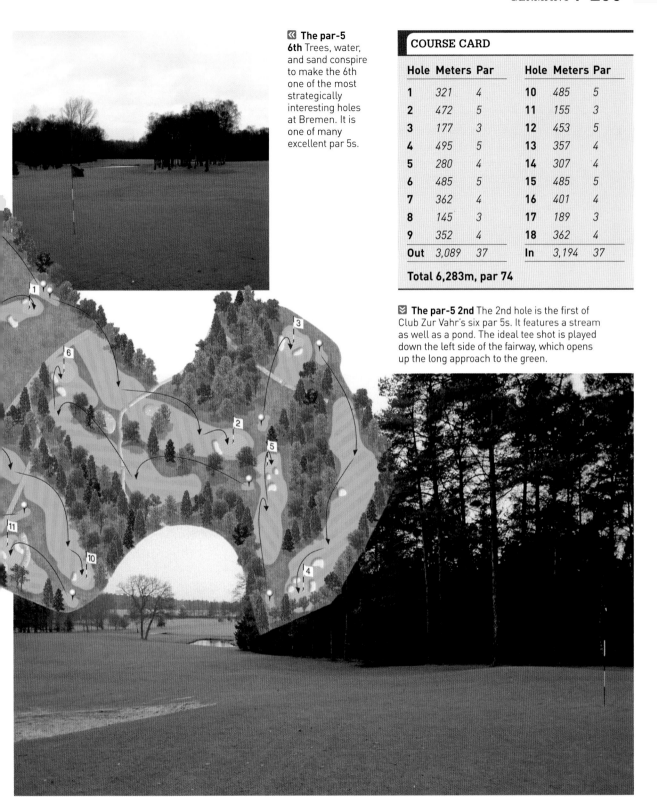

◄◄ **The par-5 6th** Trees, water, and sand conspire to make the 6th one of the most strategically interesting holes at Bremen. It is one of many excellent par 5s.

COURSE CARD

Hole	Meters	Par		Hole	Meters	Par
1	321	4		10	485	5
2	472	5		11	155	3
3	177	3		12	453	5
4	495	5		13	357	4
5	280	4		14	307	4
6	485	5		15	485	5
7	362	4		16	401	4
8	145	3		17	189	3
9	352	4		18	362	4
Out	3,089	37		In	3,194	37

Total 6,283m, par 74

▼ **The par-5 2nd** The 2nd hole is the first of Club Zur Vahr's six par 5s. It features a stream as well as a pond. The ideal tee shot is played down the left side of the fairway, which opens up the long approach to the green.

Sporting Club Berlin

NICK FALDO CHAMPIONSHIP COURSE, BAD SAAROW, GERMANY

The Faldo course at Sporting Club Berlin looks remarkably like a well-groomed Scottish links course. Designed in 1996 by the British golfer Nick Faldo, it borrows ideas from Muirfield (*see* pp.280–1), where he had won the Open.

Award-winning layout

Sporting Club Berlin is located in the town of Bad Saarow on Lake Scharmützelsee, an hour-and-a-half's drive southeast of Berlin. In November 1997, less than 18 months after the Faldo course opened, *Golf World* magazine voted it the Best New Course in Continental Europe and Best Course in Germany. The following summer, Sporting Club Berlin staged the German Open. When this proved a resounding success, the club was selected to host the 2000 World Amateur Team Championships.

The Scottish look

The use of large pot bunkers and the encouragement of brown-tinted native fescue roughs give Scottish-style definition to the fairways. As at Muirfield, trees serve as occasional boundaries. In keeping with the spirit of links golf, the only water hazard is a Scottish-style burn (stream), which introduces itself on the 1st hole. The wind is not quite as fierce as in Scotland, but Sporting Club Berlin still presents a formidable test of golf.

⏏ **The par-4 15th** One of the best holes at Sporting Club Berlin is the short 15th. Curving gently from left to right, its fairway is studded with an array of pot bunkers.

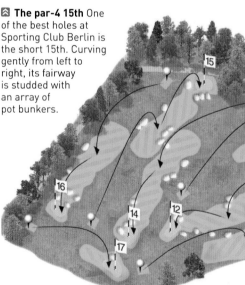

COURSE CARD

Hole	Metres	Par	Hole	Metres	Par
1	498	5	10	509	5
2	377	4	11	522	5
3	170	3	12	342	4
4	347	4	13	213	3
5	197	3	14	363	4
6	483	5	15	351	4
7	398	4	16	326	4
8	346	4	17	179	3
9	408	4	18	416	4
Out	*3,224*	*36*	**In**	*3,221*	*36*

Total 6,445m, par 72

⏏ **A hint of Scotland in Germany** This view of the links-styled Faldo course could be mistaken for Muirfield in Scotland, with its similar colors, contours, bunkering, and foliage.

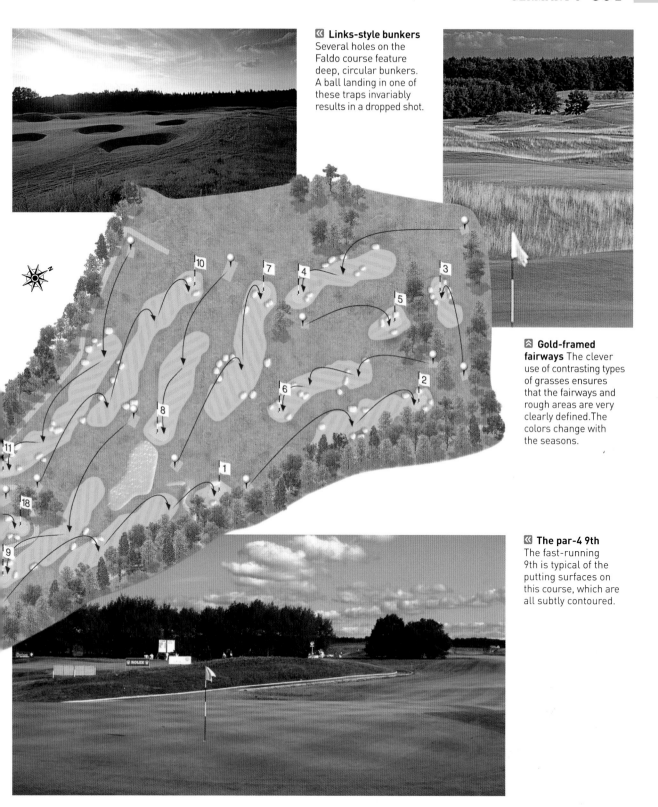

Links-style bunkers
Several holes on the Faldo course feature deep, circular bunkers. A ball landing in one of these traps invariably results in a dropped shot.

Gold-framed fairways The clever use of contrasting types of grasses ensures that the fairways and rough areas are very clearly defined. The colors change with the seasons.

The par-4 9th
The fast-running 9th is typical of the putting surfaces on this course, which are all subtly contoured.

GERMANY

For much of the 20th century, golf was viewed as an elitist sport in Germany. This image has now changed, thanks to the success and modest disposition of Bernhard Langer, Europe's 2004 Ryder Cup captain. The country's best courses are still relatively uncrowded and visiting golfers should find most clubs welcoming and accommodating.

⌂ Bernhard Langer
The proudest moment of the greatest golfer in Germany, Captain Langer with the Ryder Cup trophy in September 2004.

Feldafing

Established in 1926, Feldafing in Bavaria is one of Germany's oldest golf courses, and also one of its most splendidly situated. The course has an idyllic location nestling peacefully beside Lake Starnberg. The surrounding area was once the playground of Bavarian nobility—the castle of Maximilian II stands proudly on the edge of the course. Mature trees frame many of the fairways, and with nearby mountains providing a striking backdrop, it is difficult to believe that Munich is less than 25 miles (40km) away. By modern standards, Feldafing is a fairly short course and the fairways are quite narrow. The layout includes many challenging holes and, as many unsuspecting visitors can testify, each of the par threes is a potential card-wrecker.

» Alex Cejka Second to Bernhard Langer, Alex Cejka is Germany's most successful golfer. He has won several titles on the European Tour—including the Volvo Masters.

COURSE LOCATOR

#	Club	Location
1	**Sporting Club Berlin**, Bad Saarow
2	**Club Zur Vahr**, Garlstedt
3	**Falkenstein**, Hamburg
4	**Feldafing**, Feldafing
5	**Beuerberg**, Beuerberg
6	**Frankfurter**, Frankfurt
7	**Hubbelrath**, Düsseldorf
8	**St Dionys**, St Dionys
9	**Wittelsbacher**, Neuberg
10	**Stuttgarter**, Mönsheim

» Feldafing course
A hilly course that has been cleverly fitted into a small area, Feldafing reaches the edge of Lake Starnberg on the 2nd hole.

Falkenstein

Prior to the opening of Sporting Club Berlin in 1996, Falkenstein was generally acknowledged to be the finest course in Germany. Officially known as the Hamburger Golf Club, it was designed in the late 1920s by a team of British architects. The project lent itself to their talents as the terrain is similar to England's southern counties, where leading golf architect Harry Colt produced some of his finest work. Dotted with heather, pines, and silver birch trees, Falkenstein is a delight to play at any time of year.

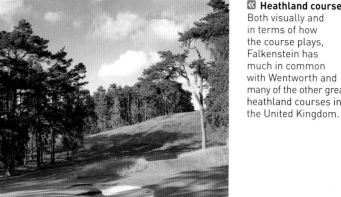

≪ Heathland course Both visually and in terms of how the course plays, Falkenstein has much in common with Wentworth and many of the other great heathland courses in the United Kingdom.

≪ Falkenstein course After WWII, the course was slightly modified by Bernhard von Limburger.

≪ Bunkers The style of the bunkers exemplifies the course's 1920s "classic" pedigree.

Alpine golf Under snow during the winter, the beautifully landscaped course at Seefeld-Wildmoos becomes a riot of color in summer. It is not Austria's most difficult course, but it is still enjoyable.

AUSTRIA/SWITZERLAND

With winter sports dominating for much of the year, the golf season is short in Austria and Switzerland. On a fine summer's day, however, there are few more enjoyable places in the world to play golf. There are around 60 courses in Switzerland and twice that number in Austria, the majority of which are set in spectacular surroundings.

Seefeld-Wildmoos

Situated 4,265ft (1,300m) above sea level and overlooked by the impressive Hohe Munde mountain, this is alpine golf at its best. Popularly shortened to Seefeld, the course was designed in the late 1960s by the US architect Donald Harradine, and is widely acknowledged to be one of the best in Austria. The fairways are framed by a dazzling array of colors as they pass over undulating terrain. A famous ski resort, Seefeld is located midway between Innsbruck and Garmisch.

Seefeld-Wildmoos course Plunging dramatically downhill, the par-3 9th is especially exhilarating.

Hohe Munde The majestic peak of Hohe Munde provides a striking backdrop to the golf course.

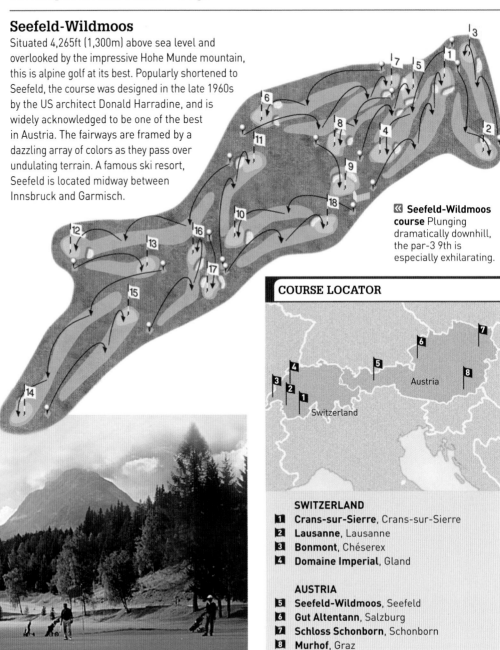

COURSE LOCATOR

Switzerland

Austria

SWITZERLAND
1 **Crans-sur-Sierre**, Crans-sur-Sierre
2 **Lausanne**, Lausanne
3 **Bonmont**, Chéserex
4 **Domaine Imperial**, Gland

AUSTRIA
5 **Seefeld-Wildmoos**, Seefeld
6 **Gut Altentann**, Salzburg
7 **Schloss Schonborn**, Schonborn
8 **Murhof**, Graz

Crans-sur-Sierre

This is the most famous of the Swiss golf clubs, thanks in large part to its hosting of the annual European Masters Tournament, one of the leading events on the PGA European Tour. The club is also one of the country's oldest, having been established in the mid-1920s. Laid out on a plateau in the Berner Alps at approximately 5,000ft (1,500m), the course enjoys breathtaking 360-degree views. Crans-sur-Sierre was once regarded as a fairly easy course but it was subsequently "toughened up" and slightly re-designed by Seve Ballesteros.

⏶ **Crans-sur-Sierre course** Seve Ballesteros's 1999 redesign lengthened the course and made the putting surfaces more challenging.

⏵ **Golf in the mountains** The Swiss Alps—including Mont Blanc—are visible in all their glory from the fairways at Crans-sur-Sierre.

⏴ **The 18th green** The venue for the European Masters since its inception, many great rounds have concluded on this green. In 1993, Jamie Spence (England) won the tournament after achieving a stunning 60 in the final round.

Kennemer

ZANDVOORT, HOLLAND

Designed by the British architect Harry Colt, and located in duneland on the Dutch coast near Zandvoort, Kennemer is regarded by many critics as the finest traditional links course in Continental Europe.

A Dutch masterpiece

Founded in 1910, the club originally played on a 9-hole inland course before moving to the coast, where Harry Colt completed its championship links in 1927. Colt's masterly layout meanders and tumbles through natural valleys framed by impressive sandhills. As at two other of Colt's great links, Scotland's Muirfield (see pp.280–1) and Ireland's Royal Portrush (see pp.274–5), the bunkers are deep and the rough is unfriendly. When the wind blows off the sea, Kennemer is a formidable test of golfing skill.

The Dutch Open

Kennemer has hosted numerous amateur and professional tournaments, including several Dutch Opens. Often staged in the week after the British Open, the Dutch Open regularly attracts a strong international field. Among past winners of the event at Kennemer are Spain's two finest golfers: Seve Ballesteros, who triumphed in 1976, and José Maria Olazabal, who won in 1989.

Clubhouse

⌃ **The clubhouse**
Kennemer has one of the finest and most distinctive clubhouses in Europe. A magnificent structure with a modern-style thatched roof, the building was designed by the acclaimed Dutch architect A. P. Smits.

» **The par-4 9th**
Kennemer's front nine concludes with a fairly difficult par 4. A left-to-right turning dogleg, its crumpled fairway is framed by large sand dunes.

GREAT ROUNDS

José Maria Olazabal: 1989 Dutch Open
Kennemer saw a vintage performance from the Spanish golfer José Maria Olazabal in the 1989 Open. He scored 67-66-68 in his first three rounds, slipped to a 76 on a very windy final day, but claimed the title when he won a sudden death playoff against Britons Ronan Rafferty and Roger Chapman.

⌃ **Thick rough** At Kennemer, the rough is typically thick and invariably difficult to recover from. Even if you can avoid the course's many deep bunkers, a good score is only possible if you stick to the fairways and greens.

◀ **The par-4 1st** The 1st at Kennemer is a well-bunkered two-shot hole that introduces the essential links character of the course. Achieving a par 4 here is a good start.

COURSE CARD

Hole	Meters	Par	Hole	Meters	Par
1	423	4	10	339	4
2	156	3	11	442	4
3	382	5	12	508	5
4	400	4	13	348	4
5	320	4	14	372	4
6	455	5	15	157	3
7	342	4	16	469	5
8	173	3	17	166	3
9	390	4	18	372	4
Out	**3,041**	**36**	**In**	**3,173**	**36**

Total 6,214m, par 72

Royal Zoute

KNOKKE HEIST, NEAR BRUGES, BELGIUM

Golf has been played at Knokke on the northern coast of Belgium since the late 19th century. A formal club was established in 1909, and patronage was bestowed by the king of Belgium in 1925.

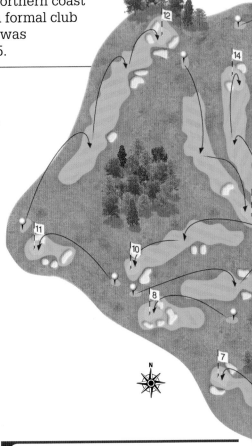

Belgium's best course

Royal Zoute, as the club became known, can be described as a links course, although it has more trees than a typical British links. Its terrain is sandy throughout, and sea breezes have a great effect. The authoritative *Peugeot Golf Guide* ranks the course as the best in Belgium. Despite its quality, however, Royal Zoute was little known outside of Belgium until the early 1990s, when it staged three successive Opens.

The Belgian Opens

The Belgian Opens of 1992–4 were a tremendous success. High-quality fields were assembled, and on each occasion Royal Zoute hosted a tournament that was won by a leading European player. Spain's Miguel Jimenez triumphed in 1992. The following year, Darren Clarke of Northern Ireland edged out the Fijian Vijay Singh and then beat England's Nick Faldo—the world number one at the time—by two strokes. In 1994, however, Faldo was victorious when he defeated the Swedish golfer Joakim Haeggman in a sudden death playoff.

⌃ **The clubhouse** As befits a championship course with royal patronage, the clubhouse at Royal Zoute is an elegant building with an imposing entrance.

⌃ **Tree-lined fairways** Some of Royal Zoute's fairways are framed by tall pine trees, which provide protection from the wind. This is quite unusual on a links course, where players are usually at the mercy of the elements.

COURSE CARD

Hole	Meters	Par		Hole	Meters	Par
1	384	4		10	351	4
2	361	4		11	191	3
3	135	3		12	486	5
4	346	4		13	408	4
5	435	5		14	329	4
6	380	4		15	446	5
7	353	4		16	167	3
8	189	3		17	499	5
9	368	4		18	350	4
Out	**2,951**	**35**		**In**	**3,227**	**37**

Total 6,178m, par 72

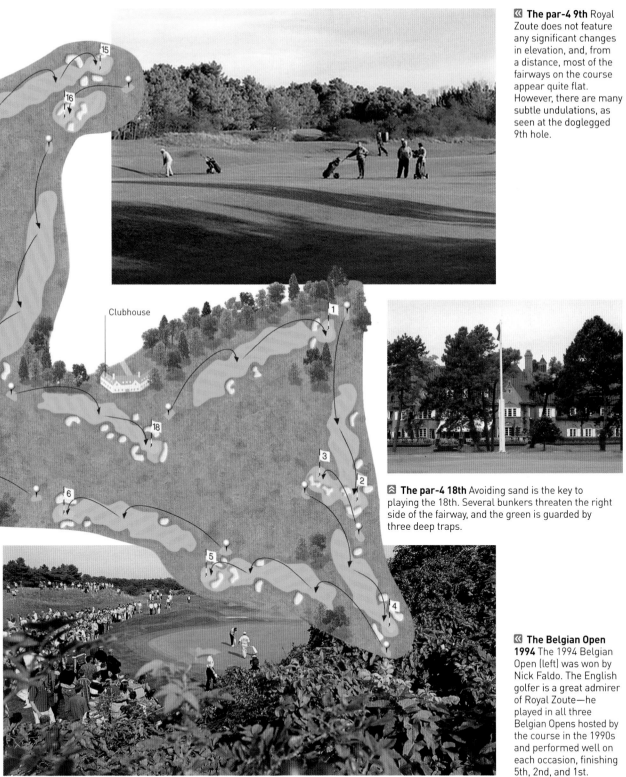

The par-4 9th Royal Zoute does not feature any significant changes in elevation, and, from a distance, most of the fairways on the course appear quite flat. However, there are many subtle undulations, as seen at the doglegged 9th hole.

Clubhouse

The par-4 18th Avoiding sand is the key to playing the 18th. Several bunkers threaten the right side of the fairway, and the green is guarded by three deep traps.

The Belgian Open 1994 The 1994 Belgian Open (left) was won by Nick Faldo. The English golfer is a great admirer of Royal Zoute—he played in all three Belgian Opens hosted by the course in the 1990s and performed well on each occasion, finishing 5th, 2nd, and 1st.

BELGIUM/HOLLAND

Without doubt, some of the finest courses in Europe are to be found in Belgium and Holland. Belgium has no fewer than 10 "Royal" golf clubs, due to the avid interest taken in the game by the country's royal family, while in Kennemer, Noordwijkse, and Haagsche, Holland has a triumvirate of links courses to rival the very best in Britain or Ireland.

Royal Belgique

Almost everything impresses the first-time visitor to Royal Belgique. Located to the east of Brussels at Tervuren, the course is situated within the grounds of the 18th-century Château of Ravenstein, which now serves as an elegant clubhouse. It was designed almost a century ago by Tom Simpson, and is fairly short by modern standards. Always beautifully maintained, perhaps the most striking aspect of Ravenstein—as many refer to the course—is the wealth and variety of trees that frame the fairways.

⊠ **Royal Belgique course** Although too short for a Major championship, the course is more than sufficiently challenging for amateur golfers.

COURSE LOCATOR

HOLLAND

1 **Noordwijkse**, Noordwijkse
2 **Kennemer**, Zandvoort
3 **Haagsche**, Wassenaar
4 **Hilversumsche**, Hilversum
5 **Utrechtse de Pan**, Utrecht

BELGIUM

6 **Royal Zoute**, Knokke-Heist
7 **Royal Antwerp**, Antwerp
8 **Royal Belgique**, Tervuren
9 **Royal Waterloo**, Ohain
10 **Royal Club des Fagnes**, Spa

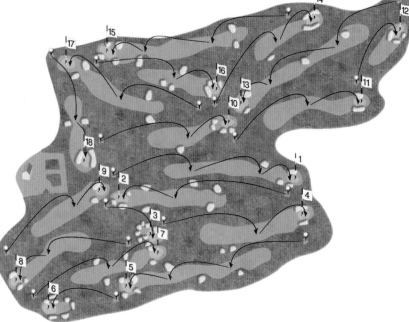

» **Nicolas Colsaerts** Born in 1982, Belgian Colsaerts is a world-class golfer. He won the Volvo World Match Play Championship in 2012 and was the first Belgian to play in the Ryder Cup.

Noordwijkse

Established in 1915, it was only in 1972 that Noordwijkse Golf Club completed a move to its present coastal site. It is a magnificent course, with 13 of the 18 holes tumbling through spectacular sand dunes and the remainder laid out in an attractive forest. The Dutch Open has been held at Noordwijkse on several occasions and winners include such illustrious players as Seve Ballesteros, Payne Stewart, and Bernhard Langer.

Dutch and Belgian players

It has been suggested by Dutch historians that golf may have been invented in Holland (*see* p.8)—a claim vehemently denied by the Scots—but there has never been a Dutch champion. There is no obvious reason for this, especially given the quality of courses in Holland and the success of South African players of Dutch descent. Belgium's golfers have fared a little better. The country's most famous golfer was Flory van Donck, who won several European titles—including five Belgian Opens—between 1935 and 1955.

A classic yet modern links course Although it has a timeless feel and the look of a traditional Scottish links course, Noordwijkse is relatively new. Designed by Frank Pennink, it is rated one of the best championship courses in continental Europe.

The clubhouse The course is laid out in two loops of nine with both the 9th and 18th greens situated close to the clubhouse. Perched on a hill, the views across the links from within the building are spectacular.

Florence Descampe Recognized as Belgium's most successful female player, Florence Descampe has won tournaments on both sides of the Atlantic and represented Europe in the women's Solheim Cup (*see* p.214).

Pevero

PORTO CERVO, COSTA SMERALDA, SARDINIA, ITALY

In the 1960s, the famously wealthy Aga Khan started to develop part of Sardinia's Costa Smeralda into a resort, and invited the acclaimed US architect Robert Trent Jones to design a golf course. Pevero, built in 1971, is the breathtaking result of their collaboration.

Italian opulence

Of the hundreds of courses that Robert Trent Jones has designed around the world, Pevero—located in one of the most opulent resort areas in Europe—is probably the most classy and scenic. It is also said to be one of the architect's favorites. The terrain is hilly and quite rocky in parts; dwarf pine trees and wild flowers are interlaced with native scrub and gorse bushes. The mountains of Corsica are visible on the horizon—a fitting backdrop to the palatial yachts cruising from bay to bay.

⌃ **The par-4 4th** Played from an elevated tee with commanding views of the coast, the course plunges into a beautiful valley at the celebrated 4th.

An architect's masterpiece

The golf course does not impose itself on the landscape; rather it melds seamlessly into it. Strong and strategically interesting holes can be found throughout the round. The most talked-about sequence, however, starts with the downhill tee shot at the 4th (where the panoramic views are magnificent), and continues until the golfer holes out on the dramatically sited lakeside green at the 7th.

⌄ **The par-4 6th** Accuracy is everything at the short, narrow 6th, where a lake threatens both the tee shot and the approach.

⌃ **The par-5 9th** One of the best opportunities to achieve a rare birdie at Pevero occurs at the relatively short par-5 9th.

COURSE CARD

Hole	Meters	Par	Hole	Meters	Par
1	376	4	10	169	3
2	350	4	11	485	5
3	474	5	12	351	4
4	351	4	13	354	4
5	175	3	14	170	3
6	305	4	15	436	5
7	166	3	16	262	4
8	339	4	17	132	3
9	454	5	18	489	5
Out	2,990	36	**In**	2,848	36

Total 5,838m, par 72

≪ Captivating views
Robert Trent Jones sited the tees and greens carefully at Pevero to offer panoramic views over the bays on either side of the course. This splendid view is from the 10th tee.

≪ The clubhouse
The prestigious clubhouse at Pevero blends harmoniously into its immediate surroundings. Balconies and a terrace overlook the bay.

⌃ The par-3 10th The second nine-hole loop starts with a well-bunkered, downhill par 3, which, typical of many holes at Pevero, is immensely scenic. It sets the tone for a memorable back nine.

Clubhouse

ITALY

Golf is not a major sport in Italy, but the quality of Italian courses is undeniable. In the far north, deep in the land of pristine lakes and snow-capped peaks, there are several extremely scenic courses. Rome is renowned for mature parkland designs, and Sardinia has a fine 18-hole course at Is Molas and a spectacular layout at Pevero (*see* pp.312–13).

Olgiata

Located to the northwest of Rome, Olgiata is a classic parkland golf course. Designed by the British architect C.K. Cotton and opened in 1961, Olgiata quickly established itself as one of the country's best tournament venues. The Eisenhower Trophy (now known as the World Amateur Team Championship) was contested here in 1964 and four years later the World Cup was staged—Al Balding sealed a victory for Canada when he eagled the penultimate hole.

There is a grand-scale feel to Olgiata—rolling, boulevardlike fairways are framed by mature oaks and elm trees, and usually lead to large greens defended by deep bunkers. There is a strong finish to the layout with the short 16th hole often cited as one of Italy's finest par-3 holes.

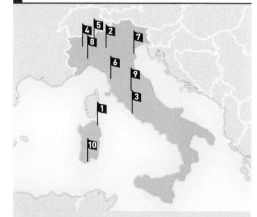

COURSE LOCATOR

1 **Pevero**, Porto Cervo
2 **Villa d'Este**, Montorfano
3 **Olgiata**, Largo Olgiata
4 **Biella le Betulle**, Biella
5 **Castleconturbia**, Agrate Conturbia
6 **Castelalfi**, Montaione
7 **Albarella**, Isolade Albarella
8 **Monticello**, Cassina Rizzardi
9 **Ugolino**, Grassina
10 **Is Molas**, Pula

⊠ **Olgiata course** There are, in fact, 27 holes at Olgiata. This map shows the layout of the club's acclaimed Championship 18.

⊠ **Costantino Rocca** Costantino Rocca, pictured left, is one of the few Italians to have played in the Ryder Cup. In the 1997 match he beat Tiger Woods.

⌃ **A classic parkland challenge** The expansive, sweeping nature of the fairways at Olgiata is clear as the golfer pitches to a large green.

Villa d'Este

Approximately 19 miles (30km) north of Milan, close to Lake Como and adjacent to the shores of Lake Montorfano, is the magnificent golf course of Villa d'Este. Designed in the 1920s by Peter Gannon, it is widely regarded to be one of the top five courses in Italy and has been rated among the top 30 courses in Europe by *Golf World* magazine. Always beautifully maintained, the fairways wend their way around a dense forest of pines, chestnuts, and birch trees. Although it once regularly hosted the Italian Open, Villa d'Este is a little short by modern tournament standards, yet it is an ideal length (and certainly sufficiently challenging) for most golfers.

⌃ The clubhouse Very few clubs in Europe can boast so splendid a clubhouse as Villa d'Este. The building overlooks one of Italy's finest and most attractive courses.

》 Villa d'Este course From 1928 to 1972, Villa d'Este staged 12 Italian Opens. Among the most famous winners were the Australian Peter Thomson and the Belgian Flory van Donck.

《 A golfing jewel Villa d'Este has an idyllic setting beside Lake Montorfano. The course is framed by beautiful trees and backed by the foothills of the Alps—a glorious location for a game.

Praia D'El Rey

PENICHE, ÒBIDOS, PORTUGAL

Situated near the medieval fortress town of Òbidos, about an hour's drive north of Lisbon, Praia D'El Rey is a relative newcomer to Portugal's golf scene. The course, designed by US architect Cabell Robinson in 1997, is the centerpiece of a luxury five-star resort.

Robinson's finest

Praia D'El Rey nestles in an attractive pine forest near Òbidos lagoon, overlooking a long stretch of beautiful beach and also the Berlengas island nature reserve. The architect Cabell Robinson—designer of many golf courses in southern Europe—described his appointment as course designer as "the opportunity of a lifetime." He certainly rose to the occasion, because Praia D'El Rey has been hailed as Robinson's greatest creation and also as one of Europe's outstanding layouts. In 2003, when the course was just six years old, *Golf World* magazine ranked it 13th best in the whole of Continental Europe.

A course of contrasts

A key reason for Praia D'El Rey's popularity is that it offers the golfer two very contrasting experiences. Several of the holes on the front nine have been carved out of the pine forest, which necessitates a precise game of "target golf."

The second nine holes are laid out over terrain that is closer to the sea and generally plays more like a links course. Between the 12th and 15th, the course runs in dramatic fashion right alongside the ocean and can be likened to Cypress Point in the US (*see* pp.226–7).

⌃ **The par-3 8th**
There is a combined woodland and parkland character to several holes on the front nine. The tee shot at the short 8th must fly across the corner of an attractively landscaped pond frequented by swans.

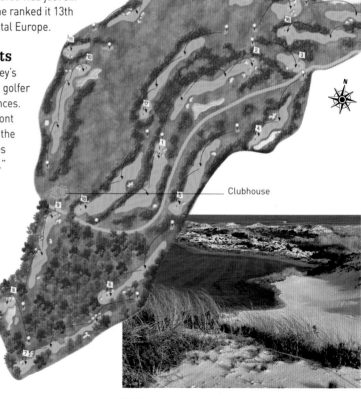

— Clubhouse

⌃ **The par-4 4th** Along with the 13th, 14th, and 15th holes, the 4th enjoys a spectacular setting that is often compared with the scenery of Cypress Point on California's Monterey Peninsula.

COURSE CARD					
Hole	Meters	Par	Hole	Meters	Par
1	385	4	10	480	5
2	463	5	11	183	3
3	167	3	12	362	4
4	304	4	13	300	4
5	441	4	14	150	3
6	361	4	15	399	4
7	519	5	16	427	4
8	168	3	17	570	5
9	393	4	18	395	4
Out	3,201	36	In	3,266	36
Total 6,467m, par 72					

San Lorenzo

QUINTA DO LAGO ESTATE, ALMANCIL, PORTUGAL

Renowned more for its natural beauty than its degree of difficulty, San Lorenzo has been described as the Queen of the Algarve. The golf course was completed in 1988 and quickly established its reputation as Portugal's premier 18-hole layout.

Magnetic appeal

The Algarve's spectacular coastline and wonderful year-round climate has made it Portugal's most popular region and the one with the greatest concentration of golf courses. Most players aspire to a round at San Lorenzo, which is located in a pine forest beside the Ria Formosa estuary on the edge of the Quinta do Lago estate.

Roller-coasting golf

After a fairly benign opening, the course steps up a gear as it heads toward the coast at the 5th. The views become spellbinding at the 6th, 7th, and 8th, which form a truly stunning, roller-coasterlike sequence. The back nine is generally more demanding, with the 12th being possibly the toughest hole on the course. Two of the finest challenges are left to the end: water threatens the left side of the 17th and 18th fairways, and practically encircles the 18th green. A dry finish is not always possible at San Lorenzo.

⌃ **Hazards at the par-5 8th** Though San Lorenzo is not a punishing course, the architect, Joseph Lee, used ample sand and water as defenses within his layout.

Sandbanks

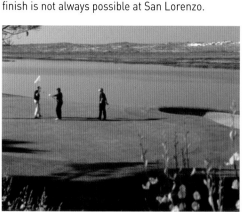

⌃ **The par-4 6th** The 6th green is sited beside the Ria Formosa estuary. Wildflowers and birdlife are among the attractions—and distractions—to golfers.

COURSE CARD

Hole	Meters	Par	Hole	Meters	Par
1	494	5	10	519	5
2	162	3	11	350	4
3	334	4	12	395	4
4	339	4	13	359	4
5	129	3	14	157	3
6	386	4	15	482	5
7	345	4	16	190	3
8	525	5	17	344	4
9	366	4	18	371	4
Out	*3,080*	*36*	**In**	*3,167*	*36*

Total 6,247m, par 72

PORTUGAL

Forty years ago there were very few golf courses in Portugal, yet today the country is beginning to challenge Spain as the favorite venue in Europe for golfing vacations. The Algarve is Portugal's version of the Costa del Sol—a golfing heartland with a superb sandy coastline—but there are also wonderful courses to the north, south, and west of Lisbon.

Penha Longa

The European design portfolio of Robert Trent Jones Jr. is not yet as extensive as that of his famous father (who produced such masterly courses as Valderrama in Spain and Pevero in Sardinia), but it is growing impressively. Penha Longa, which opened in 1993, is Jones Jr.'s first creation in Portugal and is already regarded as one of the country's top layouts. Europe's Tour pros were full of praise when the club hosted the Portuguese Open in 1994 and 1995.

Penha Longa is approximately 15 miles (25km) west of Lisbon, toward Cascais in the hills above Estoril. The area is beautiful and historic, with a stunning royal palace and 16th-century monastery nearby. Occupying undulating, heavily wooded terrain, the course offers spectacular views of the surrounding countryside. Typical of a Robert Trent Jones Jr. course, the layout features many water hazards and is expertly bunkered. Scoring well is not easy, yet very few golfers leave Penha Longa without looking forward to a return visit.

COURSE LOCATOR

1. **San Lorenzo**, Quinta do Lago estate
2. **Praia D'El Rey**, Óbidos
3. **Quinta do Lago**, Almancil
4. **Penina**, Portimão
5. **Palmares**, Lagos
6. **Penha Longa**, Sintra
7. **Troia**, Setubal
8. **Vila Sol**, Quarteira
9. **Vilamoura**, Vilamoura
10. **Estela**, Estela

» **Dramatic terrain** Bordered by trees and studded with elegantly sculpted bunkers, the fairways at Penha Longa twist and tumble through spectacular terrain. Most golfers find the challenge formidable but exhilarating.

⌃ **Water hazards** The remains of an ancient aqueduct provide a striking backdrop to the 6th and 7th holes at Penha Longa. Water hazards are a prominent and distinctive feature of the layout, and their presence on a hole will invariably dictate playing strategy.

Penina

The three-time British Open Champion Henry Cotton envisioned and largely designed Penina; he also made the course famous by living there for a period of time. Completed in 1966, Penina was the first course to open in the Algarve. Although it is now the focal point of a five-star resort, the course was formerly flat, featureless, and used for growing rice. The planting of thousands of trees transformed the site, and today Penina is one of the most attractive courses in the Algarve. It is also one of the most challenging, as proven by its selection to stage the 2004 Portuguese Open.

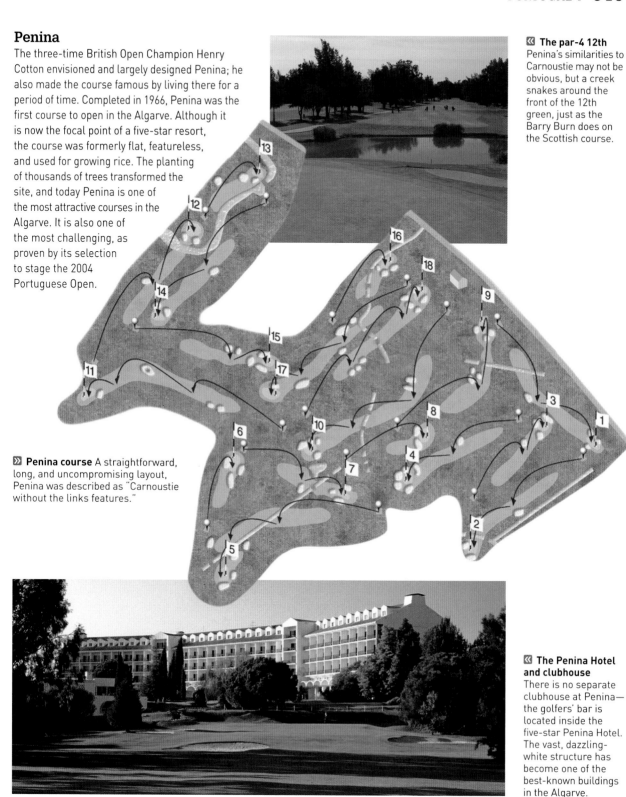

❮❮ The par-4 12th Penina's similarities to Carnoustie may not be obvious, but a creek snakes around the front of the 12th green, just as the Barry Burn does on the Scottish course.

❯❯ Penina course A straightforward, long, and uncompromising layout, Penina was described as "Carnoustie without the links features."

❮❮ The Penina Hotel and clubhouse There is no separate clubhouse at Penina—the golfers' bar is located inside the five-star Penina Hotel. The vast, dazzling-white structure has become one of the best-known buildings in the Algarve.

El Saler

EL SALER, VALENCIA, SPAIN

One of Europe's best and most extraordinary courses is to be found near Valencia on the east coast of Spain. El Saler is one of those courses that cannot decide whether it is a links or an inland course. What is indisputable, though, is that it offers a veritable feast of golf.

High quality

It is said that a measure of the quality of a course is its ability to encourage rather than resist superlative golf. This was certainly the case at El Saler in the 1984 Spanish Open, when Bernhard Langer compiled possibly the finest ever performance on the European Tour. Just a few months later, the German golfer claimed his first Major victory in the Masters.

Good design

Acclaimed Spanish architect Javier Arana built many of Spain's top golf courses, and he made imaginative use of some very contrasting terrain when he designed El Saler in 1967. Resplendent with emerald umbrella pines, parts of the course resemble great layouts on Portugal's Algarve coast. Yet where it hugs the shoreline, the course is more like a British links. And when the wind blows, those holes by the sea can be quite formidable.

Gulf of Valencia

☒ **Crowds at the par-4 8th** The Gulf of Valencia provides a striking backdrop to the 8th hole, shown here during the Seve Trophy of 2003. Major tournament golf is regularly played at El Saler.

☒ **The par-4 7th** El Saler has very sandy terrain. This is especially evident at the 7th, a hole that draws the golfer toward the ocean.

The par-3 17th One of the best holes at El Saler—indeed one of the finest holes in Spain—is the brilliantly bunkered 17th. It is a long par 3, which, like the two-shot 7th, is played directly toward the sea.

GREAT ROUNDS

Bernhard Langer: 1984 Spanish Open
Bernhard Langer produced the round of his life when capturing the 1984 Spanish Open at El Saler. His final-day 62 included an amazing 9 birdies in 11 holes from the 5th. This enabled him to win the championship, despite starting the day seven strokes behind the third-round leader.

Seve Ballesteros The great Spanish captain redesigned some of El Saler's holes.

The Seve Trophy at El Saler In 2003, the club hosted the Seve Trophy, a biennial match between the teams of Continental Europe and GB&I. The trophy is named in honor of Seve Ballesteros.

COURSE CARD

Hole	Meters	Par	Hole	Meters	Par
1	400	4	10	375	4
2	365	4	11	520	5
3	485	5	12	190	3
4	175	3	13	325	4
5	485	5	14	385	4
6	415	4	15	520	5
7	340	4	16	395	4
8	340	4	17	195	3
9	145	3	18	430	4
Out	3,150	36	In	3,335	36

Total 6,485m, par 72

Valderrama

SOTOGRANDE, CADIZ, SPAIN

Outside of the British Isles, Valderrama is probably the most famous golf course in Europe. Always kept in immaculate condition, this was for many years the home of the European Tour's flagship event, the Volvo Masters. In 1997, Valderrama hosted a memorable Ryder Cup.

A modern course

Valderrama was designed by Robert Trent Jones in 1974. The architect also made refinements to Augusta in the US (*see* pp.222–3), and Valderrama is often compared with that course. Both are associated with a Masters tournament, and have supreme conditioning and dazzling white bunkers. However, while Augusta's wide fairways are bordered by pines and there is little rough, the fairways at Valderrama are narrow, framed by cork trees, and fringed with rough. Accuracy is the key to playing well at Spain's best course.

Dramatic stage

Continually changing pace and direction, the course's routing takes advantage of the sometimes subtle, sometimes dramatic terrain. The par 3s are all very good, especially the downhill 12th. The round builds to an exciting climax at the do-or-die par-5 17th. It is a hole that smiled kindly on Seve Ballesteros and his team when, in 1997, they defeated a very strong US side to retain the Ryder Cup.

⏶ **Victorious 1997 Ryder Cup team** It was entirely fitting that Seve Ballesteros—Spain's greatest ever golfer and a player who contributed so much to the Ryder Cup—should captain the winning European side when the event was staged at Valderrama in 1997.

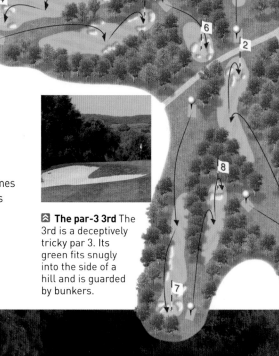

⏶ **The par-3 3rd** The 3rd is a deceptively tricky par 3. Its green fits snugly into the side of a hill and is guarded by bunkers.

⏵ **Bunkering at the par-3 6th**
Stylish bunkering is a trademark of golf course architect Robert Trent Jones. The shortest hole at Valderrama features a clutch of his best creations.

⏫ **The par-5 17th** The 17th at Valderrama is one of the best-known holes in golf. Redesigned by Seve Ballesteros for the 1997 Ryder Cup, it is almost impossible to hold in two shots. The green is wide but shallow, and slopes down to a seemingly magnetic water feature.

COURSE CARD

Hole	Meters	Par	Hole	Meters	Par
1	354	4	10	369	4
2	375	4	11	504	5
3	156	3	12	200	3
4	515	5	13	367	4
5	344	4	14	337	4
6	150	3	15	207	3
7	420	4	16	385	4
8	319	4	17	519	5
9	415	4	18	417	4
Out	3,048	35	In	3,305	36

Total 6,353m, par 71

⏩ **The par-4 14th** The 14th hole at Valderrama is played from an elevated tee, which offers splendid views over the hills of Andalucia. A relatively short par 4, this hole requires a deft approach shot to a beautifully sited green below.

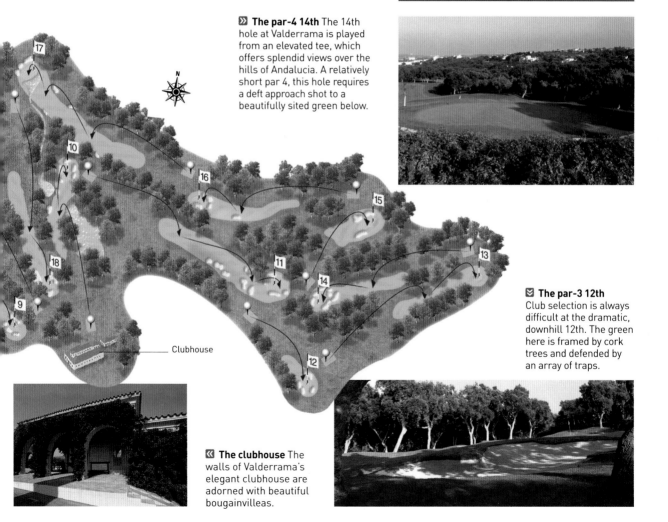

Clubhouse

⏬ **The par-3 12th** Club selection is always difficult at the dramatic, downhill 12th. The green here is framed by cork trees and defended by an array of traps.

⏪ **The clubhouse** The walls of Valderrama's elegant clubhouse are adorned with beautiful bougainvilleas.

Falsterbo

FALSTERBO, NEAR MALMO, SWEDEN

Set on the southwestern tip of Sweden is the finest golf course in Scandinavia. Falsterbo is a true links, a lonely place where a lighthouse dominates the skyline and the wind reigns supreme. Few golfers could fail to enjoy such glorious surroundings.

Splendid isolation

Founded in 1909, Falsterbo is one of Sweden's oldest golf clubs. However, the Swedish capital, Stockholm, is 10 times farther away from Falsterbo than the Danish capital, Copenhagen, so many foreign visitors arrive via Denmark. Laid out over a peninsula, the links course sometimes seems like it is about to slip into the Baltic Sea. Golfers share this isolated environment with a marvelous variety of birdlife.

Daunting hazards

Falsterbo is a very challenging course, and the inexperienced player will not prosper here. In addition to an ever-present wind, golfers must confront an array of hazards, including marshland reeds, water, trees, and nearly 100 links-style bunkers. Golfers who slice their opening drive will probably finish out of bounds; if they do the same with the final approach shot, they may land on the beach. But brave and intelligent golf is richly rewarded at Falsterbo.

The par-5 18th The final hole is a tough par 5 running next to the shore. Huge dunes hug the right side of the fairway, and a deep bunker guards the front left side of the green. The clubhouse offers some welcome respite.

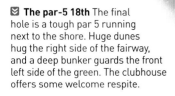

The par-4 7th At the rugged 7th, golfers emerge from marsh country and head toward classic links terrain.

The par-4 12th Falsterbo's lighthouse lies beyond the 12th hole. The tower is a landmark for those on land as well as at sea—golfers often look toward it to align their drives at the 12th.

Bird's-eye view The course at Falsterbo is often likened to Turnberry in Scotland (see pp.288–9). Indeed, the two courses lie at the same latitude, both are sited over a remote, alluring coastline, and each features a lighthouse.

Flommen Marsh

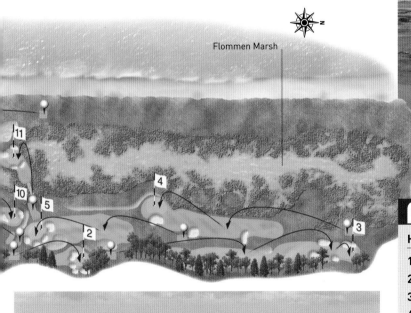

Across the links Lonely and exposed, yet hauntingly beautiful; this view toward the lighthouse was taken from the dunes beside Falsterbo's 18th green.

COURSE CARD

Hole	Meters	Par		Hole	Meters	Par
1	400	4		10	350	4
2	160	3		11	145	3
3	480	5		12	370	4
4	360	4		13	515	5
5	350	4		14	210	3
6	155	3		15	470	5
7	295	4		16	355	4
8	175	3		17	345	4
9	380	4		18	440	5
Out	2,755	34		In	3,200	37

Total 5,955m, par 71

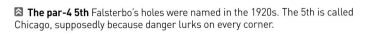

The par-4 5th Falsterbo's holes were named in the 1920s. The 5th is called Chicago, supposedly because danger lurks on every corner.

SWEDEN/DENMARK

Scandinavia has the most golfers in Europe per capita, outside Britain. The Swedes are particularly avid golfers and have recently produced several world-class players, especially women. The superb links course at Falsterbo is one of Europe's best. In Denmark, Holstebro claims similar preeminence, but Esbjerg and Rungsted also have many devotees.

Halmstad

After Falsterbo (see pp.324–5), the championship layout at Halmstad is seen as the leading course in Sweden. Located approximately halfway between Gothenburg and Malmo in the small resort town of Tylosand, Halmstad boasts two 18-hole layouts— the championship North Course and the less demanding South Course. Despite sandy terrain and proximity to the sea, it is as different from Falsterbo as Wentworth is from Carnoustie or Winged Foot from Shinnecock.

Designed in the 1930s by Rafael Sundblom, tall pines line most of the fairways and a range of hazards, from strategically positioned bunkers to ditches and a stream, ensures that the course is a challenge for even the most skillful of golfers.

COURSE LOCATOR

SWEDEN
1 **Falsterbo**, Falsterbo
2 **Halmstad**, Halmstad
3 **Barsebäck**, Löddeköpinge
4 **Ullna**, Åkersberga

DENMARK
5 **Holstebro**, Holstebro
6 **Esbjerg**, Marbaek
7 **Rungsted**, Rungsted Kyst
8 **Silkeborg**, Silkeborg

>> **A near-island green at Halmstad** A stream meanders through the center of the North Course. It has been incorporated into the design of several holes, notably the sequence between the 12th and 14th.

<< **Halmstad (North) Course** The North Course has a traditional "out and back" layout.

>> **Annika Sorenstam** One of the greatest women golfers of all time, in 2001 Annika Sorenstam became the first female player to score a 59 in an LPGA tournament.

Holstebro

Opened in 1970 and widely acclaimed as the leading course in Denmark, Holstebro reminds many visiting players of some of Britain's outstanding woodland courses. There is a hint of Blairgowrie, Scotland, and a dash of Woburn, England, at Holstebro—its picturesque, manicured fairways weave amid secluded avenues of pine trees fringed with gorse bushes and heather. Although fairways are generous, the wayward hitter will be punished, and most of the greens are protected by cunningly positioned bunkers.

There are, in fact, two courses at Holstebro—the championship 18 is complemented by a shorter, easier, 9-hole course. There are many excellent holes but among the most interesting on the championship course are the short 3rd—a beautiful par-3 in an avenue of pines; the doglegged par-3 9th; and the very long, and wonderfully flowing, par-5 16th.

« Natural setting Holstebro is surrounded by an attractive forest, and the immediate countryside abounds with wildlife.

Scandinavian players

Both Swedish and Danish players have competed for Europe in the Ryder Cup—Joakim Haegmann was the first Swede in 1993 and Thomas Bjorn was the first Dane four years later. While Scandinavian male golfers regularly win events on the PGA European Tour, no player has yet won a Major championship. The same cannot be said of Scandinavia's women golfers, several of whom have won Grand Slam events.

⌃ Holstebro course Water is not a prominent feature at Holstebro, although it fashions the par-3 17th and par-4 18th holes on the championship course.

» Thomas Bjorn Denmark's finest player has won several titles around the world, including the inaugural Loch Lomond Invitational in Scotland.

Emirates

MAJLIS COURSE, DUBAI, UNITED ARAB EMIRATES (UAE)

Built in the deserts of Dubai in 1988, the Emirates Golf Club can truly be described as a golfing oasis. The club's superb Majlis Course has been the venue for the Dubai Classic Tournament since 1989.

Unique clubhouse

The clubhouse at the Emirates is its most extraordinary feature—a glass-walled structure topped with a series of canopies that make it look like a group of huge, high-tech Bedouin tents. This amazing building overlooks two 18-hole golf courses: the original Majlis Course, built in 1988, and the Wadi Course, which opened in 1996.

Desert charms

Held in March, the Dubai Classic Tournament heralds the beginning of a new year on the PGA European Tour. The Emirates is one of the most popular venues on the golfing calendar, and the tournament always attracts a high-caliber international field. Seve Ballesteros, Fred Couples, Ernie Els, and Colin Montgomerie have all won here. The fairways on the Majlis Course seem to be a deeper shade of green than on courses elsewhere in the world—probably because they contrast so vividly with the desert surrounding the course. Rather alarmingly, the layout's myriad water hazards possess seemingly magnetic powers. The golfing challenge is tough, but immensely enjoyable.

The par-3 4th This hole seems simple from the tee, but wayward shots are punished by a combination of sand and water.

The par-3 7th The tee shot at the 7th must carry across a lake to reach the putting surface. Twin bunkers lurk at the back of the green.

The par-5 10th There are no water hazards to contend with at the 10th, but the green is completely encircled by sand. It is a genuine three-shot hole.

The original golfing oasis Though surrounded by a barren, sandy landscape, there is no shortage of water and trees on the Majlis Course. Using sophisticated irrigation systems, the Majlis was the first all-grass championship golf course to be built in the Gulf region. It was dubbed the "Desert Miracle" when it opened.

Clubhouse

COURSE CARD

Hole	Yards	Par		Hole	Yards	Par
1	458	4		10	549	5
2	351	4		11	169	3
3	530	5		12	467	4
4	188	3		13	550	5
5	436	4		14	434	4
6	475	4		15	180	3
7	186	3		16	425	4
8	434	4		17	359	4
9	463	4		18	547	5
Out	3,521	35		In	3,680	37

Total 7,201 yards, par 72

The clubhouse Situated behind the large double green that serves both the 9th and 18th holes on the Majlis Course, the Emirates' clubhouse has been rated the best golf clubhouse in the world by *Golf World* magazine.

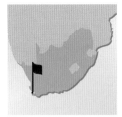

Royal Cape

WYNBERG, CAPE TOWN, SOUTH AFRICA

South Africa has a relatively small golfing population, but it has nurtured many of the game's Major champions. Royal Cape, founded in 1895, was the country's first golf club and has staged many great championships over the years, including the South African Open.

South Africa's first

Starting with a fairly crude nine-hole layout on Waterloo Green, the club moved twice in its early years before settling in its present location at Wynberg in 1905. Royal Cape is just 20 minutes from the center of Cape Town and a similar distance from the city's international airport. The majestic Table Mountain range is the backdrop to the course.

Parkland with water

Although it lies near the coast and is affected by sea breezes, Royal Cape is really a parkland course. Narrow, tree-lined fairways and well-bunkered greens offer a stern test to the golfer. There is plenty of water too, particularly at the corner of the 3rd, 4th, and 5th holes, and also at the 14th, 15th, and 16th. No fewer than 11 South African Opens have been staged here, which is proof of the high quality of the course.

◄◄ The par-3 15th Royal Cape is a scenic course. Two of its par 3s—the 4th and the 15th—are played across a pond.

Railroad track

COURSE CARD

Hole	Meters	Par	Hole	Meters	Par
1	367	4	10	322	4
2	341	4	11	442	5
3	433	4	12	312	4
4	131	3	13	170	3
5	491	5	14	401	4
6	341	4	15	148	3
7	460	5	16	485	5
8	171	3	17	379	4
9	385	4	18	352	4
Out	*3,120*	*36*	**In**	*3,011*	*36*

Total 6,131m, par 72

⌃ The par-4 14th The drive at the gently curving 14th should be steered toward the left center of the fairway to set up an easier approach. Water threatens both sides of the green.

⟨⟨ The par-4 17th
Not many golf courses can boast views that are as striking as those at Royal Cape. A splendid panorama of the mountains highlights the approach to the 17th.

Clubhouse

Connemara Road

Torrens Road

⟨⟨ The clubhouse As befits South Africa's oldest golfing institution, Royal Cape's impressive clubhouse exudes a sense of history and tradition, as well as a welcoming atmosphere.

⟨⟨ The par-4 3rd Often played into a stiff breeze or crosswind, the 3rd requires two solid, straight hits if the green is to be reached in two strokes. A par here is well-earned.

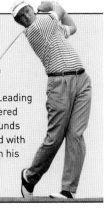

GREAT ROUNDS

Ernie Els: 1996 South African Open
The 1996 Open at Royal Cape is known as the one that Els won, lost, then won again. Leading after a first day 65, Els frittered away his advantage with rounds of 70 and 74. He then rallied with a superb closing 66 to claim his second South African title.

SOUTH AFRICA

From the tradition of Royal Cape to the razzmatazz of Sun City, and from the natural layout at the Durban Country Club to the engineering feat of the Links at Fancourt, South African golf has enormous variety—as befits the "rainbow nation." Recent years have seen a development boom with many new courses opening, especially in the Western Cape.

Durban Country Club

Described by leading architect Tom Doak as "the most isolated great golf course in the world," the Durban Country Club was designed by Laurie Waters and George Waterman in the early 1920s. Situated close to the coast, the course is affected by strong sea breezes and has many links characteristics, including undulating sandy fairways, plateau greens, and deep bunkers. The best holes are the short 2nd and the roller-coasting par-5 3rd, but from first to last, the round is full of fascinating challenges.

△ **The par-3 2nd** Running parallel to the shore, the 2nd hole is a very difficult par 3. Precision is everything at this hole, as the tee shot is played across a valley to a narrow, well-bunkered green that sits on a plateau.

COURSE LOCATOR

1. **Durban Country Club**, Durban
2. **Fancourt Resort**, George
3. **Gary Player Country Club**, Sun City
4. **Leopard Creek**, Malelanen
5. **Humewood**, Port Elizabeth
6. **Wild Coast**, Wild Coast
7. **Royal Johannesburg**, Johannesburg
8. **Royal Cape**, Cape Town
9. **Pezula Club**, Knysna
10. **Arabella**, Hermanus

▽ **Durban Country Club course** The Durban Country Club has staged numerous South African Opens. Both Gary Player (1956 and 1969) and Ernie Els (1998) have won championships here.

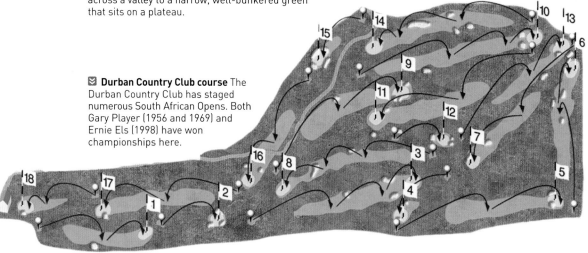

Fancourt

Rivaling Sun City for the unofficial title of "best golf resort in South Africa," Fancourt is located near the town of George, halfway between Cape Town and Port Elizabeth on the scenic Garden Route. There are no fewer than four golf courses at Fancourt: the original Montagu and Outeniqua Courses (both championship-standard parkland layouts), Bramble Hill (a "pay and play" facility), and the Links at Fancourt, designed by Gary Player and Phil Jacobs. The Links was opened in 2000 and made a dramatic tournament debut when it staged the Presidents Cup match in 2003.

» **The Links course** Unlike a typical British links course, the Links at Fancourt has water hazards—the most spectacular creates a peninsula green at the par-4 15th.

« **The 6th and 8th holes on the Montagu Course** Designed by the legendary South African golfer Gary Player, Fancourt's Montagu Course is regarded as slightly superior and more challenging than Outeniqua (see below).

☑ **The Links at Fancourt** Although it may look entirely natural, the Links at Fancourt is completely man-made. It hosted the Presidents Cup in November 2003, and the match finished in a thrilling 17–17 tie.

« **The 17th on the Outeniqua course** Also designed by Gary Player, the Outeniqua Course takes its name from the impressive range of mountains nearby.

Mission Hills

FALDO COURSE, MISSION HILLS, SHENZHEN, CHINA

Located in mountainous terrain near Shenzhen, about 90 minutes' drive from Hong Kong, this pioneering resort boasts 10 golf courses. Its premier layout is a dramatic stadium course designed by Nick Faldo.

Asian splendor

Framed by dark, forested hills, the Faldo Course at Mission Hills is characterized by bold bunkering and sweeping changes in elevation. It opened for play in 1998 and has been hailed as one of the greatest golf courses in the Asia–Pacific region.

Exhilarating holes

Outstanding features on the front nine at Mission Hills include a waste bunker at the teasingly short par-4 3rd, and a green that is like an amphitheater at the 7th. An incredible closing sequence, beginning with the curving 14th, includes a driveable, risk-reward par 4, a stunning island green, a brutal, long two-shotter, and a thrilling, reachable par 5.

» **The World Cup Course** The new Faldo Course may be Mission Hills' finest layout but the Jack Nicklaus-designed World Cup Course remains its most famous.

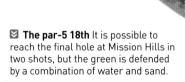

⌃ **Course designer** Nick Faldo has designed several layouts in Asia, and the stadium course at Mission Hills is his finest regional creation to date. He is pictured here with a legion of caddies on the day he officially opened the course.

COURSE CARD

Hole	Yards	Par	Hole	Yards	Par
1	550	5	10	555	5
2	448	4	11	368	4
3	324	4	12	382	4
4	492	5	13	232	3
5	371	4	14	452	4
6	197	3	15	343	4
7	388	4	16	163	3
8	185	3	17	455	4
9	471	4	18	516	5
Out	3,426	36	In	3,466	36

Total 6,892 yards, par 72

⊡ **The par-5 18th** It is possible to reach the final hole at Mission Hills in two shots, but the green is defended by a combination of water and sand.

Clubhouse

⏶ **The par-3 16th** At the short 16th, the tee shot is played downhill to an island green completely encircled by water.

⏶ **The par-4 7th viewed from the 6th green** The spectacularly bunkered two-shot 7th follows a bunkerless par 3 that is played across the edge of one of many small lakes at Mission Hills.

⏶ **Elaborate bunkering at the par-5 4th** The Faldo Course is renowned for the quality and extent of its bunkering, and also the craftsmanship that is evident in its stone walls and bridges.

Oarai

OARAI, IBARAKI, JAPAN

Designed by Seiichi Onoue, one of Japan's foremost golf architects, Oarai opened for play in 1953. This gently rolling, links-style course is situated on the Ibaraki coast, a two-hour drive east of Tokyo. It regularly hosts important tournaments, such as the Japan Open.

Ideal seaside terrain

Onoue, Oarai's architect, was given a site that was perfect for a traditional seaside course. The sandy terrain is bordered by the Pacific Ocean on one side and a dark pine forest on the other. Resisting the temptation to plant trees, Onoue decided that the golfer should be at the mercy of the elements. Another characteristic of the course is the scarcity of fairway bunkers. However, the rough is quite menacing, and the greens are defended by a combination of deep sand traps and natural slopes.

Championship golf

There are many strong holes at Oarai, among them the attractive short 4th. The three-hole finishing sequence, which comprises a long par 3 followed by two testing par 4s, is also wonderful. Oarai regularly hosts Japanese PGA Tour events, including the annual Mitsubishi Diamond Cup. In 1998, it also staged the Japan Open, which was won that year by the Japanese golfer Hidemichi Tanaka.

⊠ The par-4 9th
The strong front nine at Oarai culminates with a relatively straightforward hole, which guides the golfer back to the clubhouse.

Clubhouse

⌃ The clubhouse Oarai's clubhouse is a single-story structure, typical of 1950s Japanese architecture.

⌃ **The par-4 5th** The 5th has no bunkers and meanders through an avenue of sea pines. It is one of the few holes offering the genuine prospect of a birdie.

Pacific coast

⌃ **The par-5 10th** Oarai's back nine begins with a marvelous par 5 that runs alongside the Pacific Ocean. The hole can be reached in two shots, but the green slopes from left to right toward the sea.

GREAT ROUNDS

Todd Hamilton: 2003 Mitsubishi Diamond Cup
US golfer Todd Hamilton provided a foretaste of his ability to master a links-style golf course when he triumphed in the 2003 Mitsubishi Diamond Cup tournament at Oarai. A year later, Hamilton was the surprise winner of the British Open, following a playoff with the South African Ernie Els.

⟨⟨ **The par-4 11th**
The 11th is arguably the toughest hole at Oarai. The drive must flirt with a pond to the left of the fairway and avoid trees to the right.

COURSE CARD

Hole	Meters	Par	Hole	Meters	Par
1	398	4	10	457	5
2	467	5	11	370	4
3	370	4	12	385	4
4	151	3	13	407	4
5	421	4	14	164	3
6	311	4	15	545	5
7	539	5	16	224	3
8	196	3	17	421	4
9	411	4	18	407	4
Out	**3,264**	**36**	**In**	**3,380**	**36**

Total 6,644m, par 72

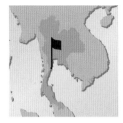

Blue Canyon

CANYON COURSE, MAI KHAO, THALANG, PHUKET, THAILAND

The Blue Canyon Country Club on the Thai island of Phuket—the name itself conjures up images of a tropical paradise. The golf itself does not disappoint, either. The Canyon Course is world-class, and the club hosts the Johnnie Walker Asian Classic on a regular basis.

Canyon Course

Located about 19 miles (30km) from Phuket Town, the club is set in a lush valley by Nai Yang Beach, with a backdrop of mountains and sea. There are two 18-hole courses—the original championship Canyon Course, which opened in 1991, and the Lakes Course, built in 1999. The Canyon Course is widely regarded as Thailand's best golf course. Designed by Yoshikazo Kato on a former rubber plantation, it guides the golfer through a stunning landscape of rugged canyons and tranquil lakes. While each hole is memorable, the 14th and 17th—both of them spectacular par 3s—are the most celebrated.

A tournament venue

Blue Canyon first hosted the Johnnie Walker Asian Classic Tournament in 1994. Since then, many of the world's greatest golfers have come to play at the club. Two occasions have been of particular note. Greg Norman captured the 1994 tournament after a brilliant final round of 64. Then, in 1998, Tiger Woods came from nine shots behind to tie Ernie Els before defeating the South African in a sudden death playoff.

COURSE CARD

Hole	Yards	Par		Hole	Yards	Par
1	390	4		10	392	4
2	218	3		11	600	5
3	449	4		12	440	4
4	407	4		13	390	4
5	398	4		14	194	3
6	556	5		15	586	5
7	205	3		16	357	4
8	412	4		17	221	3
9	561	5		18	403	4
Out	**3,596**	**36**		**In**	**3,583**	**36**

Total 7,179 yards, par 72

The par-4 3rd The Canyon Course is rightly famed for its outstanding par 3s, but there is also a selection of good two-shot holes, including the tree-lined 3rd.

GREAT ROUNDS

Tiger Woods: 1998 Johnnie Walker Classic
One of the greatest encounters between long-time rivals Tiger Woods and Ernie Els took place at Blue Canyon in 1998. Starting his final round nine strokes behind Els, Woods shot a fine 65 and then clinched the title with a birdie.

The par-3 17th With trees to the left and water to the right, the 17th demands a bold and precise tee shot. It is rated as one of the best short holes in Asia.

The par-3 14th Played from a very elevated tee, the short 14th features a boomerang-shaped island green. Making a par 3 here is a great achievement.

Clubhouse

Green at the par-4 18th The 18th finishes off the litany of great golf holes on the Canyon Course. Superb golf played in lush, tropical surroundings is a golfing paradise.

The clubhouse As the centerpiece of Thailand's (and possibly Asia's) finest 36-hole golf course, Blue Canyon's clubhouse is a luxurious fusion of Western and Thai styles.

Kingston Heath

MELBOURNE, VICTORIA, AUSTRALIA

The Australian Open has been played seven times at Kingston Heath, placing this course among the world's greatest golf venues. It is sited within the Melbourne sandbelt and ranks as Australia's second course, after its neighbor Royal Melbourne.

Creativity on a small scale

Australian pro Dan Souter completed Kingston Heath's layout in 1925; the course's bunkering was designed a few years later by the great Scottish golf architect Alister MacKenzie. Souter's work is often overlooked in comparison with MacKenzie's. However, like Merion in the US (see pp.230–1), Kingston Heath is a great example of how to build a world-class course on a relatively small parcel of land. Amazingly, the 18 holes, clubhouse, and practice area together occupy just 127 acres (51ha).

Champions of the Heath

The 2000 Australian Open was won by rising Australian star Aaron Baddeley, his second successive victory in the event. Baddeley followed a string of celebrated winners of the Open at Kingston Heath: Greg Norman won his fourth home-country title here in 1995; the underrated Peter Senior, also an Australian, triumphed in 1989; and seven-time champion Gary Player from South Africa was victorious in 1970.

The par-4 6th The 6th has prodigious fairway and greenside bunkering, which is not immediately apparent from the tee, and catches out many golfers.

Clubhouse

The clubhouse Kingston Heath's elegant, single-story clubhouse is situated close to both the 6th and 18th greens.

⌃ The par-3 10th The 10th is short, but intimidating. Only a small portion of the putting surface is visible from the tee. In between is a sea of native scrub and sand, which a shot must carry over to reach the green.

COURSE CARD

Hole	Meters	Par	Hole	Meters	Par
1	418	4	10	127	3
2	351	4	11	380	4
3	269	4	12	509	5
4	357	4	13	324	4
5	173	3	14	516	5
6	393	4	15	142	3
7	462	5	16	391	4
8	398	4	17	421	4
9	330	4	18	391	4
Out	3,151	36	**In**	3,201	36

Total 6,352m, par 72

Huge bunker at the 15th

⌃ The par-3 15th One of the greatest par 3s in Australia, the slightly uphill 15th at Kingston Heath features a huge bunker that starts just in front of the tee and snakes all the way to the green.

⏵ Fairway at the par-4 18th A brave drive down the left side of the fairway, just inside the large bunker, provides the best line for approaching the final green.

Royal Melbourne

COMPOSITE COURSE, MELBOURNE, VICTORIA, AUSTRALIA

The Composite Course at Royal Melbourne—Australia's premier golf club—features 12 holes from Alister MacKenzie's West Course and six from Alex Russell's East Course. By common consensus, this constitutes the finest 18 holes of golf in the southern hemisphere.

Perfect golf

Royal Melbourne was founded in 1891, but the wonderful layout seen today dates from the 1920s. To create their 36-hole masterpiece, the club's owners wisely engaged the finest architect of the time, Scottish-born Alister MacKenzie (see p.227), and teamed him with Australian Open champion Alex Russell, whose genius for course design was about to be discovered. The club occupies the best site in the Melbourne sandbelt, where several other great Australian clubs are located. Gently rolling throughout, the terrain might be described as a cross between linksland and heathland.

Championship venue

The idea of assembling the Composite Course was conceived when the 1959 Canada Cup was held at Royal Melbourne. While MacKenzie's West Course is acknowledged as the better course, the addition of some of the best holes from the East strengthens the layout. The club has since staged numerous Australian Opens. In 1998, it hosted the Presidents Cup, when the Internationals inflicted a crushing defeat on the US, winning by 20.5 to 11.5.

» **The famous par-3 5th** At Royal Melbourne's 5th, the tee shot is played across a valley to a severely contoured green, which is defended by deep traps to the left and right. Making a par 3 at this hole is a good achievement.

⌂ The par-4 6th The 6th is one of the greatest par 4s in golf, featuring a swinging, left-to-right dogleg, then a sloping green.

The par-4 8th
One of the most cunning holes at Royal Melbourne tempts players to drive over a vast fairway bunker.

Clubhouse

GREAT ROUNDS

Greg Norman: 1987 Australian Open Greg Norman won two of his Australian Open titles at Royal Melbourne. His first victory in 1985 came in a tournament reduced to 54 holes. With a total of 273, his 10-stroke triumph in 1987 established a new record for an Open at Royal Melbourne.

COURSE CARD

Hole	Yards	Par	Hole	Yards	Par
1	324	4	10	396	4
2	461	5	11	304	4
3	161	4	12	402	4
4	391	4	13	350	4
5	135	3	14	153	4
6	285	4	15	520	4
7	416	3	16	395	3
8	435	4	17	392	5
9	401	4	18	439	4
Out	**3,009**	**35**	**In**	**3,351**	**36**

Total 6,360 yards, par 71

Green at the par-4 6th Royal Melbourne is renowned for the quality and character of its putting surfaces. They are traditionally very quick and full of subtle contours.

Royal Sydney

ROSE BAY, SYDNEY, NEW SOUTH WALES, AUSTRALIA

Established in 1893, with royal patronage bestowed four years later, Royal Sydney is one of the oldest clubs in Australia. The course is located in the fashionable suburb of Rose Bay, a mere 15 minutes from downtown Sydney, and is a popular venue for major events.

Evolving course

Royal Sydney is renowned for its narrow fairways and strategic bunkering. No single designer created the layout—it has evolved over the years. Alister MacKenzie, the architect of Royal Melbourne (*see* pp.342–3), was chiefly responsible for the impressive bunkering. In the 1920s, Royal Sydney had a links feel, and was more affected by sea breezes than today's essentially parkland venue.

Famous Opens

The Australian Open has been played at Royal Sydney on 11 occasions, and the most extraordinary of all Open rounds took place here. In 1994, Robert Allenby played the first 14 holes of his final round in seven under par, but was five over par for his last four holes. Allenby held on to win by a single stroke when his closest challenger, Brett Ogle, also dropped three shots in his final four. Royal Sydney has a demanding finish!

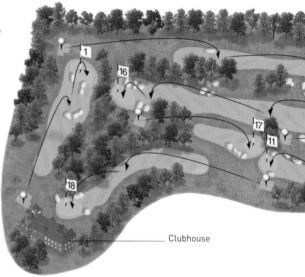

Clubhouse

☑ **Perfect finish at the par-4 18th** Royal Sydney has one of the finest finishing holes in Australian golf. The second shot is played slightly uphill to a green sloping back to front and right to left. Needing "four to win the Open" is never easy here.

☑ **The par-4 11th** A view from beside the 11th green illustrates Royal Sydney's essentially parkland layout. In its early years, the course had a more rugged look and there were fewer trees.

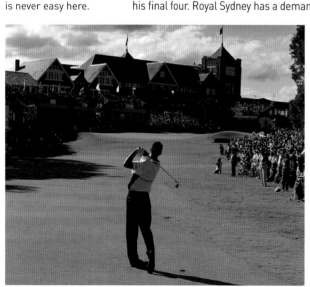

The par-4 4th
One of the best holes on the front nine—especially when played into the wind—is the doglegging 4th, with its downhill tee shot and uphill approach.

The par-3 14th Dramatic bunkering on the 14th makes it hard to believe that Robert Allenby was seven under par for his round when he walked from this green on the last day of the 1994 Australian Open.

The par-4 9th The undulating 9th is sited at the far end of the course. Royal Sydney has an old-fashioned layout, rather than the "two loops of nine" typical of many newer courses.

COURSE CARD

Hole	Yards	Par	Hole	Yards	Par
1	277	4	10	419	4
2	549	5	11	438	4
3	182	3	12	384	4
4	427	4	13	514	5
5	435	4	14	194	3
6	154	3	15	443	4
7	563	5	16	563	5
8	302	4	17	210	3
9	359	4	18	402	4
Out	3,248	36	In	3,567	36

Total 6,815 yards, par 72

Index

Index

Acknowledgments

Dorling Kindersley would like to thank Deeksha Saikia, Esha Banerjee, Neha Gupta, Priyaneet Singh, and Sonam Mathur for editorial assistance.

The publisher would like to thank the following for their kind permission to reproduce their photographs:

KEY:
a=above; b=below; c=center; f=far; l=left; r=right; t=top.

2: Corbis/John Henley; 4: Corbis/ Carl Schneider; 6–7: Corbis/Tony Roberts; 8: Hobbs Golf Colllection (b); 9: Hobbs Golf Colllection (t); 10: Hobbs Golf Colllection (bl, cfr, t); 11: Hobbs Golf Colllection (tr, b); 12: Hobbs Golf Colllection (tl); 12–13: Hobbs Golf Colllection; 14: Phil Sheldon (tl); 15: Corbis/Tim McGuire (b); 15: Phil Sheldon (tr); 16–17 Getty Images/ Thinkstock Images; 18: Getty Images/ Scott Halleran (bl); 18–19: Empics Ltd/ Tom Ward; 20: Action Plus/Leo Mason (tl); 24: Phil Sheldon (tl); 27: Phil Sheldon (tr); 28: Action Plus/Glyn Kirk (cla); 32:Getty Images (tl); 34: Getty Images/Ross Kinnaird (bl); 35: David Towersey (tr); 37: Callaway Golf (tl), Matthew Harris/The Golf Picture Library (bl); 38: burrowsgolf.com (cr); 39: Action Plus/Glyn Kirk (tr), Foresight Sports (bl, br); 44–5: Getty Images/ Mike Powell; 46: Action Plus/Glyn Kirk (bl); 47: Action Plus/Glyn Kirk (t), Action Plus/Mike Hewitt (br); 48: Action Plus/Chris Barry (tl), Action Plus/Glyn Kirk (b); 49: Action Plus/Neil Tingle (br); 50: Action Plus/Glyn Kirk (car), Action Plus/Neil Tingle (bl); 51: Action Plus/Neale Haynes (br), Matthew Harris/The Golf Picture Library (t); 52: Matthew Harris/The Golf Picture Library (bl); 53: Action Plus/Neil Tingle (b), Getty Images/Steve McDonough/ Taxi (tl); 54–5: Corbis/Simon Dearden; 60: Getty Images/Tim Sloan/AFP (br); 62: Richard Simmons (cl, cr, bl), (br); 82–3: Getty Images/Dave Cannon; 82: Getty Images/Dave Cannon (tr, br, cfr); 94–5: Getty Images (c); 95: Action Images/Richard Heathcote (tr, br, cfr); 102–03: Action Images/Richard

Heathcote; 102: Action Images/Richard Heathcote (tr, br, cfr); 112–13: Getty Images/Andy Lyons; 112: Richard Simmons (tr, br, cfr); 120–1: Corbis/ Michael S Yamashita; 120: Corbis/ Franco Vogt (br), Corbis/Mark E Gibson (tr); 121: Royalty Free Images/Corbis (tr); 126: Getty Images/Darren England (crb); 140–1: Corbis/Patrick Giardino; 140: Action Images/Richard Heathcote (tr, cr), Richard Simmons (br); 142: Getty Images/Jonathan Ferrey; 144: Getty Images/Sports Illustrated; 145: Getty Images/Martyn Hayhow/AFP (br); 146: Getty Images/Stuart Franklin (tl); 147: Getty Images/Jeff Gross (b); 148: Action Plus/Glyn Kirk (bl); 149: Action Plus/Mike Hewitt (b), Corbis/ Underwood and Underwood (tr); 150: Getty Images/Jonathon Wood; 151: Getty Images/Ian Walton (t), Getty/ Stuart Franklin (br); 152–3: Action Plus/Neale Haynes; 154: Phil Sheldon (tr); 154–5: Getty Images/David Cannon/ALLSPORT; 156: Empics Ltd/Jon Buckle (b), Empics Ltd/Mike Egerton (tr); 157: Empics Ltd/John Walton (tl), Getty Images/Alexander Joe/AFP (br); 158: Corbis/Don Mason (bl), Empics Ltd/Jon Buckle (cra); 159: Empics Ltd/Jon Buckle (b), Phil Sheldon (cra); 160: Empics Ltd/Mike Egerton (tl); 160: Action Plus/John Biever/Icon (b); 161: Empics Ltd/Mike Egerton (tl), Getty Images (bc); 162: Getty Images/Dennis Oulds/Central Press/Hulton Archive (tl); 162–3: Action Plus/Glyn Kirk (b); 163: Empics Ltd/ Matthew Ashton (tc), Empics Ltd/Mike Egerton (cl); 164: Corbis/Bruce Smith/ Fratelli Studio (tr), Empics Ltd/Adam Davy (bl); 165: Empics Ltd/Mike Egerton (tc), Getty Images/Stephen Dunn /Allsport (bl); 166: Empics Ltd/ Neal Simpson (b), Matthew Harris/The Golf Picture Library (tl); 167: Empics Ltd/Terry Firma/Fotopress (cl), Phil Sheldon (tr); 168: Empics Ltd/Mike Egerton (bl), Getty Images (br); 169: Phil Sheldon (cr, tr); 170: Matthew Harris/The Golf Picture Library (tl, b); 171: Empics Ltd/John Marsh (tl), Phil Sheldon (br); 172: Empics Ltd/Michael Steele (b); 173: Getty Images/Warren Little (br), Matthew Harris/The Golf Picture Library (t); 174: Action Plus/

Glyn Kirk (tl), Corbis/Bettmann (b); 175: Action Plus/Glyn Kirk (b), Matthew Harris/The Golf Picture Library (tl); 176: Corbis/Tony Roberts (b), Matthew Harris/The Golf Picture Library (tl); 177: Empics Ltd/Simon Barber (br), Action Plus/Glyn Kirk (cra); 178: Getty Images/Arthur Tilley (cl); 179: Corbis/ Peter Finger (b), Getty Images (tc); 180–1: Getty Images/David Cannon; 182: Phil Sheldon (tl, cra, bl); 183: Action Images/Bob Martin (b), Phil Sheldon (tl); 184: Phil Sheldon (bcl); 184–5: Action Images/Bob Martin (b); 185: popperfoto.com (tl); 186: Getty Images/Steve Munday (tr), Phil Sheldon (bl); 187: Getty Images/David Cannon (tc), Phil Sheldon (cl); 188: Phil Sheldon (tl, bc); 189: Empics Ltd/Alpha (b); 190: Phil Sheldon (tl, cra, bl); 191: Getty Images/Steve Powell/Allsport (b); 192: Action Images/Andy Couldridge (br), Action Images/Richard Heathcote (tl); 193: Action Images/Stuart Franklin (tc), Phil Sheldon (cl); 194: Phil Sheldon (tl, br); 195: Getty Images/Carl Iwasaki/ Time Life Pictures (bc), Phil Sheldon (tr); 196: Phil Sheldon (tl); 198: Pa Photos (bl), Corbis/Shaun Best/Reuters (br); 199: Phil Sheldon (cl), Action Images/Brandon Malone Livepic (tc); 200: Empics Ltd (bc), Empics/Jon Buckle (tl); 201: Topfoto.co.uk (tc), Action Images/Stuart Franklin (b); 202: Getty Images/Allsport UK / Allsport (bc); 203: Getty Images/Jamie Squire/Allsport (bl), Phil Sheldon (tc); 204: Getty Images/Jamie Squire (tr), Reuters (bc); 205: Empics Ltd/Jon Buckle (cl), Corbis/Robert Galbraith Reuters (tl); 206: Action Images/ Richard Heathcote 2002 (tl), Corbis/ Hulton-Deutsch Collection (br); 207: Getty Images/Mills/Hulton Archive (tl), Phil Sheldon (b); 208–09: Matthew Harris/The Golf Picture Library (b); 208: popperfoto.com (tl); 210: Action Images/Stu Forster (tl), Phil Sheldon (b); 211: Action Images/Brandon Malone (tr), Action Images/Richard Heathcote 2002 (cl); 212: Action Images/Stuart Franklin Darren Clarke, Northen Ireland (cl); 213: Empics Ltd/ JAM Media (br), Getty Images/Harry How (bl); 214: Matthew Harris/The Golf Picture Library (b), Phil Sheldon (tl);

215: Action Images/Stuart Franklin (tl), Pa Photos (tcr); 216: Action Images (bl), Sporting Pictures (UK) Ltd (cra); 217: Empics Ltd/Tom Ward (bc), sportsphoto.co.uk (tl), Phil Sheldon (tr); 218: Getty Images/Stuart Franklin (tl), Matthew Harris/The Golf Picture Library (bc), United States Golf Association (cra); 219: Getty Images/ Ted West/Central Press (bc), Action Images/Brandon Malone (tl); 220–1: Banff Springs Golf Course; 223: Corbis/ Tony Roberts (tr), Action Images/Bob Martin (br), Corbis/Tony Roberts (cr); 224: Empics Ltd/Jon Buckle (br), Matthew Harris/The Golf Picture Library (bl); 225: Action Images/Tim Matthews (tc), Action Images (cra), Phil Sheldon (bl); 226: Phil Sheldon (crb); 227: Phil Sheldon (b), Corbis/Tony Roberts (tc, cl), Phil Sheldon (tl); 228: Corbis/Tony Roberts (br); 229: Phil Sheldon (tl), Corbis/Tony Roberts (br), Matthew Harris/The Golf Picture Library (bl), Corbis/Reuters/Matt Sullivan (tr); 230: Corbis/Tony Roberts (crb); 231: Phil Sheldon (bl), Action Plus/Brian Morgan (tc), Action Plus/ Brian Morgan (cla), Corbis/Bettmann (tcl), Getty Images (cr). 232: Action Plus (br), Phil Sheldon (bl). 233: Corbis/Tony Roberts (bl), Matthew Harris/The Golf Picture Library (tr), Phil Sheldon (tl); 234: Matthew Harris/The Golf Picture Library (bl, car); 235: Matthew Harris/ The Golf Picture Library (cr, tc), Phil Sheldon (bc); 236–7: Empics Ltd (b); 237: Pa Photos/Empics (br), Action Images/Brandon Malone (cla), Matthew Harris/The Golf Picture Library (tl), Phil Sheldon (cra); 238: Matthew Harris/The Golf Picture Library (br); 239: Phil Sheldon (tl), Matthew Harris/ The Golf Picture Library (cra, bc), Phil Sheldon (bc) (Donald Ross); 240: Phil Sheldon (b); 241: Phil Sheldon (cr), Corbis/Tony Roberts (tl, br), Phil Sheldon (bl); 242: Matthew Harris/The Golf Picture Library (ca), Phil Sheldon (b); 243: Action Images/Brandon Malone (tl), Empics Ltd/SportsChrome (br), Matthew Harris/The Golf Picture Library (cr), Phil Sheldon (bl); 244: Action Images (cra), Action Images/ Stuart Franklin (b); 245: Action Images (tl), Action Images/Brandon Malone (br, cr), Phil Sheldon (bl); 246: Phil Sheldon (cra), Phil Sheldon (b); 247: Hobbs Golf Colllection (tr), Phil Sheldon (cr, bl); 248: Corbis/Tony Roberts (cra), Getty Images/David Rogers/Allsport (br); 249: Phil Sheldon (tl), Corbis/Tony Roberts (b, cfr), Getty Images/David Cannon/Allsport (tr); 250: Banff Springs (cla, b); 251: Banff Springs (br, tl, bl), Corbis/Gunter Marx Photography (tr); 252: Empics Ltd/Zuma Press (cla), Glen Abbey (b); 253: Getty Images/Harry How /Allsport (tr), Glen Abbey (br, bl), Phil Sheldon (tc); 254: Getty Images/David Cannon (cra), Getty Images/David Cannon (tr), Getty Images/Stephen Munday /Allsport (br); 255: Ganton (tl); 256: Eric Hepworth (cra, br); 257: Eric Hepworth (b), Eric Hepworth (cr); 258-9: Empics Ltd/Eric Hepworth (b); 258: Matthew Harris/The Golf Picture Library (cr); 259: Empics Ltd/Eric Hepworth (tl), Eric Hepworth (bc); 260: Action Images/Nick Potts (cra), Pa Photos/Empics (cla), Getty Images/David Cannon/Allsport (bc); 260-1: Action Plus/Eric Hepworth (b); 261: Empics Ltd/Eric Hepworth (tl, crb), Sporting Pictures (UK) Ltd (cra); 262: Matthew Harris/The Golf Picture Library (bl), Sporting Pictures (UK) Ltd (br); 263: Empics Ltd/Eric Hepworth (tl, tr), Matthew Harris/The Golf Picture Library (bc); 264: Matthew Harris/The Golf Picture Library (cra), Phil Sheldon (bl), 265: Action Images/Richard Heathcote (tr), Matthew Harris/The Golf Picture Library (tl, b); 266: Getty Images/Robert Laberge (cra); 267: Empics Ltd/Steve Mitchell (cla), Matthew Harris/The Golf Picture Library (br), Empics/PA/Rebecca Naden (tl), Action Images/Stuart Franklin (tr), Matthew Harris/The Golf Picture Library (tr); 268: Matthew Harris/The Golf Picture Library (cra); 268-9: Eric Hepworth (b); 269: Action Images/David Davies (tr); 270: Matthew Harris/The Golf Picture Library (cla, cra), Phil Sheldon (b); 271: Matthew Harris/The Golf Picture Library (tl, bl, c), Topfoto.co.uk (tr); 272: Matthew Harris/The Golf Picture Library (cra, cla); 273: Royal County Down (b), Matthew Harris/The Golf Picture Library (tl, cr); 274: Phil

Sheldon (cra), Getty Images/Paul Severn/Allsport (b); 275: Corbis/Michael St Maur Sheil (cr), Matthew Harris/The Golf Picture Library (bl), Phil Sheldon (t); 276: Corbis/Bettmann (br), Empics Ltd/Eric Hepworth (bl); 277: Action Plus/Neil Tingle (tl), Matthew Harris/The Golf Picture Library (b, tr, cl); 278: Action Images/Scenic (br), Loch Lomond (cla); 279: Action Images/Franklin (b), Getty Images/Gary Newkirk/Allsport (cfr), Matthew Harris/The Golf Picture Library (tr), Loch Lomond (tl); 280: Getty Images/Stephen Munday (cla); 281: Getty Images/David Cannon/Allsport (br), Action Images/Andy Couldridge Digital (cb), Empics Ltd/Eric Hepworth (cr), Getty Images (tr); 282: Getty Images/David Cannon (cra), Phil Sheldon (b); 283: Phil Sheldon (bl), Corbis/Tony Roberts (tl, cr), Phil Sheldon (tr); 284: Empics Ltd/Eric Hepworth (br), Getty Images/David Cannon (cra); 285: Action Images (tl), Empics Ltd/Eric Hepworth (cr, b), Empics/John Walton (tr); 286: Matthew Harris/The Golf Picture Library (tl), Sporting Pictures (UK) Ltd (br); 287: Action Plus/Glyn Kirk (tl), Action Plus/Mike Hewitt (tr), Getty Images/David Cannon (cb), Phil Sheldon (bl); 288: Action Images (br); 289: Action Plus/Glyn Kirk (b), Action Images/Bob Martin (cr), Matthew Harris/The Golf Picture Library (tc); 290: Action Plus/Brian Morgan (br, clb); 291: Action Plus/Brian Morgan (bl), Action Plus/Brian Morgan (tl, bl), Vision Golf (br); 292: Action Images/Richard Heathcote (cla), Action Plus/Brian Morgan (b, cl); 293: Action Plus/Brian Morgan (cr, b), Getty Images/Stuart Franklin (tl); 294: Action Plus/Glyn Kirk (c); 295: Les Bordes Golf Club (tr), Phil Sheldon (b); 296: Getty Images/Warren Little; 297: Action Plus/Neil Tingle (tr), Getty Images (b); 298: Action Plus (cla), Getty Images/Andrew Redington (b); 299: Action Plus/Brian Morgan (b), Action Plus/Brian Morgan (tl); 300: Stefan V Stengel (cra, br); 301: Getty Images/Tim Matthews/Allsport (b), Matthew Harris/The Golf Picture Library (tl), Stefan V Stengel (tr); 302: Getty Images/Roberto Schmidt/AFP

(tl), Reuters/Alexandra Winkler (cl); 303: Falkenstein Golf Club (tc, bl); 304: Seefeld-Wildmoos Golf Club (tl, bl); 305: Action Plus/Brian Morgan (tr, bl); 306-7: Action Plus/Brian Morgan(b); 306: Action Plus/Brian Morgan (bc, cla); 307: Action Plus/Brian Morgan (tl), Getty Images/David Cannon/Allsport (cr); 308: Royal Zoute (bc, cla); 309: Getty Images (bl), Royal Zoute (tl, cr); 310: Getty Images/Pierre Verdy/AFP (br); 311: Action Plus/ Brian Morgan (cr, tc), Getty Images/Gary Newkirk/Allsport (bl); 312: Pevero (bl, cra), Action Plus/Brian Morgan (bc); 313: Phil Sheldon (tc), Pevero (cl, c); 314: Getty Images/David Cannon/Allsport (br), Visions in Golf (bc); 315: Action Plus/Brian Morgan (tr, bl); 316: Action Plus/Brian Morgan (br); 319: Action Plus/Brian Morgan (bl), Getty Images/Stuart Franklin (tc); 320: Action Plus/Brian Morgan (br), Getty Images/Ross Kinnaird (bl); 321: Action Plus/Brian Morgan (tl), Getty Images/Ross Kinnaird (bl), Popperfoto.com (tr), Corbis: George Tiedemann (crb); 322: Action Images/Stuart Franklin (cla), Empics Ltd/Matthew Ashton (cr, br); 323: Empics Ltd/Matthew Ashton (bl,tl, cra, br); 324: Falsterbo (br, bl); 325: Falsterbo (tr, cla, bl), Phil Sheldon (cr); 326: Action Plus/Neil Tingle (br), Blamstead Golf Club (cb); 327: Action Plus/Neil Tingle (br), Holsterbo Golf Club (tc); 328: Empics Ltd/Matthew Ashton (bc, br); 329: Empics Ltd/Matthew Ashton (b, tr, tc); 330: Royal Cape (ca, br); 331: Royal Cape (tl), Getty Images/Andrew Redington/Allsport (br), Matthew Harris/The Golf Picture Library (bl), Royal Cape (cr); 333: Getty Images/David Cannon (cr), Fancourt Hotel and Country Club Estate; 334: Mick Edmund (br), Mick Edmund (clb), Getty Images/Steve Munday/Allsport (c); 335: Mission Hills (t), Mick Edmund (br); 336: Oarai (br, bl); 337: Getty Images/Scott Halleran (cra), Oarai (bl, cr); 338: Blue Canyon, Thailand (br), Getty Images/Andrew Redington/Allsport (bc); 339: Phil Sheldon (tr), Blue Canyon, Thailand: (tl, br, bl); 340: Getty Images/Ryan Pierse (br), Matthew Harris/The Golf Picture Library (bl); 341: Matthew Harris/The

Golf Picture Library (tl, cr, br); 342: Matthew Harris/The Golf Picture Library (bc), Action Images/Brandon Malone (br); 343: Corbis/Tony Roberts (tl), Getty Images/William West/AFP (cra), Phil Sheldon (br); 344: Reuters (bl), Matthew Harris/The Golf Picture Library (br); 345: Corbis/Tony Roberts (tr), Action Plus/Brian Morgan (tl), Matthew Harris/The Golf Picture Library (bl).

Jacket images: *Front and Back:* Dreamstime.com: Mack2happy (grass). *Front:* Corbis: Simon Dearden (flag); Momatiuk - Eastcott (sky). Dreamstime.com: Bowie15 (golf course). Tim Loughhead: c. *Back:* Tim Loughhead: c.

Every effort has been made to trace the copyright holders. Dorling Kindersley apologizes for any unintentional omissions and would be pleased, in such cases, to add an acknowledgment in future editions.

All other images © Dorling Kindersley. For further information see: www.dkimages.com